SADOMASOCHISM AND THE BDSM COMMUNITY IN THE UNITED STATES

Sadomasochism and the BDSM Community in the United States: Kinky People Unite chronicles the development of sadomasochistic sexuality and its communities in the United States from the post-war period to the present day.

Having evolved from scattered networks of sadomasochists to a coherent body bound by shared principles of "safe, sane, consensual," activists worked to transform popular perceptions of their community, end its routine harassment by law enforcement and win inclusion in American society. Often paralleling the work of LGBTQ activists, people who engaged in BDSM (Bondage and Discipline, Dominance and Submission, and Sadism and Masochism) transformed both their own sexual practices and how outsiders perceived them, successfully changing popular perceptions of them from fascists, murderers, and outlaws to people living an alternative lifestyle. The development of this community highlights the interactions of people of different sexual orientations within a sexual community, the influence of various campaigns for sexual freedom, and the BDSM community's influence on popular perceptions of sexuality and sexual freedom. The text's historical perspective gives depth and texture to a specific dimension of American history of sexuality.

This book will be of interest to students and scholars in the history of sexuality. Its clear and direct approach offers an important and useful chronology of a movement that has long been neglected.

Stephen K. Stein is Associate Professor of History at the University of Memphis, USA. He works in the histories of the US military, technology, and sexuality.

SADOMASOCHISM AND THE BDSM COMMUNITY IN THE UNITED STATES

Kinky People Unite

Stephen K. Stein

Routledge
Taylor & Francis Group
NEW YORK AND LONDON

First published 2021
by Routledge
52 Vanderbilt Avenue, New York, NY 10017

and by Routledge
2 Park Square, Milton Park, Abingdon, Oxon, OX14 4RN

Routledge is an imprint of the Taylor & Francis Group, an informa business

Library of Congress Cataloging-in-Publication Data
A catalog record for this title has been requested

ISBN: 978-0-367-47681-6 (hbk)
ISBN: 978-0-367-47680-9 (pbk)
ISBN: 978-1-003-03582-4 (ebk)

Typeset in Bembo
by codeMantra

To Carolyn

CONTENTS

ACKNOWLEDGMENTS

Several archivists helped me over the course of my research, unearthing rarely seen documents, including Shawn Wilson and Liana Zhou at the Kinsey Institute, and Rick Storer and Mel Leverich at the Leather Archives and Museum in Chicago, and Viola Johnson guided me through the holdings of the travelling Carter Johnson Leather Library. A Catherine and Charles Freeburg Fellowship allowed me to take a semester off and complete this book. I am particularly grateful to the many members of the BDSM community who spoke to me over the years, particularly Vince Andrews, Victoria Baker, Gerrie Blum, Pat Bond, Rafe DeCoito, Mark Frazier, Laura Goodwin, Johnny Gray, Jan Hall, Chuck Higgins, Sallee Mallard Huber, Viola Johnson, Mitch Kessler, Jan Lyon, Lee from NLA Austin, George Nelson, Pyxy, Bill Miranda Salzman, Seraphina, Artemis Silverowl, Vik Stump, Cecilia Tan and many others. Jan Hall shared her records of the SSCA, and Vince Andrews shared NLA records not held at the Leather Archives and Museum. My special thanks go to Nancy Ava Miller who not only discussed the Dallas Conference and early years of PEP with me, but also contributed this book's cover photo, which she took at the 1987 March on Washington.

ABBREVIATIONS

AOL	America Online
APA	American Psychiatric Association
APEX	Arizona Power Exchange
ASS	Atlanta SM Solidarity
B&D	Bondage and Discipline
BDSM	A combination of B&D, D&S and S&M
CDG	Chicagoland Discussion Group
CHC	Chicago Hellfire Club
CMC	California Motor Club
COSMOS	Council of SM Organizations
DADS	Denver Area Dominants and Submissives
D&S	Dominance and Submission
DSM	Diagnostic and Statistical Manual (of the APA)
FFA	Fist Fuckers of America
GDI	God Damn Independent
GMSMA	Gay Male SM Activists
HELP	Homophile Effort for Legal Protection
IML	International Mr. Leather
IMsL	International Ms. Leather
ISC	Interim Steering Committee of the SSCA
LAAM	Leather Archives and Museum
LGBTQ	Lesbian, Gay, Bisexual, Transsexual, Queer
LIL	Living in Leather
LSM	Lesbian Sex Mafia
MAsT	Masters and slaves Together
NCSF	National Coalition for Sexual Freedom
NEA	National Endowment for the Arts

NELA	New England Leather Alliance
NGLTF	National Gay and Lesbian Task Force
NLA	National Leather Association
NOW	National Organization for Women
ORGASM	Oregon Guild Activists of SM
PEP	People Exchanging Power
RACK	Risk Aware Consensual Kink
SDG	Seattle Dungeon Guild
SOBNET	Sexually Oriented Board Network
SSC	Safe, Sane, Consensual
SSCA	Safe, Sane, Consensual Adults
TCC	The Tri-State Couples Club
TES	The Eulenspiegel Society (later officially renamed TES)
VASM	Vancouver Alliance for SM
WAP	Women Against Pornography
WIITWD	What It Is That We Do

INTRODUCTION

E.L. James' 2011 novel *Fifty Shades of Grey* surprised critics—both by its contents, a sadomasochistic relationship between billionaire Christian Grey and recent college graduate Anastasia Steele, and its record-breaking success. Apparently, sadomasochistic sex appealed to millions of readers. This should not have come as a surprise. Surveys showed about ten percent of Americans experimented with spanking or bondage or other forms of what practitioners labeled BDSM, a condensed abbreviation of the most common terms describing sadomasochistic sexuality: bondage and discipline (B&D), dominance and submission (D&S or D/S) and sadism and masochism (S&M, S/M, or SM). Comedians like Stephen Colbert joked about it. Gags, safe words and other BDSM jargon and paraphernalia figured in their punch lines. Popular television shows ranging from *CSI* and *Law & Order* to *Castle, Frasier,* and *Will and Grace* featured BDSM-themed episodes. This sexual knowledge, which facilitated *Fifty Shades*' success, resulted from a concerted, decades-long effort by BDSM activists to organize sadomasochists into a distinct community, reshape their sexuality and end its pejorative characterization by legal and medical authorities. By presenting BDSM as "safe, sane, and consensual" they changed popular perceptions. Instead of dangerous sociopaths, criminals and fascists, sadomasochists became "just another alternative lifestyle," as Rosie O'Donnell declared them in *Exit to Eden* (1994), a film based on Anne Rice's novel.

***

BDSM is a sexual practice that combines varying degrees of strong—even painful—sensation, dominant/submissive role-playing, and bondage or other restraint. We owe the terms masochism (the enjoyment of pain) and sadism (the enjoyment of inflicting pain), and sadomasochism (a combination of the two) to nineteenth-century sexologist Richard von Krafft-Ebing who assiduously categorized sexual activity, demarcating between the normal and the perverse, the latter including fetishism, masochism, sadism and a host of other practices.[1]

Since then, sadomasochists have pushed back against the pathologization of their sexual desires, sought to reclaim these terms and offered their own terminology and definitions. In the early 1980s, members of Atlanta S&M Solidarity (ASS) agreed "the term S&m or SM or sadomasochism in its broadest sense" meant "erotic (sexual) role play involving a dominant ('top') and a submissive ('bottom') that may involve psychological or physical components or both." A decade earlier, Rick Leathers argued the "essence of S&M is the ritual enactment of dominance and submission" involving "pain, humiliation, trust/responsibility exchanges, and controlled assaults on the body to achieve a high intensity of experience." Jay Wiseman, author of *SM 101*, defined it as "the use of psychological dominance and submission, and/or physical bondage, and/or pain, and/or related practices in a safe, legal, consensual manner in order for the participants to experience erotic arousal and/or personal growth."[2]

Writing in mid-1970s as popular awareness of sadomasochism grew, Michael J. Mitchell warned it was a mistake to evaluate sadomasochists "based solely on what is observed." Not only do they make "extensive use of fantasy," but in the "controlled conditions" of their scenes, pain melds with pleasure, "giving sadomasochistic activities a strange, but often exciting sweet and sour quality," a combination of "agony and ecstasy." Pain and subjugation, "played for their erotic value," become "extremely personal forms of communication and interaction," requiring mutual trust and confidence between participants. The submissive (also called bottom, M, slave and other terms) establishes limits. "Some scenes have no pain at all, instead exploring bondage, humiliation, or other techniques." Actions are deliberate, careful and halted by "code words or signals," if needed. "No other expression of passion and intellect," Mitchell claimed, matches sadomasochism "in its capacity to reveal both the saint and the sinner in each individual."[3]

Numerous sexual activities fall under the rubric of BDSM, so many that it would be impossible for all—or even most—to feature in a single BDSM encounter or scene, as they are generally termed. Nonetheless, the above definitions indicate the most common practices: restraint of the bottom by the top, infliction of pain through flagellation or other means, and a hierarchy of dominance and submission. As Anne McClintock notes, BDSM often "plays social power backwards." Sadomasochists assume the roles of CEOs, police officers, teachers and other authority figures and submit to "punishment" inflicted by their social subordinates. Similarly, "SM theatrically flouts the edict that manhood is synonymous with mastery, and submission a female fate." Sadomasochists, Pat Califia declared, were "probably the first group of people in human history who have said power doesn't have to be an evil thing, and the only factor that determines whether or not a sexual act is moral or ethical is consent."[4] BDSM scenes are usually negotiated in advance—often in quite rigorous detail—as tops and bottoms discuss their interests and establish limits.

In many ways, BDSM is sexual theater. Appearance and symbolism are as important as the experience of pain and other sensations. The context in which scenes take place may be as important as the activities involved. This may include elaborate costuming and detailed role-play. Often, they are essential for bottoms to eroticize imbalances in power and transmute pain into pleasure. Pain outside of an erotic context simply hurts. Psychologist Roy Baumeister determined masochists were not self-destructive. They "may seek pain but they try hard to avoid injury." Most were rather "ordinary people" and no more interested in visiting the dentist than anyone else. On the other hand, sex without elements of BDSM is simply "vanilla." BDSM complicates sex, which BDSM activist Brenda Howard noted, "is why we like it."[5]

Sadomasochists have offered numerous explanations for BDSM's allure. The film *Exit to Eden* connects adult BDSM desires to a childhood spanking, a common trope perhaps originating with philosopher Jean-Jacques Rousseau who in his *Confessions* (1782) connected his adult interest in flagellation to childhood beatings. Some contemporary sadomasochists make similar connections, though recent surveys indicate BDSM interests generally develop at a mature age. Some sadomasochists find catharsis through intense BDSM stimulation. Others have ecstatic, spiritual or transcendent experiences. Some find it healing or transformative. For many, psychiatrist Robert Stoller concluded, "SM games" can be "acts of freedom" in which "earlier traumatic, frustrating experiences . . . are reconstructed and mastered in the theater of pain." Most sadomasochists simply find it intensifies the sexual experience, in part, by decentering pleasure from the genitals and deeply involving the mind. People engage in BDSM for enjoyment. They find it fun and playful—so much so they are as likely to refer to the elaborately outfitted rooms in which they orchestrate BDSM scenes as playrooms rather than dungeons, to their equipment—no matter how painful—as toys, and the scenes themselves as play, or play parties, if many people are involved. As Staci Newmahr suggests, BDSM is "serious leisure."[6]

Beginning in the early 1970s with the first BDSM organizations, sadomasochists struggled to find palatable terms describing their sexual activities. Most rejected sadomasochism, a term redolent of serial killers and nonconsensual violence, as well as S&M, which seemed too close to sadomasochism. Some suggested SM or S/M, while others preferred dominance and submission (D&S or D/S), which avoided association with sadism and masochism, terms often used pejoratively to imply sadomasochists were either victims or their abusers. Many professional dominants favored B&D (bondage & discipline), a term used commonly in pornographic magazines and personal ads. Discussions over terminology—sometimes heated—continued into the 1990s, driving some sadomasochists to give up in frustration and adopt the acronym WIITWD (What It Is That We Do). Over the same period, the terms "kink" and "kinky" previously applied to any non-normative sexuality became increasingly associated—though never solely—with BDSM.

When they named their organizations, sadomasochists usually avoided these terms entirely. A few, like the Chicago Hellfire Club, hinted at their sexual nature, but most chose names that hid their purpose, such as Briar Rose, The Eulenspiegel Society (TES) and Society of Janus. Some, like the National Leather Association, used the term "leather" to identify with the larger leather subculture, while hiding their BDSM identity to most outsiders. In later years, many conferences and events also used the term leather, such as the Leather Leadership Conference, even though they focused almost exclusively on BDSM and its practitioners. Embracing the term leather let people avoid publicly declaring their sadomasochism. Similarly, there are numerous leather awards and contests, such as the Leather Leadership Award, and the International Mr. and Ms. Leather contests, most of whose winners are sadomasochists, but no Mr. or Ms. S&M or BDSM award.

This was, in part, a political decision. BDSM practitioners were acutely conscious of their minority status. Even as their organizations grew in size and number, they remained a small, isolated community. As Tony DeBlase, a leading BDSM educator and publisher, explained, identifying as leather allowed him to appeal to a broad sexual population, running the gamut from men who adopted leather and other macho styles of presentation (cowboy, military, police, etc.), but restricted themselves to "vanilla" sex, through men into "rough sex," and on to those into BDSM.[7] This, of course, caused confusion. Some used leather to signal BDSM interests; for others, it was just macho sexual display.

For David Kloss, who won the first International Mr. Leather contest in 1979, leather represented "something that's on the edge," offering "the element of danger by pushing the limits. It represents maximum gratification," while encompassing "a tribal feeling."[8] As a descriptive term, though, leather is both overly broad and too limited. It includes gay and lesbian sadomasochists who identify with a larger leather subculture, but excludes most heterosexual sadomasochists who do not. Leather is best seen as a distinct subcultural identity "centered on the fetishization of leather" with rules for dress, cruising and other behaviors, which create the tribal identity Kloss and other leatherfolk find alluring. Some of them engage in BDSM. Most do not.[9]

In contrast, BDSM is a set of sexual practices involving bondage, pain and dominant/submissive role play, which an increasingly organized BDSM community has shaped around a discourse of consent and safety. Modern BDSM practice is the result of this intense and intimate social construction of sadomasochistic sexuality. While some people who engage in BDSM claim it as part of their sexual identity and see themselves as part of a BDSM community, many do not. Nonetheless, the BDSM community's discourses on consent and safety have influenced these sadomasochists, as well as contributing to mainstream discourse on sexuality and sexual consent.

For simplicity, I have used the term BSDM in this book, even though the term did not enter common use until the mid-1990s—and even later for many gay and lesbian sadomasochists who preferred to identify as leathermen or leatherdykes. BDSM is, nonetheless, the most commonly used term at the time of this writing and has the advantage of including all its practitioners, regardless of gender or orientation. For lack of a better term, the lack of general agreement on a preferred term within the BDSM community and because BDSMer does not roll trippingly off the tongue, I refer to people who engage in BDSM as either sadomasochists or BDSM practitioners.

Appropriate terminology for gay and lesbian community has also changed over time, reflecting growing inclusiveness from lesbian and gay to lesbian, gay, bi- and transsexual, and today's LGBTQ, which includes queer. In that regard, I have tried to use the term in general use at a particular time to avoid implying an inclusiveness not necessarily present in the past—an inclusiveness desperately sought by BDSM activists. Similarly, several prominent members of the BDSM community, such as Pat (later Patrick) Califia, have changed names. I have endeavored to use the name these people used at a particular time.

★★★

While long studied by social scientists, particularly anthropologists and sociologists, sadomasochists have received only passing mention in historical studies of sexuality. Social scientists, in turn, have focused mostly on contemporary BDSM practice, without delineating how it changed over time. Even those who focus their attentions on particular organizations, such as TES or Society of Janus, the world's oldest public BDSM organizations, describe play parties and other contemporary events, but say little about their history.[10] They describe BDSM activities and explain the values promoted by the BDSM community, but do not explore how these developed and changed over time.

This book, *Sadomasochism and the BDSM Community in the United States: Kinky People Unite*, is the first comprehensive history of the BDSM community and BDSM organizations in the United States. It draws on the rich literature of the BDSM community, including books, magazines, newsletters and various amateur publications, as well as the records of major BDSM organizations and activists, particularly Tony DeBlase, a leading figure in several important BDSM organizations and publisher of *Drummer, DungeonMaster* and other important magazines. It explores the development of the BDSM community, which emerged from scattered, loosely networked enthusiasts in the 1950s and developed into a cohesive subcultural community linked by hundreds of local BDSM organizations, annual conventions and a vibrant literature in the 1990s. These organizations facilitated the education and socialization of BDSM practitioners, shaped BDSM practice to emphasize safety, negotiation and consent, and led a surprisingly successful effort to win mainstream acceptance of their sexual activities.

People have engaged in BDSM activities for centuries. Renaissance philosopher Giovanni Pico della Mirandola had friends who enjoyed flagellation. In John Cleland's *Memoirs of a Woman of Pleasure* (1748), "unmerciful" flagellation drives Mr. Barvile wild with passion. Some erotic works, such as *Exhibition of Female Flagellants* (circa 1777) and *Venus Schoolmistress, or Birchen Sports* (circa 1788), focus entirely on flagellation. By the late nineteenth century, brothels specializing in flagellation operated in cities across Europe. Flagellation literature, the specialty of several British and French publishers, flourished as a subgenre. Sadomasochists occasionally shared their fantasies in the correspondence columns of popular magazines.[11]

How many people engaged in BDSM in these years is uncertain. Historian Lawrence Stone uncovered group sex and sadomasochism among several eighteenth-century families in Norwich, England.[12] Anne McClintock and other scholars have explored the nineteenth-century relationship of Hannah Cullwick and Arthur Munby who engaged in costumed, master/slave role-play, flagellation and other forms of BDSM.[13] Clearly, sadomasochists in these years occasionally found one another outside the walls of brothels and enjoyed long relationships. Yet, they were too few and too poorly organized to form a community. That changed after World War II, as a growing literature catering to their tastes encouraged correspondence networks among sadomasochists. Surprisingly, it was in the United States, not Great Britain or continental Europe, where loose affiliations of sadomasochists first developed into public organizations.

In late 1970, Pat Bond advertised in several New York underground papers, seeking fellow sexual masochists. The respondents met in his apartment and their meetings developed into The Eulenspiegel Society (TES), the world's first publicly advertised BDSM organization. TES, which soon met weekly, became a model for other organizations, particularly the Society of Janus, which formed in San Francisco in 1974. TES, Janus and other BDSM organizations offered places for sadomasochists to meet, learn from one another and build a community based on a shared interest in BDSM, a growing body of knowledge about its practices, and codes of conduct emphasizing consent, negotiation and safety.

A growing BDSM literature, including books and magazines, helped sadomasochists explore their interests and connect with one another. Larry Townsend's *Leatherman's Handbook* (1972) guided gay sadomasochists to leather bars to seek like-minded men. These bars provided a foundation for BDSM sex clubs, which emerged in the 1970s. Several of these, such as New York's Mineshaft, gained international reputations. A multi-room establishment crowded with hot, sweaty men, the Mineshaft offered a venue for every imaginable kink. Places like the Mineshaft attracted people who saw themselves as sexual outlaws who tolerated no barriers between themselves and fulfilling their sexual passions. They offered one of the purist expressions of French philosopher and historian Michel Foucault's conception of *ars erotica* in which the truth of sex is "drawn from pleasure itself, understood as a practice and accumulated as experience." It was in clubs like the Mineshaft the people developed "new possibilities of pleasure with strange parts of their body—through the eroticization of the body."[14]

Sadomasochism, of course, is just one of the sexual categories that anthropologist Gayle Rubin placed outside the "charmed circle" of acceptability in her landmark essay "Thinking Sex."[15] Activities at the Mineshaft and similar clubs involved many of the others, as well. The participants—mostly men—reveled in these intense, sexual environments, enjoying their outlaw status and the combination of fear and arousal they provoked in others. Most people, though, had trouble reconciling the outlaw image presented by sadomasochists and the reality of their sexual activities, which—contrary to expectations—were generally fairly safe. Journalists, medical professionals and others routinely presented negative portrayals of sadomasochists, describing them as dangerous, murderous or suicidal. So, too, did filmmakers such as William Friedkin whose 1980 film *Cruising* portrayed sadomasochists as serial killers.

Increasingly, BDSM activists sought to tame this outlaw, pleasure-focused world. Resolving the tension between enjoying BDSM as outlaw sexuality and keeping its participants safe occupied much of their attention into the 1990s. They also hoped to win mainstream acceptance—or at least end the routine harassment of BDSM practitioners by legal authorities. Changing popular perceptions of BDSM required erasing BDSM's outlaw image, which further encouraged activists to codify BDSM practice, establishing behavioral norms and rules to follow. They introduced what Foucault labeled *scientia sexualis* to BDSM practice, which they measured, constrained and packaged as wholesome, safe, sane and consensual fun. Instead of intimidating bars and sex clubs, this new generation of BDSM activists offered newcomers a safe, welcoming environment, which prioritized education and socialization over immediate sexual gratification.

Contemporary BDSM sexuality is the result of an intense and dedicated social construction over the past 50 years.[16] In the past, BDSM newcomers sought out experienced practitioners and learned from them, often as submissives. By the late 1980s, though, newcomers were more likely to learn specific skills, such as flagellation, piercing or fancy rope bondage, alongside dozens of others at demonstrations presented by local BDSM organizations or the workshops of BDSM conferences. In the 1990s, they benefited from a growing BDSM literature, including club newsletters, magazines and increasingly specialized books on BDSM techniques ranging from bondage and flogging to electrical devices, pony play, and cock and ball torture (CBT). Several books explored the intricacy of BDSM relationships, ranging from casual play partners to intense, full-time master/slave commitments. Today, of course, one can find a vast amount of practical BDSM information on the Internet. The encouragement for education and the status derived from mastering BDSM techniques is such that Race Bannon, a popular BDSM educator and writer, recently suggested "we're the most overeducated subculture around." Mirroring contemporary debates on college education, Bannon argued for less lecture and more hands-on instruction.

Sadomasochists had lost the "visceral joy" of BDSM and become "slaves to technique." *Scientia sexualis* had displaced *ars erotica*.[17]

★★★

The development of the BDSM community highlights the interactions of people of different sexual orientations within a sexual community, as well as the influence of various campaigns for sexual freedom on the BDSM community, and that community's influence on mainstream perceptions of sexuality and sexual freedom. Operating on society's sexual fringes, often suspect and ridiculed, the BDSM community tests the limits of sexual freedom and expression in both mainstream society and within LGBTQ community, which for many years excluded sadomasochists from its events.

In fact, the BDSM community offers a microcosm of disputes within the LGBTQ community over whether to silence its flamboyant elements to ease integration with mainstream society or insist mainstream society accept their community's diverse members as they are. Seeking acceptance from the larger LGBTQ community, BDSM activists faced the same choices. Should they enforce changes in behavior and appearance to gain acceptance or maintain an unrestrained, outlaw image, which disturbed outsiders? BDSM activists chose the former. Proclaiming BDSM was "safe, sane, and consensual," they systematically reinvented BDSM practices, transformed the BDSM community and worked to change popular perceptions of BDSM.

The BDSM community demonstrates how a minority sexual community can pursue sexual citizenship. A concept introduced by David Evans and advanced by Jeffrey Weeks and others, sexual citizenship involves the interaction of sexual and political life and bridges private and public spheres. While sexual activities themselves are often consummated in private, finding sexual partners is necessarily a public act. It requires free sexual expression, the ability to publicly state one's desires and seek those who share them. No matter how private, sexual activity requires some level of public acceptance.[18] As Evans explained, for most sexual minorities, "commitment to their sexual citizenship rights is chiefly expressed through their 'out' participation in commercial 'private' territories."[19]

Sadomasochists were systematically denied sexual privacy and thus sexual citizenship. Police raided their parties, gathering places and even private homes, arresting participants. Revelation of BDSM interests costs sadomasochists jobs—and even custody of their children. The popular reaction against BDSM was such that psychologists Darren Langdridge and Trevor Butt suggested BDSM is "too sexual" and "too transgressive of normative sexual expectations" to earn citizenship.[20]

Yet, BDSM activists sought exactly that. Paradoxically, as Jeffrey Weeks notes, winning the right to engage in private sexual activities of one's choice requires going public and presenting sustained "transgressive challenges" to institutions and traditions excluding sexual minorities.[21] So, BDSM activists encouraged people to openly declare their sadomasochistic interests and unite together across lines of gender, orientation and sexual interest. They lobbied government and politicians, engaged in public demonstrations and worked to make their case for inclusion and sexual citizenship. This book chronicles and analyzes this surprisingly successful effort. While negative characterizations of sadomasochism remain common in movies and television, they are balanced by positive portrayals in popular show ranging from *CSI* to *Will and Grace*. E.L. James' BDSM-centered novel *Fifty Shades of Grey* (2011) not only shattered all sales expectation, but helped launch entire categories of "steamy romances" featuring various intensities of BDSM activities.

★★★

Proceeding chronologically, this book traces the development of sadomasochistic practice and the development of a distinct BDSM community in the United States from the end of World War II to the first decades of the twenty-first century. Chapter 1 covers the period from 1946 to 1969 when the first sadomasochistic periodicals appeared and dedicated leather bars emerged. Both facilitated contacts and networking among sadomasochists, which intensified in the 1960s due to growing media coverage and contact magazines, which encouraged sadomasochists to emerge from the shadows.

Chapter 2 explores the 1970s when the first BDSM organizations formed, leather bars flourished and distinct BDSM venues opened. Four foundational BDSM organizations formed in these years: the Chicago Hellfire Club, The Eulenspiegel Society (TES) in New York, and the Society of Janus and Samois in San Francisco. They attracted members from beyond their immediate regions and served as models for the numerous new BDSM organizations formed in the 1980s. Covered in Chapter 3, these new organizations—more than 200 my mid-decade—displaced leather bars as the primary centers of BDSM education and socialization and facilitated the creation of annual BDSM conferences.

BDSM organizations worked together to end police harassment and win political rights, efforts highlighted in Chapter 4 by their appearance at the 1987 March on Washington for Lesbian and Gay Rights and the creation of a national organization to lobby on their behalf. By the mid-1990s, most American cities had at least one BDSM organization, which offered educational seminars on BDSM technique, and social gatherings and play parties for members. These organizations reshaped BDSM activities to emphasize consensuality and safety and forged sadomasochists into a coherent, intersectional sexual community whose members fought to legitimize their sexual behavior, end their harassment by the government and win acceptance from LGBTQ organizations and mainstream society.

Political activism by BDSM organizations peaked in the 1990s, the subject of Chapter 5. Working together, BDSM organizations lobbied the American Psychiatric Association to reclassify "sexual masochism" and "sexual sadism" in less pejorative terms in its *Diagnostic and Statistical Manual of Mental Disorders*, raised for funds for sadomasochists facing criminal charges, and worked to change the public image of BDSM by emphasizing these activities were "safe, sane, and consensual." These efforts proved largely successful. In the new millennium, police harassment of BDSM events declined as did pejorative depictions of BDSM. Positive—or at least neutral—portrayals increased in movies and television. Generally, American society evinced a greater understanding of BDSM and its norms, particularly the use of safe words to halt activities in the event of emergency or when pleasure ceased. The growing acceptance of BDSM, combined with the ease of access to information and potential sex partners provided by the Internet, reduced the need for dedicated BDSM organizations and publications. Many disappeared. This paradox of mainstream acceptance and organizational decline is the subject of Chapter 6, the book's final chapter. Surviving BDSM organizations depoliticized and focused almost entirely on the immediate social and educational needs of their members.

Notes

1 Richard von Krafft-Ebing, *Psycopathia Sexualis* (New York: Stein & Day, 1965).
2 Atlanta S&M Solidarity, "General Statement of Purpose," Leather Archives and Museum (hereafter LAAM), DeBlase Papers, Box 39; Jay Wiseman, *SM 101: A Realistic Introduction* (San Francisco, CA: Greenery, 1996), 139; and Rick Leathers, "Leather vs S/M," *Growing Pains*, November 1980, 2–3.
3 Michael J. Mitchell, "Erotic S&M Among Gays," *Gay News*, 2 December 1976, 16–7.
4 Anne McClintock, "'Maid to Order' Commercial S/M and Gender Power," *Social Text* 37 (Winter 1993), 87 & 105–7 and "A Chat with Pat Califia," *Black Sheets* 6 (1995), 18.
5 Roy F. Baumeister, "The Enigmatic Appeal of Sexual Masochism," *Journal of Social and Clinical Psychology* 16 (1997), 147. Gloria G. Brame and William D. Brame, *Different Loving Too: Real People, Real Lives* (British Columbia: Moons Grove Press, 2015), 84.
6 Gary Taylor and Jane Ussher, "Making Sense of S & M: A Discourse Analytic Account," *Sexualities* 4, no. 3 (2001), 302–6; Ummni Khan, "Sadomasochism in Sickness and in Health: Competing Claims from Science, Social Science, and Culture," *Current Sexual Health Reports* 9 (2015), 53; Dossie Eaton and Janet Hardy, *Radical Ecstasy: SM Journeys to Transcendence* (San Francisco, CA: Greenery, 2004); Robert J. Stoller, *Pain & Passion: A Psychoanalyst Explores the World of S & M* (New York: Plenum, 1991), 290; and Staci Newmahr, "Rethinking Kink: Sadomasochism as Serious Leisure," *Qualitative Sociology* 33 (2010), 313–31.
7 Fledermaus [DeBlase] to JD, *Drummer* 103 (1987), 4 and Michael Grumely, *Hard Corps: Studies in Leather and Sadomasochism* (New York: EP Dutton, 1977), *Chapter* 1.
8 Roy DeLaMar, "Twenty-five Years of Leather," *The Advocate*, 13 May 2003, 16.
9 Peter Hennes, *Faeries, Bears, and Leathermen: Men in Community Queering the Masculine* (Chicago, IL: University of Chicago Press, 2008), 213 footnote 2.
10 See for example Staci Newmahr, *Playing on the Edge: Sadomasochism, Risk, and Intimacy* (Bloomington: Indiana University Press, 2011) and Margot Weiss, *Techniques of Pleasure: BDSM and the Circuits of Sexuality* (Durham, NC: Duke University Press, 2011). Other important studies include Thomas Weinberg, *S and M: Studies in Dominance and Submission* (Buffalo, NY: Prometheus, 1995); Peggy Kleinplatz and Charles Moser, *Sadomasochism: Powerful Pleasures* (London: Routledge, 2006); Meg Barker and Darren Langdridge, *Safe, Sane and Consensual: Contemporary Perspectives Sadomasochism*

(London: Palgrave Macmillan, 2008); David M. Ortmann and Richard Sprott, *Sexual Outsiders: Understanding BDSM Sexualities and Communities* (Lanham, MD: Rowman & Littlefield, 2012); Danielle Lindemann, *Dominatrix: Gender, Eroticism, and Control in the Dungeon* (Chicago, IL: University of Chicago, 2012); and Ariane Cruz, *The Color of Kink: Black Women, BDSM, and Pornography* (New York: NYU Press, 2016).

11 Julie Peakman, "Initiation, Defloration, and Flagellation: Sexual Propensities in Memoirs of a Woman of Pleasure," in Patsy S. Fowler and Alan Jackson (eds.), *Launching Fanny Hill: Essays on the Novel and Its Influences* (New York: AMS Press, 2003), 160–70.

12 Lawrence Stone, "Libertine Sexuality in Post-Restoration England: Group Sex and Flagellation among the Middling Sort in Norwich, 1706–1707," *Journal of the History of Sexuality* 2, no. 4 (1992), 511–26.

13 Anne McClintock, *Imperial Leather: Race, Gender, and Sex in the Colonial Contest* (New York: Routledge, 1995); Diane Atkinson, *Love and Dirt: The Marriage of Arthur Munby and Hannah Cullwick* (New York: Macmillan, 2003); and Liz Stanley (ed.), *The Diaries of Hannah Cullwick, Victorian Maidservant* (New Brunswick, NJ: Rutgers University Press, 1984).

14 Michel Foucault, *The History of Sexuality, Volume 1* (New York: Vintage, 1978), 57 and *Ethics: Subjectivity and Truth* (New York: The New Press, 1994), 165.

15 G. Rubin, "Thinking Sex," in Carol Vance (ed.), *Pleasure and Danger: Exploring Female Sexuality* (Boston, MA & London: Routledge & Keegan Paul, 1984), 281.

16 Other scholars have noted this, but without tracing its history. See, for example, Taylor and Ussher, "Making Sense of S & M: A Discourse Analytic Account."

17 Brame and Brame, *Different Loving Too*, 105–6.

18 David T. Evans, *Sexual Citizenship: The Material Construction of Sexualities* (London: Routledge, 1993); Jeffrey Weeks, "The Sexual Citizen," *Theory, Culture and Society* 15, no. 3–4 (1998), 35–52; and David Bell and John Binnie, *The Sexual Citizen: Queer Politics and Beyond* (Cambridge: Polity, 2000).

19 Evans, *Sexual Citizenship*, 63.

20 Darren Langdrige and Trevor Butt, "A Hermeneutic Phenomenological Investigation of the Construction of Sadomasochistic Identities," *Sexualities* 7 (2004), 44.

21 Weeks, "Sexual Citizen," 37.

1

BUILDING BDSM NETWORKS, 1946–69

Bizarre, a new, digest-sized magazine appeared on North American newsstands in 1946. It contained photographs, stories, readers' letters and illustrations featuring corsets, tight-lacing and women with extraordinarily narrow waists; women wearing long, black leather gloves and thigh-high boots with six-inch heels; women restrained by chains, manacles, rope and assorted bondage devices, including a scold's bridle, which fit around the head like a cage and gagged the woman; piercing; tattooing; erotic wrestling; and a woman hooked up to a stationary bicycle with a device that whips her rear if she stops pedaling. The cover illustration of the next issue, a scantily clad woman in high heels manacled by her ankles, wrist and neck, promised even more daring contents. Along with effusive prose, it offered illustrations of women in revealing outfits and extreme bondage, and the first episode of Sweet Gwendoline, a cartoon serial. Regularly captured and tied up by Sir Dystic D'arcy and other villains, Gwendoline ended many episodes "struggling madly" against tight, "cruel cords." But things never went farther. While revealing and often skin-tight, clothing stayed on, and breasts and genitals remained covered. Other than describing the pleasurable sensations imparted by bondage, flagellation and tight corsets, no sexual activity occurred.[1]

Bizarre was the first magazine focusing entirely on consensual, erotic sadomasochism. The publisher, John Coutts, used the pseudonym John Willie, as well as several others, and produced most of the contents of the early issues, and almost all the photographs and illustrations in the magazine's 11-year run.

By the mid-1950s, *Bizarre* had more than a thousand subscribers, a total circulation of 15,000, and sold on major city newsstands throughout the United States and Canada. Its success encouraged Irving Klaw, Leonard Burtman and others to launch similar publications targeting fetishists and sadomasochists. These publishers benefited from relaxed post-war censorship standards, which facilitated the proliferation of "girlie" magazines during and after the war. Some, such as

Robert Harrison's *Whisper* and *Flirt*, featured occasional fetish content, including illustrations by Coutts. While fetish publishers risked obscenity prosecution, they generally found ways to operate within the law while satisfying their customers' desires—customers they sometimes helped connect with one another.

As historian Martin Meeker notes, the emergence of gay male and lesbian communities in twentieth-century United States resulted from changes in how "individuals could connect to knowledge about homosexuality" and to one another.[2] The same proved true for sadomasochists. The increasing availability of fetish and BDSM magazines, which by the 1960s included personal advertisements, encouraged people to explore these interests and seek those who shared them. Most BDSM and fetish magazines targeted heterosexuals, but a growing number focused on gay men. Some gay sadomasochists joined the motorcycle clubs or frequented leather bars, and therein found men who shared their interests. Bar patrons, motorcycle club members and the publishers, readers and advertisers of BDSM magazines developed contacts with one another that spread from city to city. While hidden from the public eye, these networks grew in the 1950s and 1960s, provided a foundation for the emergence of public BDSM organizations and a visible BDSM community in the 1970s.

Before *Bizarre*

Sadomasochism was hardly new in 1946. *Fanny Hill* (1748), the *Lustful Turk* (1828) and other nineteenth-century erotic works included scenes of flagellation. *The Merry Order of St. Bridget* (1857) focused entirely on flagellation. Along with other late-nineteenth-century sexologists Richard von Krafft-Ebing categorized, defined and named sexual practices. In the fifth edition of *Psycopathia Sexualis* (1890), he described sexual fetishes linked to various body parts, materials or objects, and coined the terms sadism and masochism, after the Marquis de Sade, famed for his violent sexual and political polemics, and Leopold von Sacher-Masoch, in whose novel *Venus in Furs* (1870) Severin, a stand-in for Sacher-Masoch, submits to Wanda who wears furs and beats and humiliates him at his request. Krafft-Ebing argued sadism resulted from "an innate desire to humiliate, hurt, wound, or even destroy others" for sexual pleasure. While Havelock Ellis pointed to sadomasochistic couples who were deeply in love, most sexologists agreed with Krafft-Ebing. More importantly as Michel Foucault notes, they won general acceptance of their categorizations of sexual activities as normal or pathological and placed sadomasochism firmly in the latter category.[3]

The volume of fetish and flagellation literature increased in the nineteenth century and spread to several general interest magazines. *The Englishwoman's Domestic Magazine*, in particular, opened its correspondence column to fetishists in the late 1860s and early 1870s. Readers engaged in faux debates over the values of tight-laced corsets, strict discipline and corporal punishment while relating fantasies of these and other BDSM activities. A generation later, *The Family Doctor* published a similarly flurry of BDSM content, as did *Photo Bits*. Between 1909 and 1912, *Photo Bits* "became thoroughly fetishized," running "a broader and more bizarre spectrum of fetishes than any previous magazine," which James Joyce noted in his novel *Ulysses* (1922). It featured regular fetish columns written by "the Amorist" and "Cosmopolite" whose topics included flagellation, female domination, tight-lacing, and satin and rubber fetishism. Both frequently referenced Krafft-Ebing.[4]

After the First World War, *London Life*, a "cheaply priced, lavishly illustrated magazine" appeared. At first glance, it differed little from similar racy magazines featuring movie studio publicity stills, photographs of art nudes and bathing beauties along with "gossip and fashion columns, racy fiction, and expository essays." Those with fetish interests, though, noticed *London Life*, catered to "readers of a limited taste," disproportionately featuring fetish content. It developed a worldwide following.[5]

London Life added a correspondence column in 1923 and afterward printed not just readers' letters, but also their stories, illustrations and photographs. Descriptions of "kink" activities filled growing pages, accounting for most of its content by 1939. While much of this involved corsets and tight-lacing, other popular topics included amputees, bondage, cross-dressing, female boxing and wrestling, flagellation, high heels, human ponies, lingerie, long hair, piercing, rubber, spanking, stockings and tattooing. "Advertisers in *London Life* reached a global market, offering corsets, high heels, personal portraits, birth control, photographs, and racy books." German bombing damaged *London Life's* warehouse and wartime paper shortages reduced its publishing schedule. In October 1941, its editors ended its correspondence column and fetish content disappeared from its pages.[6]

While Americans could purchase *London Life* at major city newsstands, most books and magazines featuring fetishism and sadomasochism sold under the counter. Nonetheless, publishers of flagellation and fetish literature, such as Gargoyle Press, advertised in pulp magazines. Issues of *Snappy Romance* contained ads for flagellant literature including *The Merry Order of St. Bridget, Tender Bottoms* and *A Scarlet Pansy*. Dorothy Spencer, reputedly a Tucson, Arizona housewife, advertised and sold her "Spencer Spanking Plan," which encouraged wives to discipline their husbands.[7]

Fetishists and sadomasochists searching for like-minded companions found them through vendors of fetish paraphernalia, carefully disguised personal ads in newspapers and magazines, and—if gay—in a handful of bars or bathhouses, such as New York's Everard and St. Marks baths, "the safest and most stable gay institutions" of the era.[8] Others patronized the few big city brothels that offered flagellation and related services. Charles Guyette, later famous as the "G-string King" for outfitting burlesque performers, proved an important point of contact for many American fetishists and sadomasochists.

Guyette sold high-heeled footwear and fetish costumes along with conventional lingerie and showgirl and burlesque costumes. He also sold erotic photographs, both his own work and photos he acquired from European producers.

Guyette advertised in *London Life*, and connected select clients and friends with one another, becoming the center of a growing network of fetishists and sadomasochists. Among them was Greg Day, a New York socialite who hosted elaborate BDSM parties in his home. Convicted in 1935 for mailing "obscene and lewd" fetish photographs, Guyette served a year in prison. On release, he focused on his clothing business, which flourished in the 1940s, earning him his nickname. With the exception of female boxing and wrestling, Guyette stopped selling photographs directly to customers. Instead, he licensed them to fetish publishers who reprinted them.[9]

William Moulton Marston, who created the *Wonder Woman* comic, purchased fetish clothing from Guyette. Marston once belonged to a small circle of BDSM enthusiasts and later played BDSM games with his partners Elizabeth Holloway and Olive Byrne for whom he purchased Guyette outfits. While fans praised *Wonder Woman* comics, critics derided them for what seemed an opulence of bondage. Frederick Wertham, in particular, singled out Wonder Woman in his anti-comics crusade, noting bondage, spanking and similar subjects accounted for a quarter of some issues' page count. Yet, *Wonder Woman* was not unique. Sadomasochists found much that titillated them in *Flash Gordon, Prince Valiant* and *Terry and the Pirates.*[10]

John Coutts and *Bizarre*

In 1946, John Coutts, a British merchant sailor, illustrator and photographer, launched the most influential post-war fetish and BDSM magazine, *Bizarre*. A *London Life* reader, Coutts moved to Sydney, Australia in the 1930s where he met other fetishists and sadomasochists, among them his future wife, Holly Anna Faram, whom he photographed in bondage and fetish attire. Working with McNaught's, a specialty shoe company that advertised in *London Life*, Coutts sold a photo catalog of women in high-heeled shoes and boots to customers throughout the English-speaking world. Some of his customers also wanted shoes, so for a time Coutts worked as a cobbler. This mail-order businesses connected Coutts with fetishists around the world, among them John Bringman, an American photographer and costume maker who worked with Guyette. Like many of its readers, Coutts wrote to *London Life*, which published some of his illustrations, though censoring the images by removing whips and chains. The editors rejected his letters extolling the joys of tying up women as too racy. Annoyed by *London Life's* limitations, Coutts determined to launch his own magazine, but the 1939 outbreak of World War II forestalled his plans.[11]

After the war, Coutts moved to Canada, where he published the first four issues of *Bizarre* before moving to New York. There, Bringman introduced him to Guyette and other fetishists and sadomasochists. They helped Coutts promote his photo business and connected him with publishers, including Robert Harrison who purchased Coutts' illustrations and comics. Coutts collaborated with several fetish photographers and publishers, but none of these business partnerships lasted long. A BDSM enthusiast who loved tying up women, Coutts was suspicious of anyone who entered the field solely for profit.[12]

In 1952, Harrison launched *Confidential*, the decade's leading celebrity gossip and scandal magazine. Before then, Harrison published a collection of cheesecake magazines, including *Beauty Parade, Eyeful, Titter, Wink* and *Whisper*. The post-war climate proved congenial to sexual topics. As Harrison faced growing competition, Edythe Farrell, his editor, encouraged him to read Karfft-Ebing, purchase costumes and props from Guyette, and experiment with fetish content. Before joining Harrison, Farrell edited *The Police Gazette* where she boosted circulation with sadomasochistic imagery.[13]

While never a dominant theme, and often presented as a humorous burlesque, fetish and sadomasochistic photographs and illustrations increased in Harrison's magazines: "girls in bondage, girls wrestling, and girls chained by their evil slave masters." Issues featured "Shackled Sirens," "Corset Cuties," "High Heel Honeys," "Booted Babes," "Dominant Damsels" and "Fighting Girls." *Titter's* December 1949 issue featured an illustration of a man spanking a woman, explaining "no matter how sweet and demure" they appear, "Babes Like it Rough!" Episodes of Coutts' "Adventures of Sweet Gwendoline" appeared in *Wink*. While this content boosted circulation, *Confidential* proved wildly successful. Profits soared, and Harrison shut down his cheesecake titles one by one.[14]

Coutts, whose business relationship with Harrison soured over late payments, relaunched *Bizarre* with issue 6 in 1951. A labor of love, Coutts produced most of its articles, illustrations and photographs. *Bizarre* was soon available on newsstands in major cities across the United States, and sold as many as 15,000 copies per issue. In its pages, Coutts discussed and illustrated a variety of BDSM fantasies, bondage positions, knots and more, exploring BDSM in more explicit detail than any of its predecessors or competitors. He always covered breasts and genitals, but provided detailed drawings of BDSM equipment and fetish costumes.

Coutts captioned some images of bound women with variations of the warning "don't let this happen to you, learn jiu-jitsu." This failed to fool critics, one of whom complained *Bizarre* was "filth," a magazine for "real, textbook type sadists, who can only achieve sexual satisfaction in the act of inflicting pain, preferably on helplessly bound, half-nude girls." Bookstores, he noted, displayed *Bizarre* "side-by-side" with "*The History of Flagellation, Sexual Perversion through the Ages*, and similar pseudoscientific books whose explicitly detailed passages are a joy and delight for the twisted minds of perverts." Association with this material, he warned, inevitably led to violent crime.[15]

Bizarre's readers wrote to share their adventures and fantasies, their letters and photos occupying growing space, and Coutts devoted two issues entirely to them. Some letters indicate *Bizarre* readers met one another, but no formal organizations developed from these encounters. One reader, an advertising executive who later adopted the name Fakir Musafar, wrote about his body modifications and rituals, which he termed "modern primitivism." Musafar wrote for several later fetish publications, developed a corset business, popularized body piercing, and became an important resource for San Francisco's BDSM community in the 1970s.[16]

Coutts proved a better artist and photographer than a publisher. He continued to sell illustrations and photographs through the mail to 5,000 customers, his "solid citizens," but producing a magazine on schedule overwhelmed him. Friends stepped in to help, and in 1956, Coutts sold *Bizarre* to one of them. Identified only as REB, he published six more issues of *Bizarre* before shutting it down in late 1959.[17]

Coutts moved to Los Angeles where he focused on photography and illustration. His mail-order business flourished. He shot and sold numerous new photo sets, as well as Sweet Gwendoline comics. Despite his cautious advertising, which avoided "bondage," "gag," "flagellation" and similar words, U.S. Postal Inspectors questioned him in May 1961. Fearing prosecution and recently diagnosed with brain cancer, Coutts shut down his business, destroyed his mailing list, negatives and other records, and moved to the United Kingdom where he died the following year.[18]

Thanks to his international contacts, Coutts proved an integrative figure, disseminating BDSM information and technique through *Bizarre*, his photo business, and extensive correspondence, which included American soldiers stationed in Japan. Coutts both influenced and was influenced by BDSM enthusiasts around the world, including Japan where *Kitan Club*, a bondage magazine, began publication in 1947. A friend stationed in Okinawa sent Coutts several of its issues, and *Bizarre* and *Kitan Club* influenced one another. More immediately, Coutts demonstrated a demand for BDSM and fetish content, on which other publishers capitalized, particularly Irving and Paula Klaw and Leonard Burtman.

Irving and Paula Klaw

In 1939, brother and sister Irving and Paula Klaw began selling movie stills, celebrity photos and pin-ups from their Manhattan bookstore. Paula's husband, Jack Kramer, joined the business, which they renamed Movie Star News. Unlike Coutts, the Klaws had no fetish or sadomasochistic interests. They simply responded to customer requests for photos of bondage and spanking, which they began selling in 1947. The Klaws purchased photos from Coutts, Guyette and others, but increasingly arranged their own photo shoots with models, many of whom also worked for Harrison. Guyette provided costumes. The Klaws also published comic serials by Eric Stanton, Gene Bilbrew and other artists, and short fiction booklets, accompanied by photos or illustrations.[19]

The Klaws advertised in Harrison's magazines and mailed detailed catalogs of their offerings to several thousand customers who, in turn, sent the Klaws suggestions for photo shoots. The 1948 catalogs offered photos of "Long, Long Hair Girls," "Silk Stocking and High Heel Poses," "Lingerie Models," "Girls in Extreme High Heels," "Curvaceous Corset Cuties," "Slave Girls" and "Dominant Female Sirens." Over time, the Klaws became more daring, offering "Specially

Posed Bound and Gagged Models," "Tightly Laced Corset Photos," "Girls Being Spanked" and "Fettered Poses." Cartoon serials included *Bound in Leather, Captives of Madame La Bondage, Mrs. Tyrants' Finishing School, Princess Elaine's Terrible Fate, Rubber Queen's Captives* and many others.

Between 1947 and 1964, the Klaws released about 350 short 8 mm and 16 mm films, 100 illustrated books and comics serials, and tens of thousands of photographs, making them the leading producers of fetish and bondage media. Many featured their favorite model, Bettie Page. Lauded by fans, one critic described her as a "sadist's delight," the "favorite pin-up in magazines appealing to fetishists and perverts." Page also appeared in the Klaws' two burlesque feature films, *Varietease* (1954) and *Teasarama* (1955). Headlined by Lili St. Cyr and Tempest Storm, two of the era's most popular burlesque performers, these avoided fetish content.[20]

The Klaws carefully censored their photos and illustrations. They eliminated nudity, covered up cleavage, and insisted models wear two pairs of underwear so no pubic hair showed. Unlike Harrison, they avoided overt suggestions of sexual activity and never posed women with men. Nonetheless, their large publishing operation attracted attention from both the government and Citizens for Decent Literature, an anti-pornography organization, which highlighted Klaw publications in its alarmist film *Perversion for Profit* (1964).

In 1950, the Post Office threatened to block the Klaws' mail. The Klaws stood firm, and the Post Office failed to execute its threat, but it successfully pressured magazines to reject their ads. Pressure mounted on the Klaws in 1955 when Senator Estes Kefauver formed his Subcommittee to Investigate Juvenile Delinquency. Kefauver assisted the Post Office by helping pass a law allowing obscenity prosecutions in the jurisdiction mail was received, rather than from which it was sent. This allowed prosecutors to file cases where community standards were less tolerant of sexual material. Compared to *Playboy*, which by the mid-1950s displayed topless women, the Klaws' offerings were demure, but their sadomasochistic content attracted government investigators. As one Texas postmaster declared, "almost all sex criminals prove to have a long record of obsession with pornographic and sadistic material."[21]

Irving Klaw exercised his Fifth Amendment right to avoid testifying to the Kefauver committee, which extended its mandate from juvenile delinquency and comic books to pornography, claiming adult titles fell into teenagers' hands. In 1956, the Post Office claimed the Klaws had sold more than a million dollars of pornographic material and began withholding mail addressed to their storefront address. Government prosecutions increased afterward, but Klaw successfully defended himself in court, in part because definitions of obscenity left the status of fetish and bondage content unclear. As one district attorney complained, the contents of *Bizarre* and similar magazines were "the filthiest material ever peddled," but they did not "come under the legal definition of pornography."[22]

Klaw also confused authorities by moving his mail-order operation to New Jersey and operating under different names, including Ikay Products, Jani Sales

Company and Nutrix. The latter became famous for illustrated story booklets, which often showed "an obsessional interest in mechanical detail," and a techno-fetishism for complex "instruments designed for torture and punishment."[23] Klaw was convicted in 1959, but the verdict was overturned on appeal. Convicted again on 18 March 1964 for "conspiring to use the U.S. mails to send obscene materials" (several Nutrix booklets), Klaw and Kramer, his co-defendant, again won on appeal. Nonetheless, the legal battles wore out the Klaws and made it difficult for them to pursue legal action against other fetish publishers like Edward Mishkin who plagiarized their books and magazines. They closed Nutrix, curtailed their other fetish operations, and burned many of their negatives. Irving died in 1966, but Paula continued operating Movie Star News. Like Guyette, she found it safer to sell bondage photographs to other publishers, whose reprints sustained Bettie Page's popularity.[24]

Finding BDSM Partners

Locating sexual partners who shared one's sadomasochistic interests proved difficult in the 1950s. The most reliable means were personal introductions or carefully coded personal ads. Business owners, including Guyette, Coutts and the Klaws, proved important points of contact and facilitated meetings between favored customers. The Klaws, in particular, maintained a dialog with their customers and benefitted from their experience. One of them, "Little John" (John Coutts was "Big John"), coached the Klaws in the intricacies of bondage and rope-tying, provided equipment and costumes, staged photo shoots, and introduced them to potential customers, artists and photographers.[25]

Samuel Steward, a literature professor who later wrote gay erotica as Phil Andros, cruised bars and bathhouses for sadomasochistic partners, but with limited success. Few men were interested in flagellation and even fewer enjoyed the heavy beatings Steward liked to receive and dish out. So, Steward sought out "rough trade," sex with working class men whose attitude towards homosexuals was so unclear "you never knew if you were going to get a blow job or get beaten up."[26]

Steward took serious risks, but only occasionally found a man who satisfied his sadomasochistic desires. In 1947, though, he answered an ad in the *Saturday Review of Literature*, which harkened back to corporal punishment letters in *Englishwoman's Domestic Magazine*. Placed by Hal Baron it read: "Should flogging be allowed? Ex-sailor welcomes opinions and replies."[27]

Baron introduced Steward to other men who answered his ads. Willing to dominate or submit as needed, Steward formed a growing network of gay sadomasochists. He hosted a BDSM orgy in his home in 1949 and 28 more over the next eight years. Steward was among the first to acquaint Alfred Kinsey with BDSM and sent the pioneering sexologist accounts of his sexual encounters and duplicates of home-made whips. In one memorable encounter, Steward beat a man, whipped him, twisted his nipples, clamped a wrench to the head of his penis, and "pissed in his mouth."[28] A perfectionist, Steward wrote outlines of

BDSM scenes he wished to enact, and presenting lists of his desires to potential partners. One of them, "What This Particular M Likes," read:

1 Please remember that he is your absolute slave.
2 Make him undress you.
3 Order him to take off your shoes and socks and kiss and lick your feet.
4 Make him suck your balls.
5 Piss in his mouth (a little, not too much, make him swallow it by holding your hand over his mouth and pinching his nose shut).
6 Make him swallow your come. (He may try to spit it out.)
7 Put dog collar on him. Pull him by leash.
8 It is not necessary YOU come every time. Make him jerk off in front of you.
9 Spit in his face.
10 Beat him in the face with your hard cock. Straddle his chest.
11 Talk mean and nasty to him. Call him a dirty cocksucker.
12 Wear dirty socks. Cram them in his mouth.
13 Give him a few whacks on the ass with your belt. Or use whip if one present.
14 Pinch his tits, or other tender spots.
15 Make him lie on the floor, and piss some on him.
16 Do NOT ask him to rim you (tongue in ass). Many M's are afraid of getting hepatitis this way or yellow jaundice.
17 Make him lick your armpits, the sweatier the better.
18 If you want to, make him give you a tongue-bath all over, or do whatever gives you pleasure.
19 In general, be as hard on him as want to be.
20 Remember, he is your ABSOLUTE slave![29]

A few other mainstream magazines, such as *Hobby Directory*, ostensibly a model railroad magazine covering various related hobbies, published coded personal ads, which used phrases like "leather and Levis" to indicate BDSM interests. The same was true of big city newspapers, such as the *New York Times* in which a gentleman who "liked to collect flags," actually sought flagellation.[30] The budding sadomasochist's best option, though, was *Justice Weekly*, a Canadian tabloid.

Launched in 1946 by Philip H. Daniels, *Justice Weekly* was available by subscription and on many North American newsstands. By the early 1950s, its 16 pages included personal ads, readers' letters, a gossip column, and lurid crime reports, its nominal subject matter. Its "morally conservative editorial stance" concealed provocative content. Oblique at first, sexual ads referenced "modern parties," "Greek Culture," "English Arts" and "subjects discussed in these pages." Ads from couples often suggested "weekend get-togethers." While *Justice Weekly's* lurid headlines condemned deviant sexuality, its readers' letters, like those of *Englishwoman's Domestic Magazine* a half century earlier, debated the pros and cons of spanking and corporal punishment.[31]

In the 1950s, Daniels expanded *Justice Weekly's* coverage of corporal punishment, "discipline," homosexuality, and other sexual topics outside the mainstream. By 1960, *Justice Weekly's* circulation exceeded 25,000. Ads filled a quarter of its pages. The majority of them—and many letters from readers—referenced cross-dressing, clothing fetishes, "discipline" (or similar euphemisms), swinging and other unorthodox sexual desires. Advertisers indicated they traveled widely, referenced interests in art, literature and theater, and otherwise signaled their comfortable socioeconomic status. Placed by men and women, gay and straight, fetish and BDSM sex ads became central to *Justice Weekly's* finances.

In 1962, one woman advertised for an athletic, "real he-man" who shared her interest in "Levis and leather." Other ads searched for people who were "broad-minded," "uninhibited," and interested in the "bizarre" and "exotic." None used the terms sadist, masochist, sadomasochism or any abbreviation for these, yet were nonetheless direct: "Widow of 35 experienced in corporal punishment and petticoat discipline would like to hear from gentleman of pleasing appearance and submissive nature. Have extensive wardrobe of restraint garments." Readers' letters described their sadomasochistic activities, which provoked ads from people interested in meeting them. Ads and letters became more explicit and focused on BDSM to such extent that by 1962, other personal ads explained they had "no interest in discipline."[32]

In the early 1960s, Nan Borrows (aka Mistress Nan) answered a *Justice Weekly* ad for "discipline devotees" and met a succession of people who shared her interests. So, too, did journalist Michael Leigh who described the swingers, sadomasochists and fetishists he met in his alarmist book, *The Velvet Underground.* Some *Justice Weekly* ads mentioned clubs for "discipline devotees," but these were likely professional dominatrices or similar commercial establishments, such as "Madame de Sade's" club, which claimed American and overseas members.[33]

New publishers steadily entered fetish and BDSM publishing in the 1950s, carefully crafting restrained magazines aimed directly at fetishists and sadomasochists with little traditional sexual content. Most avoided the breadth of *Bizarre*, instead targeting narrowly defined subgenres, such as cross-dressing, fetish clothing, high heels and female domination. They never mentioned sexual activity and kept breasts and genitals fully covered.

Photographer Leonard Burtman, financed by Benedict Himmel, proved the most successful of these. While a fetishist and sadomasochist himself, Burtman did not let personal interests distract from business. He displayed a better sense of the market than Coutts or the Klaws and produced a slew of narrowly targeted fetish and BDSM photo sets, magazines, illustrated booklets and 8mm films. The most popular in the late 1950s was *Exotique.* Subtitled "a new publication of the bizarre and unusual," *Exotique* celebrated fetish clothing and dominant women. In stories, illustrations and photos, its three-dozen issues repeated two themes: a woman dominating a man, often involving cross dressing, or a more experienced woman guiding a younger woman into the joys of fetish clothing. A member of Guyette's social circle, Burtman briefly worked as a photographer for the Klaws before striking out on his own. He collaborated with Coutts on a few photo shoots in 1953, and employed a number of artists and models who also worked for the Klaws, including Gene Bilbrew, Eric Stanton and Bettie Page. Burtman's social circle grew with his magazine empire and came to include a number of women who worked as professional dominants and appeared in his publications.[34]

Burtman built a mailing list of over 10,000 customers, offering content titillating enough to satisfy them, but sufficiently restrained to emerge victorious from obscenity prosecutions. Like the Klaws, Burtman used different business names and avoided nudity and showing men and women together. His legal team examined his magazines before publication and recommended changes, which he implemented. Burtman monitored the changing legal climate, and his BDSM magazines became more daring in the 1960s. Operating as Selbee Associates, he launched new magazines, including *Bizarre Life*, *Corporal*, *Connoisseur*, *Exotica*, *High Heels*, *New Exotique* and *Unique World*. The costumes became skimpier, but breasts and genitals remained covered until the decade's end when he introduced nudity to fetish publications.

Perhaps inspired by *Justice Weekly's*, Burtman's new magazines accepted personal ads. So, too, did *Fantasia*, published in Los Angeles by Lucian Press, and other competitors. Personal ads became common features in fetish and BDSM publications. Like *Justice Weekly*, they assigned advertisers code numbers and for a small fee forwarded letters to their intended recipients. Several newsletters specialized in BDSM contact ads, including *The Capricians*, *The Whipping Post* and *La Plume*, billed as "The Correspondence Medium Devoted to the Connoisseur of the Unusual." *La Plume* appeared as separate bimonthly U.S. and British editions with about 500 ads per issue. By the late 1960s, these included a few ads for small, informal gatherings of fetish enthusiasts, including a "rubber fashion and discipline club seeking new members." These ads were probably placed by professional dominants who often advertised their brothels as "clubs." For a time, *La Plume* sold specially crafted, tiger's eye pins to allow readers to recognize one another. There is no indication this proved successful.[35]

Dedicated fetish magazines with contact ads displaced *Justice Weekly*, which ceased publication in April 1972. These new publications facilitated contacts among sadomasochists who formed a growing network. Even those not answering ads learned from them. There were people around the world who shared their sexual interests. These ads also standardized common abbreviations: B&D (bondage and discipline), D&S (dominance and submission) and S&M (sadism and masochism).

The Emergence of Leathermen

Gay sadomasochists also connected through personal ads, but they developed other ways to find one another. Motorcycle films like *The Wild One* (1953), which starred Marlon Brando offered gay men a new sartorial aesthetic. Brando, who looked "so magnificent" in his black leather jacket, "sunglasses and leather cap cocked so rakishly over one eye that he quickly became the sullen mascot of the fledgling gay leather movement." These men adopted his outfit and hypermasculine image, which subverted "the prevailing stereotypes of effeminate homosexuals." Some formed motorcycle clubs, becoming the "saintly motorcyclists" Allen Ginsburg venerated in *Howl*. Brando's attire also influenced gay artists, particularly Tom of Finland (Touko Valio Laaksonen), whose work drew on World War II illustrations and posters of bare-chested soldiers and sailors. His iconic, heavily muscled men first appeared in physique magazines beginning with Bob Mizer's *Physique Pictorial* in 1957. Aimed at gay men, physique magazines pushed the bounds of censorship, portraying mostly naked men in increasingly erotic poses and situations. Gladiators, cowboys, lumberjacks and bikers featured prominently. Whips, chains and other sadomasochistic props crept into pictorials, as artists and photographers developed the leatherman's iconography.[36]

These leathermen adopted "biker styles" as "a way of articulating their particular outlaw forms of desire," and a subset of gay bars emerged catering to them. As anthropologist Gayle Rubin notes, leather was not synonymous with sadomasochism. Leather developed as a broader category that included "gay men who do S/M, gay men who are into fisting, gay men who are fetishists, and gay men who are masculine and prefer masculine partners." It became "a multivalent symbol" with "different meanings to different individuals and groups." As an identifying category for gay men, leather encompassed fashion (leather, Levis, western), sex (rough, raunchy and/or kinky) and community (motorcycle clubs, preferred bars and other hangouts).[37]

Most leathermen were not sadomasochists, but sadomasochists found leathermen's attire and habits congenial. They cruised the same bars and joined the same clubs. "The S&M crowd" gravitated to leather groups because they understood their desires. While not necessarily sharing them, neither were they shocked by them.[38]

Dress codes varied among bars and clubs, but all rejected traditional stereotypes of gay attire, which leathermen derided as "fluff." A sign at the Tool Box, San Francisco's premier leather bar, warned "no tennis shoes allowed." Fuzzy sweaters and polo shirts were also discouraged. Leather bars required "macho" attire, with leather, cowboy/western and uniforms particularly encouraged, though work boots, a t-shirt and button-fly Levi's were often sufficient. Wearing more leather came to indicate more seriousness and commitment. With rare exceptions, leather bars excluded women.

The first gay motorcycle club, the Satyrs, formed in Los Angeles in 1954. The concept spread slowly, first in California, where Oedipus (1958), The Warlocks (1960) and California Motor Club (CMC, 1963) formed. The concept spread in the 1960s. Empire City (1964) formed in New York, Border Riders (1969) in Seattle and the Rocky Mountaineers (1968) in Colorado. The latter's co-founder, Jim Kane, was a former Catholic priest and frequent sex partner of Samuel Steward. Numerous new clubs formed in the 1970s in the United States, Canada and Western Europe. By the mid-1970s, New York City alone had 14 gay motorcycle clubs. In the United Kingdom, MSC (Motor Sport Club) London grew to 400 members by 1974. The larger clubs organized runs, annual gatherings to which other clubs were invited, such as the CMC's Carnival, which attracted 10,000 men in 1977.[39] Larger events gave attendees commemorative pins or buttons. Worn on their vests, large collections of run pins became symbols of commitment and status.

The clubs adopted the trappings of mainstream motorcycle clubs, such as leather jackets or vests with a large patch of the club's logo (colors) displayed on the back, hence the term "backpatch club." They also adopted many of the practices of fraternal organizations, such as requiring potential members to petition to join, be sponsored by existing members, and undergo "pledge" periods. Leather attire (vests, chaps, caps and pants) became the norm for members who—even if not sadomasochists—enjoyed being associated with rough sex. The connection to motorcycles and leather was as much social as erotic—often more so. They fostered a "sense of camaraderie," which novelist John Rechy found "rare in other segments of the gay world." Sexual activities among members were mostly conventional. Demonstrating a combination of attraction and repulsion that complicated leathermens' relationships with the larger gay community, Rechy insisted that while their sexual activities ranged "from the power-oriented to the loving, even gentle," they were "not contingent on pain or gay humiliation" and "therefore outside the penumbra of S & M," which he derided.[40]

The first dedicated leather bars developed in New York and Los Angeles, followed by Chicago and San Francisco. They emerged as much through osmosis, as leathermen joined one another at favorite haunts, as they did from bar owners' intentions. Always few in number, the 1965 edition of Damron's Address Book listed almost 60 San Francisco gay bars, only three of which were leather.

Among the best-known leather bars in the early 1960s were The Stud in New York, Chicago's Gold Coast, and San Francisco's Tool Box. The latter opened in 1961. Frequented by members of the CMC, it was featured in 1964 in *Life* magazine. Gay rights activist and Mattachine Society member Hal Call arranged for *Life* to take photos there, hoping the bar's famous Chuck Arnett mural of cruising leathermen would counteract stereotypes of gay men as weak. In addition to the mural's two-page spread, *Life* offered several articles on San Francisco's gay community and a brief interview of Tool Box owner Bill Reque. While *Life* disparaged Reque's customers as "the far-out fringe of the gay world," its photos signaled aspiring leathermen that San Francisco, with its "brawny young men in their leather caps, shirts, jackets, and pants," was the place to be. Aspiring leathermen like Jack Fritscher read it "as an invitation to come to San Francisco and be a man's man."[41]

Two years earlier, *Confidential* explored the Arcade, a New York leather bar identified as the Raven in the article. A leather-clad doorman kept out those inappropriately dressed and the owner paid prostitutes to sit at the bar to deter police harassment. Little sexual activity took place in the bar, but the home of bar owner F. Oleson (aka "The Master") boasted a well-equipped room with "chains, leg irons, pins, racks, cat-o-nine tails, whips, sticks," and "lots of rope." The "greatest orgies" took place there. Oleson explained he was just one of a several New Yorkers hosting BDSM parties in well-equipped home dungeons. "There's always been folks into S&M." Among them were publisher Bob Milne and artist Mike Miksche, who drew sadomasochistic and leather art under the name Steve Masters.[42]

Miksche guided Kinsey though New York's BDSM scene, and Kinsey reciprocated by introducing Miksche to Sam Steward. The two allowed Kinsey to film their encounter in which Miksche, dressed in brown leather, beat Steward heavily before sex.[43] Kinsey assigned letter codes to the sexual activities his interviewees described: S for sadism, M for Masochism, etc. This may—through the agency of Miksche, Steward and other interviewees—have popularized the use of the abbreviations S, M and S&M among sadomasochists.

Charles Clark had his first sadomasochistic encounter in New York in the early 1950s with a man who picked him up at the Fawn Bar on West Street. He cruised Central Park and the bars, particularly Keller's, one of the first dedicated leather bars. Like other budding leathermen, he developed ways to signal his interests. By the 1960s, his favorite spot for sexual encounters was "The Trucks," the underpass of the West Side Highway near disused piers where commercial trucks parked at night. It became an active cruising ground with the back of unlocked trucks providing private space for flagellation and rough sex. Bars increasingly differentiated themselves, making his cruising easier. Men signaled interest with visible key chains or handcuffs carried in leather jacket epaulets. Several bathhouses became popular with leathermen, including St. Marks, which "had a reputation for heavy sex scenes," which discouraged "proper queens," and the Everard, which "was more acceptable because the S/M sex was done behind closed doors."[44]

In Chicago, Chuck Renslow operated Kris Studio, which published physique magazines and pictorials. After Steward introduced him to sadomasochism, its themes infiltrated *Mars, Rawhide* and other Kris magazines. In 1959, Renslow bought the Gold Coast bar and completed its transformation to a leather bar, altering its décor and employing leathermen whose attire signaled its preferred clientele. Renslow, who eventually operated a host of profitable bars, cabarets, gyms and bathhouses, became the center of a growing network of sadomasochistic gay men. These included several artists and writers including his lover and business partner, Dom Orejudos, a popular leather artist under the name Etienne. Travelers to Chicago called Renslow, who connected them with men who shared their sexual tastes.[45] While most cities lacked impresarios like Renslow, gay sadomasochists increasingly found one another in leather bars, baths and motorcycle clubs.

The Business of Sadomasochism

On 21 December 1965, Newark, New Jersey police raided the 16-room Victorian home of professional dominatrix Monique von Cleef, and arrested her.

Von Cleef's 2,000-name client list purportedly included high-placed government officials. She charged $50 for initial consultations and as much as $500 for full BDSM sessions involving elaborate role play, her specialty. Von Cleef's arrest made the cover of *Confidential*. Newspapers around the country covered the raid and trial in lurid detail, displaying photographs of von Cleef's home and the tools of her trade seized by the police: "chains used as restraining devices, including one bearing a legend on the metal face, 'Slave Samuel. Property of Monique;' several dildos; a leather paddle; a strait jacket; various types of belts; padded clothes and other devices," as well as BDSM books, equipment catalogs, films, magazines and photographs. Convicted, von Cleef served four months in prison for "conspiring to maintain a building for purposes of lewdness," committing "acts of lewdness," and possessing obscene publications.[46]

Four years later, the U.S. Supreme Court reversed her sentence, ruling the top-to-bottom search of her home unconstitutional because police lacked a search warrant. By then, von Cleef had returned to Amsterdam where she wrote her memoirs and continued to attract high-paying clients. Before leaving the United States, she presented BDSM demonstrations at Coke's, a San Francisco strip club.

Before coming to the United States, Von Cleef worked as a professional dominant in the Netherlands. On her arrival in 1963, she advertised her services in contact publications. She became friends with Burtman and appeared regularly in his magazines. Her ad in *La Plume*, accompanied by her photo, was short and to the point: "N.Y.C. Exotic Miss, 30 yrs. 36-26-36. Extremely interested in rubberwear, satin, French lingerie, discipline, etc.; Anxious to experiment. Will correspond with all. Write descriptively. Photo appreciated." Von Cleef's frequent ads and appearances in fetish publications, attracted the attention of postal inspectors who tracked her down and arranged for Newark police to raid her home. She was just one of dozens—probably hundreds—of dominatrices operating in American cities in the mid-1960s.[47]

Von Cleef's legal troubles highlighted those of another celebrated dominatrix, Mariella Novotny, "known on both sides of the Atlantic" as the "Mistress of Fetish." According to *Bizarre Life*, she controlled "an international ring of girls who are not allowed to refuse any form of deviation." At various times, Novotny worked as a stripper, brothel owner and professional dominant. She hosted celebrity sex parties in Britain, one of which, the "Man in the Mask" party, attracted media attention for the eponymous man, purportedly a British nobleman, who greeted guests at the door naked and was later tied between two posts and flogged. In 1961, New York police found Novotny's luxury apartment filled with "wall shackles, chains secured to the ceiling, handcuffs, leg irons," and various torture devices. Prosecution proved impossible, though, since she was overseas.[48]

Professional dominants worked in European brothels as far back as the sixteenth century, perhaps earlier. They were well established by the Victorian Era, and Herbert Spencer Ashbee recounted stories of several famous ones, including Theresa Berkeley. His *Index Librorum Prohibitorum* (1877) included an illustration of Berkeley's specially constructed spanking bench. By the turn of the century, many of London's professional dominants advertised their services as "massage parlors," and this subterfuge spread to the United States.[49]

When professional dominants first plied their trade in the United States is uncertain, but certainly before the 1920s. In 1936, police raided Dr. Anna Swift's 17-room Danish Massage Institute on West 70th Street in New York. They found a library of pornographic books and "whips and prison chains" used in strange "erotic rites." Emma Bond, her bookkeeper and phone operator for 11 years, described several customers including "a man we called 'Pig' who was regularly tied up." Other customers included "Red Gloves," "Nice Fish," "Sara," "Wolf" and "Edward." Swift's client book listed customers' proclivities and favorite "nurse," with whom Swift split their $20 fee. In contrast, "Jenny the Factory" earned as much as $200 for a flagellation session at her San Francisco "torture house." San Francisco police reported they found BDSM equipment in almost every house of prostitution they raided.[50]

Justice Weekly and BDSM contact magazines facilitated the careers of professional dominants who emerged as a distinct type of sex worker, selling sexual services, but withholding sex itself. Von Cleef, for example, offered to whip the undercover detective who later arrested her, but repeatedly refused him sex. Thanks to BDSM contact publications, professional dominants became well-known figures—even celebrities—in the BDSM press. The men who purchased magazines to find professional dominants and the dominatrices who advertised in them provided the bulk of their revenue. Xaviera Hollander, the era's "Happy Hooker," estimated ten percent of her clients were masochists seeking corporal punishment. Male hustlers reported similar ratios.[51]

Successful professional dominants developed networks of contacts, which overlapped those of fetish publishers. Burtman surrounded himself with dominant women, including Anne Laurence, a professional dominatrix who, like Von Cleef, advertised and appeared in his magazines. Her friend Jean Fisher posed for some of Coutts's illustrations.[52] Professional dominants taught BDSM skills to newcomers they hired, shared tips and referred clients to one another, developing national and even international contacts. These women, along with some male hustlers, offered another option for men seeking BDSM—men who generally kept their kinky activities secret from others in their lives.

The requirements of their businesses made professional dominants important customers for BDSM equipment and fetish clothing makers. Guyette retired around 1960, but businesses making and selling bondage gear and fetish clothing increased in number. Among the best known was Uncle Sam's Umbrella Shop. Along with umbrellas, its nominal specialty, it sold canes and whips, several of which had soft tails designed for use on people rather than animals. Von Cleef bought a whip from Uncle Sam's store on New York's west side shortly after arriving in the United States and became a regular customer. Most people, though purchased by mail, ordering from the store's brochures, which offered an "excellent selection of unique items not meant to hurt . . . merely frighten. Especially if the animals you are riding are in charge of the situation." These items included bullwhips, paddles, a cat-o-nine tails, and other "popular riding accessories" not generally applied to horses.[53]

Growing numbers of businesses catered to the interests of growing numbers of sadomasochists. On the West Coast, Discipline Supply in San Diego sold the finest, "handmade English canes." Fakir Musafar's H-G Specialty Company in Palo Alto made corsets for tight-lacing enthusiasts. Luis Avila, offered a complete line of leather goods, including high-heeled shoes and boots, corsets, hoods, whips and belts from his workshop in Guadalajara, Mexico. Several entrepreneurs operated fetish clothing stores from the back rooms of leather bars, such as Febe's in San Francisco where A Taste of Leather opened in 1966.[54]

Sadomasochism in Literature and Film

The Supreme Court steadily narrowed the definition of obscenity in a decade of successive rulings following the 1957 decisions in *Butler v. Michigan* and *Roth v. United States.* The latter upheld the convictions of both Samuel Roth, who published erotic classics (sometimes without permission) and David and Violet Alberts, a California couple who published bondage magazines. Perhaps, as historian David Allyn argues, the courts simply reflected changing attitudes and marketplace demand for erotica.[55] In *Butler,* the Court ruled against Michigan laws so restrictive they would restrict adults "to reading only what is fit for children." *Roth* required a work's "dominant theme taken as a whole" to appeal to "the prurient interest" of an "average person, applying contemporary community standards." This was a major change from the earlier *Hicklin* criteria. Based on *Queen v. Hicklin,* an 1868 British case, it considered works obscene, regardless of literary merit, if any part seemed likely to "deprave and corrupt" readers "whose minds are open to such immoral influences." After *Roth,* courts evinced a greater openness to sexual portrayals, particularly normative of heterosexual intimacy. While publishers of gay and sadomasochistic literature also won important victories, their path to legal acceptance was much more treacherous. Nonetheless, sadomasochistic erotica became easier to publish and purchase, and sadomasochistic themes spread to pulp novels, low-budget films and other media.

Post Office officials pushed back against the Court's permissiveness, promising a "war to the finish" against smut peddlers. Postal inspectors raided the offices of Chuck Renslow, H. Lynn Womack and other physique publishers. They "confiscated mailing lists," and searched them for other people to charge or coerce into testifying. Renslow was acquitted but Womack, publisher of *MANual,* was convicted in 1960. Womack appealed his case to the Supreme Court, which in *MANual Enterprises v. J Edward Day* (1962) issued its first ruling on physique publications. Justice John Marshall Harland, writing for the majority, declared them "tawdry," but not obscene or "patently offensive." The case established the legality of the gay physique pictorials, which flourished afterward, reaching monthly sales of 750,000 by 1965. Womack expanded into book publishing and published several of Steward's Phil Andros novels under his Guild Press imprint. Renslow and other publishers offered increasingly daring photos and illustrations, some of which hinted at sadomasochism with ropes, chains and whips in the background.[56]

In 1966 in *Memoirs v. Massachusetts*, the Supreme Court ruled the novel *Fanny Hill* did not meet the *Roth* standard. To be obscene, a work must fail all three principles articulated in *Roth*. It must appeal to prurient interest, be patently offensive, and "utterly without redeeming social value." Tom Lehrer celebrated the decision in his song "Smut." Yet, that same year the Supreme Court constrained this broad standard by sustaining a lower court ruling against Edward Mishkin for publishing *Swish Bottom, Mistress of Leather*, and *So Firm and Tightly Packed*. Material could be obscene if designed to appeal to the prurient interest of particular deviant sexual groups, in this case gay men and sadomasochists. Emboldened, police raided several physique publishers, which provoked Times Square pornographic booksellers to clear out titles depicting sadomasochism or fully nude men.[57]

These rulings created a legal environment through which gay and BDSM publishers stepped carefully. Rather than Justice Potter Stewart's famous 1964 declaration in *Jacobellis v. Ohio* that he knew pornography when he saw it, the Mishkin ruling expressed a consumerist understanding of pornography. Who purchased and was aroused by it mattered as much as what was shown. Most BDSM publishers already recognized this. For the courts, audience mattered as much as content. Scantily clad men with bulging muscles were fine in bodybuilding magazines, but not in one of Renslow's physique magazines. Similarly, a woman tied to a chair, her clothing disheveled to reveal large swaths of flesh, was fine for the covers of mass market novels or detective magazines, but not in one of Irving Klaw's photo booklets. Publishers remained careful, and many editions of *Fanny Hill* omitted the novel's two flagellation scenes.

Over the next several years, "the Court cleared every book that passed before it." In *Stanley v. Georgia* (1969), it established the right to own pornography and read it in the privacy of one's home. Yet, historians John D'Emilio and Estelle Freedman overstate matters to suggest this indicated "nothing warranted the label obscene." Rather, the court cleared books, but handled magazines, pictorial matter and movies differently. As D'Emilio and Freedman note, while "a gay subculture took root in American cities" in these years, "American society responded by raising the penalties that lesbians and gay men faced."[58] This included harassing gay magazine publishers. Sadomasochism was treated much the same. Books were acceptable, but not magazines or anything with pictures. These risked obscenity prosecution. Nonetheless, the courts could not simultaneously open the door to vanilla heterosexuality while repressing non-normative sexuality. The legal climate slowly improved for these publishers, as well.

In 1965, Grove Press published the first American edition of Paulene Reage's (Anne Desclos) *Story of O*. Before then, Americans wishing to read it either purchased it in Europe, or bought copies smuggled into the United States. Several

French publishers specialized in erotica for overseas markets, particularly Olympia Press, whose Traveler Series featured numerous sadomasochistic titles, including Diane Bataille's *Whip Angels* (1955) and *The Image* (1956) by Catherine Robbe-Grillet (writing as Jean De Berg). Robbe-Grillet became famous for the BDSM parties she hosted in Paris. Decades later they still "made *Fifty Shades of Grey* seem like a Disney movie." Olympia's most popular writer was Angela Pearson who wrote *The Whipping Club* and other flagellation novels.[59]

First published in France in 1954, *Story of O* follows the sadomasochistic romance of O who submits to increasingly heavy BDSM scenes at the hands of her lover Renée and his half-brother Sir Stephen. A stern master, he promised never to love O, yet she pines for him when they are apart. O wears a ring on her finger identifying her as sexually available to members of an elite, secretive BDSM society, Roissy, to which O is taken in the novel's opening. Afterward, O grants Renée and Sir Stephen the right to use

> her body however they wished, in whatever place or manner they should choose, the right to keep her in chains, the right to whip her like a slave or prisoner for the slightest failing or infraction, or simply for their pleasure.

O is beaten and humiliated, yet repeatedly challenges Sir Stephen to push their relationship to greater extremes. Her only respite is at Samois, an advanced training academy for submissive women run by Anne-Marie. There, O is beaten only once, as an initiation on her first night, though she is branded with Sir Stephen's initials before her departure.

Story of O, won the prestigious Prix de Deux Magots prize, created a brief sensation due to its female authorship, and became the best-selling contemporary French novel outside France.[60] Its American publication, historian David Squire argues, marked "the end of any coherent restrictive application of the concept of pornography to books," granting "mainstream audiences access to sexually explicit literature."[61] No American prosecutor pursued an obscenity case against *O*. Grove followed *O* with more sadomasochistic novels, and other publishers released a slew of cheap pulp novels on previously forbidden themes, particularly homosexuality and sadomasochism. New editions of Victorian Era stories were popular, as were pseudonymous works that imitated them, such as John Glassco's *Harriet Marwood, Governess* (1967). As the *New York Times* noted, sadomasochistic books became "large sellers."[62]

Many of these novels featured in sadomasochists' fantasies and inspired their BDSM role-play. William Carney's *The Real Thing* (1968), though, stood out among them. Over the course of this epistolary novel, its protagonist, an experienced BDSM master, teaches his young apprentice about the technical and psychological issues of constructing sadomasochistic scenes. In addition to lessons in technique, Carney offered readers precise guidelines in presenting themselves as leathermen. "Never wear a sweater." Never mix black and brown leather or bronze and steel adornments. Limit chains and other accessories. "Wear colors sparingly." Keep clothing snug. "Boots proclaim the man." "Never wear in daytime what ought to be seen only at night." Use belt buckles, keys and other "hardware" to signal intention: "left side is sinister, sadist, top man, teacher, master, shepherd, S; right is dexter, masochist, bottom man, bad boy, slave, mutton." Carney's book was an instruction manual in novel form. "For some people in the scene," anthropologist Edgar Gregerson noted, it achieved the "status of scripture."[63]

Despite its repeated warnings of the dangers of BDSM activities, and the apparent demise of the novel's narrator, Carney presented sadomasochism as not only hot, but the ultimate expression of male sexuality—the sex of "real men" who "channeled aggression," and "bypassed that asocial behavior of the normal run of queen, fairy, hustler, and hood." Sadomasochists were "a band of initiates who remain apart." Men for whom "the act of sex" was "merely the concluding benediction of an elemental rite" they "severely observed and mercilessly performed." Other gay BDSM novels followed in its wake, their publishers purchasing growing ad space in *The Advocate*.[64]

Sadomasochistic themes also spilled into mainstream literature. Robert E. Howard, famous for his Conan stories, had an extensive collection of books on flagellation, which featured in some of stories.[65] Mickey Spillane's character Mike Hammer, the era's most hardboiled detective, regularly encountered—and sometimes engaged in—sadomasochism. In *One Lonely Night* (1951), Spillane's fourth novel, Hammer seduces and later whips a treasonous heiress working for "the Reds." Hammer's communist enemies, in turn, capture, strip, bind and whip Hammer's trusty secretary Velda. He rescues her just in the nick of time. In his previous novel, *Vengeance is Mine* (1950), Hammer similarly found Velda hanging by her wrists naked while the villain whipped her.

Ian Fleming's James Bond trumped all other manly heroes for sadomasochistic content. In *Casino Royale* (1953), his first Bond novel, the villainous Le Chifre, a "flagellant" tortures Bond, whose female partner is captured by having her skirt thrown up and tied around her arms, a technique from Coutts' *Bizarre* magazine. In *From Russia With Love* (1957), which U.S. President John F. Kennedy described as one of his favorite books, Bond's partner, Darko Kerim, recounts how he kept a woman captive, tied under his table, feeding her scraps until she fell in love with him—a scenario adopted by BDSM pornography. Enough of Fleming's sadomasochism transitioned to film for reviewer Richard Whitehall to describe *Dr. No* (1962), the first Bond film, as "the headiest box-office concoction of sex and sadism ever brewed in a British studio" and "the perfect film for a sadomasochistic society"—criticisms previously aimed at Fleming's novels.[66]

Sadomasochists themselves, Fleming and his wife Ann, discussed their BDSM play in steamy letters Ian warned her to keep hidden. Ann longed for Ian to whip her, writing "I love being hurt by you and kissed afterwards."[67] Fleming, in turn, increased the sadomasochistic content of his Bond stories. In "007 in New York" (1963), Bond considers going to a bar that is a "rendezvous for sadists and masochists of both sexes." He knows the dress code: "black leather jacket and leather gloves. If you were a sadist, you wore the gloves under the left shoulder strap. For the masochists it was the right." While waiting for his target to appear in "The Living Daylights" (1962), Bond reads a pornographic novel chosen for its "spectacular jacket of a half-naked girl strapped to a bed." In *Her Majesty's Secret Service* (1963), when Bond first meets Contessa Teresa di Vicenzo, his future wife, "their eyes met and exchanged a flurry of masculine/feminine master/slave signals."

Perhaps inspired by Leonard Burtman, whose brief flirtation with feature filmmaking began (and ended) with *Satan in High Heels* (1962), sexploitation filmmakers discovered sadomasochism. Burtman's film played in drive-ins across the United States, but apart from the protagonist's provocative outfits and sexual manipulation of men, it lacked sadomasochistic content. Other filmmakers proved more daring.

In 1964, producer George Weiss and director Joseph Mawra made *White Slaves of Chinatown* (1964). It starred Audrey Campbell as Olga Petroff, a cruel, drug dealing communist brothel owner who exploited, whipped and tortured numerous women along with the occasional man. It proved so popular they made and released *Olga's House of Shame* and *Olga's Girls* that same year. Campbell's portrayal attracted adoring fans and inspired imitators who produced *Body of a Female* (1964), *Tortured Females* (1965), *Maidens of Fetish Street* (1966), *Invitation to Ruin* (1967), *The Bizarre Ones* (1968), *The Ultimate Degenerate* (1969) and two more Olga films: *Madame Olga's Massage Parlor* (1965) and *Olga's Dance Hall Girls* (1969). Joe Sarno, perhaps the best-known sexploitation filmmaker, featured sadomasochism in several films, as did Jess Franco, a popular European director whose titles often referenced sadomasochistic literature: *Marquis de Sade: Justine* (1968); *Venus in Furs* (1968); and *Eugenie, The Story of Her Journey into Perversion* (1968). Unlike Klaw's starlets, who "paddled each others' bottoms daintily," Franco's villainous dominatrices "laid on the whip with a wicked vindictiveness."[68]

Several rock groups referenced sadomasochism in their music, including the New York Dolls' "Red Patent Leather," The Vibrators' "Whips and Furs," and "Venus in Furs" by The Velvet Underground, a group named for the alarmist novel. In 1969, sadomasochism entered the theater with *Oh! Calcutta!* The play featured two extended bondage scenes, which *Bondage Life* magazine described in rapturous detail. BDSM had finally made the big time. *Newsweek* magazine declared the play's nudity proof America was finally becoming sexually liberated.[69]

Apart from an occasional spanking scene, such as those delivered by John Wayne in *Donovan's Reef* (1963) and *McLintock* (1963)—both regularly praised by spanking aficionados—sadomasochism remained confined to sexploitation films and a few underground films, such as Kenneth Anger's *Scorpio Rising* (1963), which fetishized bikers and leathermen. Two notable exceptions, both produced in Europe, were the British television show *The Avengers* (1963–68) and French director Roger Vadim's *Barbarella* (1968). The latter's plot resembles those of Klaw's Nutrix serials, particularly the finale in which Barbarella (Jane Fonda), captured by villainous Durand, is put through her paces in a number of mechanistic torture devices, culminating in the "Exsexive Machine," which shorts out thanks to her superheroic orgasmic capacity.

The Avengers became famous for the tight leather outfits worn frequently by its first female lead, Honor Blackman (1962–64), and less often by her successor Diana Rigg (1965–68). Both were frequently tied up by villains. The Blackman episodes did not air in the United States until many years later, but Blackman, a "leather-clad fury" in "leather breeches and jerkin and high black boots" outlining her figure "like no other material," received voluminous mail from British fans. These fans, she said, made her an expert on "the kinks," a notoriety she and co-star Patrick MacNee poked fun at by recording the song "Kinky Boots." American broadcasters refused to air Rigg's most fetishistic episode, "A Touch of Brimstone," in which she appeared in a leather corset, spiked collar, high heels, and little else. British censors allowed it to air, but deleted a 38-second scene in which the villain lashed Rigg with a bullwhip. Later episodes shied away from such overt sadomasochism, put provided enough fetishistic titillation that sadomasochists remembered them fondly year later.[70]

***

While Kinsey's data complications indicated as many as ten percent of men and women fantasized about BDSM activities, most experts did not welcome BDSM as a sexual practice. Several contemporary sex manuals encouraged explorations stretching traditional sexual boundaries, but drew the line at sadomasochism.[71] *The Sensuous Woman* (1969), whose author found oral sex "delicious," warned readers to "get professional help" if boyfriends exhibited interests in bondage or wanted "to resort to whips and chains."[72] Erwin Goldstein and Martin Haeberle in *Sex Book: A Modern Pictorial Encyclopedia* (1971) and David Reuben in his best-selling *Everything You Wanted to Know About Sex* (1969) issued similar, though somewhat contradictory, warnings. Reuben dismissed most heterosexual sadomasochists as "timid" and unable to "obtain gratification from grownup sex." They were "harmless folks who have fun with each other." Despite "the whips, belts, ropes, and leg irons," rarely did anyone get hurt. "If they did, they wouldn't come back next week for more games." Only a "rare few" were "rapist-murderers" intent on "killing and mutilating their victims," but they had "no relationship emotionally to the part-time, week-end sadist/masochist."[73]

Reuben provided no means of distinguishing the two and placed all gay sadomasochists in the dangerous category. They thrived on danger and it was "part of their sexual ritual." While murder was exceptional, "assault, robbery, and blackmail" were common among gay sexual partners. Yet, even these danger-seeking men feared the "subcategory of homosexual known as the 'S and M.'" Only a rare few would "knowingly pick up an 'S and M'" for sex. These "S and M" men, Reuben warned, were "among the cruelest people who walk this earth." In the past, they worked "as professional torturers and executioners. More recently they filled the ranks of Hitler's Gestapo." They specialized in "luring other homosexuals to their apartments, trapping them, and torturing them." Thankfully, "fear of arrest and punishment" kept most of them in line.[74]

As these warnings indicate, increasing tolerance for BDSM publications did not lead to tolerance for sadomasochists as a group. Medical and legal authorities routinely condemned them. While prosecutions of BDSM publishers declined in the 1960s—and those prosecuted were often acquitted—the same was not true of sadomasochists themselves. Police regularly raided professional dominants, arresting them and the occasional client. They also arrested people engaged in non-commercial BDSM activities. In 1967, California court convicted Marvin Samuels, a friend of Kenneth Anger, for assault based on a film showing him whipping another man. That man had responded to an ad Samuels placed and consented to both the filming and whipping. Samuels appealed, claiming both consent and his intention to send the film to the Kinsey Institute, but judges held "consent of the victim" was not a legitimate defense "to assault or battery, except in a situation involving ordinary physical contact or blows incident to sports such as football, boxing or wrestling." BDSM activities fell outside those categories. After all, one noted, "it is a matter of common knowledge that a normal person in full possession of his mental faculties does not freely consent to the use, upon himself, of force likely to produce great bodily injury." Someone who did was not sane and the insane lack the self-awareness to consent.[75]

The ruling's twisted logic rested on legal definitions that, as Gayle Rubin argued, held sexual activities to a different standard and penalized them. It was exceptionally rare for a sadomasochistic scene to produce the level of injuries common in boxing matches or football games. Yet, boxers and football players were sane while sadomasochists were not.[76]

Nonetheless, Kinsey's sex surveys helped shift "public discourse from justifying or repressing sexual behavior on the basis of religious edicts or medical advice to statistical distribution." If enough people engaged in particular sexual acts, Kinsey argued, their behavior should be considered normal and natural.[77] This became a touchstone for later BDSM activists who worked to normalize sadomasochism by pointing to sex surveys indicating many Americans engaged in BDSM, the tropes of which were so well known that Tom Lehrer lampooned them in "The Masochism Tango" (1960), describing, burning, piercing, trampling, whipping and marking a submissive with the dominant's initials. Condemned by the courts and medical professionals, most sadomasochists feared exposure, social censure and prosecution. They kept their activities secret.

Yet, enough sadomasochists sought out others for networks among them to flourish and grow in the 1950s and 1960s. Contact publications, professional dominants, leather bars and business owners helped BDSM enthusiasts connect, building networks crisscrossing the nation and extended into other countries. As a result, people with BDSM interests slowly developed from consumers of BDSM publications, clothing and equipment to a community with shared interests, values and political objectives. While Samuel Steward celebrated the outlaw nature of BDSM and complained to friends about the institutionalization of its culture, his was a lonely voice.[78] The increasing connectedness of sadomasochists in the 1960s provided the foundation for a specialized literature focused on their needs and the emergence of distinct BDSM organizations, and an increasingly public BDSM community, in the 1970s.

Notes

1 Eric Kroll, *The Complete Reprint of John Willie's Bizarre* (Koln: Taschen, 1995). *Bizarre*'s first issue was actually numbered "two" to establish the pretense of a successful publication.
2 Martin Meeker, *Contacts Desired: Gay and Lesbian Communications and Community, 1940s–1970s* (Chicago, IL: University of Chicago Press, 2006), 1.
3 Krafft-Ebing, *Psycopathia Sexualis* (New York: Stein & Day, 1965), 53; Havelock Ellis, *Love and Pain* (1903); and Michel Foucault, *The History of Sexuality, Volume 1* (New York: Vintage, 1978), 57.
4 Margaret Beetham, "'Natural but Firm': The Corset Correspondence in The Englishwoman's Domestic Magazine," *Women: A Cultural Review* 2, no. 2 (1991), 163–7; David Kunzle, *Fashion and Fetishism: Corsets, Tight-Lacing and Other Forms of Body Sculpture* (Phoenix Mill: Sutton Publishing, 2004), 160–1, 169–74, and 197–8; Valerie Steele, *The Corset: A Cultural History* (New Haven, CT: Yale University Press, 2003), 88–93; and Robert Vincent Bienvenue, "The Development of Sadomasochism as a Cultural Style in the Twentieth-Century United States" (PhD Dissertation, Indiana University, 1998), 45–50.
5 Kunzle, *Fashion and Fetishism*, 212 and G. Latimer, "Appeal to Silent Readers," *London Life*, 24 August 1935, 26, quoted in Lisa Z. Sigel, "Fashioning Fetishism from the Pages of 'London Life'," *Journal of British Studies* 51, no. 3 (July 2012), 668.
6 J.B. Rund, *Possibilities: The Photographs of John Willie* (New York: Belier Press, 2016), 16–8, and 442; Sigel, "Fashioning Fetishism," 665 and 670; and Kunzle, *Fashion and Fetishism*, 208.
7 Peter Haining, *The Classic Era of the American Pulp Magazine* (London: Prion, 2000), 98; Jay Gertzman, *Bookleggers and Smuthounds: The Trade in Erotica, 1920–1940* (Philadelphia: University of Pennsylvania Press, 1999), 75–6; and Dorothy Spencer to Lenora Frost, 28 September 1940, Vertical File, Sadomasochistic Erotica Producers, Kinsey Institute for Research in Sex, Gender, and Reproduction Archives (hereafter Kinsey Institute).
8 George Chauncey, *Gay New York: Gender, Urban Culture, and the Making of the Gay Male World, 1890–1940* (New York: Basic Books, 1995), 223–4.
9 Bienvenue, "Development of Sadomasochism," 71–8, 89, 97–9; Rund, *Possibilities*, 189; and Richard Pérez Seves, *Charles Guyette: Godfather of American Fetish Art* (New York: CreateSpace, 2017), 144–53.
10 Jill Lepore, *The Secret History of Wonder Woman* (New York: Vintage, 2015), 118–9; Tim Hanley, *Wonder Woman Unbound: The Curious History of the World's Most Famous Heroine* (Chicago, IL: Chicago Review Press, 2014), chapters 5 and 6; Pérez Seves, *Charles Guyette*, 153–5; and Harold Cox, "Review of My Private Life: Real Experiences of a Dominant Woman," *Checkmate* 12 (August 1995), 4.
11 Rund, *Possibilities*, V–VII, 16 and Bienvenue, "Development of Sadomasochism," 76 & 89–91.
12 Rund, *Possibilities*, 17 and 182 and Seves, *Charles Guyette*, 154.
13 Samuel Bernstein, *Mr. Confidential: The Man, His Magazine & the Movieland Massacre That Changed Hollywood Forever* (New York: Walford Press, 2006), 17–9 and 30–1 and Seves, *Charles Guyette*, 148 & 152.
14 Henry E. Scott, *Shocking True Story: The Rise and Fall of Confidential, "America's Most Scandalous Scandal Magazine"* (New York: Pantheon, 2010), 15–7 and Rund, *Possibilities*, VIII and 182.

15 Julia Pine, "In Bizarre Fashion: The Double-Voiced Discourse of John Willie's Fetish Fantasia," *Journal of the History of Sexuality* 22 (January 2013), 1–33 and "You Can't Print that Stuff in a Magazine," *Behind the Scene*, May 1956, 56–8, Sadomasochism Clipping File, Kinsey Institute.
16 Kroll, *John Willie's Bizarre*; John Willie, *The Adventures of Sweet Gwendoline*, 2nd ed. (New York: Belier Press, 1999), V-XII and 20–4; and Bienvenue, "Development of Sadomasochism," 89–97, 100–1, 161–4.
17 Rund, *Possibilities*, 187–9 and 232–5; Kroll, *John Willie's Bizarre*; and Willie, *The Adventures of Sweet Gwendoline*, V–XII and 20–4.
18 Rund, *Possibilities*, 232–5.
19 Rund, *Possibilities*, 17 and 182–3; *Cartoon and Pin-Up Parade* 48, Kinsey Institute; and Bienvenue, "Development of Sadomasochism," 106–8 & 145–7.
20 J.B. Rund, *Bizarre Comix 2* (New York: Belier Press, 1976); "Interview with Paula Klaw," *The Irving Klaw Years, 1948–1963* (North Hollywood, CA: Harmony, 1976), 9–14 & 54–6; and "You Can't Print that Stuff in a Magazine," *Behind the Scene*, May 1956, 27 & 57, Sadomasochism Clipping File, Kinsey Institute.
21 Bienvenue, "Development of Sadomasochism," 150–3 and David A. Johnson, *Buying Gay: How Physique Entrepreneurs Sparked a Movement* (New York: Columbia University Press, 2019), 137.
22 Rund, *Bizarre Comix 2*, 1–2; "Dealer's Mail Blocked," *New York Times*, 17 July 1956, Sadomasochism Clipping File, Kinsey Institute; and "You Can't Print that Stuff in a Magazine," *Behind the Scene*, May 1956, 27, Sadomasochism Clipping File, Kinsey Institute.
23 Maurice North, *The Outer Fringe of Sex: A Study in Sexual Fetishism* (London: Odyssey Press Ltd, 1970), 140.
24 Rund, *Bizarre Comix 2*, 1–2; "Klaw vs. United States of America," Irving Klaw Vertical File, Kinsey Institute; "You Can't Print that Stuff in a Magazine," *Behind the Scene*, May 1956, 27 & 54–57, Sadomasochism Clipping File, Kinsey Institute; Bienvenue, "Development of Sadomasochism," 150–60, 214, & 217; and Gilliam Freeman, *The Undergrowth of Literature* (London: Nelson, 1967), 2.
25 Rund, *Possibilities*, XV and Bienvenue, "Development of Sadomasochism," 106.
26 Justin Spring, *Secret Historian: The Life and Times of Samuel Steward, Professor, Tattoo Artist, and Sexual Renegade* (New York: Farrar, Straus and Giroux, 2010), 59.
27 Samuel M. Steward, "Dr. Kinsey Takes a Peak at SM: A Reminiscence," in Mark Thompson (ed), *Leatherfolk: Radical Sex, People, Politics, and Practice* (Boston, MA: Alyson, 1991), 83.
28 Spring, *Secret Historian*, 59–60, 102–3, 117, 130, & 139–40.
29 Spring, *Secret Historian*, 288–9.
30 Meeker, *Contacts Desired*, 23–5 and Gayle S. Rubin, "Valley of the Kings: Leathermen in San Francisco, 1960–1990," PhD diss., University of Michigan, 1994, 91–2.
31 Mary Alison Jacques, "Justice Weekly: The Story of a Canadian Tabloid," PhD diss., McGill University, 2014, 7, 18, 59, & 85–90.
32 *Justice Weekly*, 29 September 1962, 7; Rubin, "Valley of the Kings," 92–4; Freeman, *Undergrowth of Literature*, 170–4; and Jacques, "Justice Weekly," 59, 141, 144–7.
33 Mistress Nan, *My Private Life: Real Experiences of a Dominant Woman* (Los Angeles, CA: Daedalus, 1995), 15–22; Edward Shorter, *Written in the Flesh* (Toronto: University of Toronto Press), 217; Federman, *Undergrowth of Literature*, 58; and Michael Leigh, *The Velvet Underground* (New York: MacFaddan Books, 1963).
34 Kim Christy, *The Complete Reprint of Exotique: The First 36 Issues* (Cologne: Taschen, 1998); Rund, *Possibilities*, 186; and Bienvenue, "Development of Sadomasochism" 167–9.
35 Gerald and Caroline Greene, *S-M: The Last Taboo: A Study of Sado-Masochism* (New York: Grove Press, 1974), 139–41; Gerhard Falk and Thomas S. Weinberg, "Masters, Slaves, and Bitch-Goddess Classes: The Social Organization of Sadists and

Masochists," unpublished paper, 1978, Kinsey Institute; and North, *The Outer Fringe of Sex*, 95–98, and 112, footnote 4.

36 Daniel Harris, *The Rise and Fall of Gay Culture* (New York: Ballentine, 1997), 181; F. Valentine Hooven, Durk Dehner, and S. R. Sharp, *Tom of Finland: Life and Work of a Gay Hero* (Berlin: Bruno Gmünder, 2012); and Taylor, "Looking for Mr. Benson," 125.

37 Rubin, "Valley of the Kings," 28–9 and Gayle S. Rubin, *Deviations: A Gayle Rubin Reader* (Duke University Press Books, 2011), 308.

38 Joe Parisi, "Stereotyping," *The Advocate*, 27 August 1975, 26–7.

39 Rubin, "Valley of the Kings," 252–3; "NYC Bike Clubs," *Drummer* 16 (1977), 75; "The Leather Scene," *SMG News*, September 1974, 4 and "CMC Carnival," *Drummer* 20 (1977), 74–7.

40 Peter Hennen, *Faeries, Bears, and Leathermen: Men in Community Queering the Masculine* (Chicago, IL: University of Chicago Press, 2008), 135 and John Rechy, *The Sexual Outlaw: A Documentary* (New York: Grove Weidenfeld, 1977), 254.

41 "Homosexuality in America," *Life*, 26 June 1964, 66–80; Fritscher, "Artist Chuck Arnett" in Thompson, *Leatherfolk*, 107; Meeker, *Contacts Desired*, 159, 170–3, and 221; and Rubin, "Valley of the Kings," 197.

42 Lenny George, "Tattle-Tape Goes to a 'Suffer Club', America's Strangest Sin Club," *Confidential*, February 1962, 28–30 & 64–8, Sadomasochism Clipping File, Kinsey Institute; Robert Watson Wood, *Christ and the Homosexual: Some Observations* (New York: Vantage Press, 1960), 33–4; and Rubin, "Valley of the Kings," 98.

43 Steward, "Dr. Kinsey Takes a Peak at SM" in Thompson, *Leatherfolk*, 85–6 and Spring, *Secret Historian*, 139–43.

44 W. Charles Clark, "Stonewall and the S/M-Leather Lifestyle 2: Growing up in the Gay S/M Scene in the 1950s" *Checkmate* 14 (February 1996), 8–9, 19: and Clark, "Stonewall and the S/M-Leather Lifestyle 3: The Brambles, the Baths, the Bars, and the Trucks," *Checkmate* 15 (May 1996), 8–9 & 18.

45 Rubin, "Valley of the Kings," 416; Bienvenue, "Development of Sadomasochism," 255–7; Tracy Baim and Owen Keehnen, *Leatherman: The Legend of Chuck Renslow* (Chicago, IL: Prairie Avenue Productions, 2011), 75–6 & 87–9; Spring, *Secret Historian*, 274–7; Joe Parisi, "Chicago's Renslow," *The Advocate*, 2 June 1976, 41–3; Lawrence Mass, "Coming to Grips with Sadomasochism," in Weinberg and Kamel, *S and M: Studies in Sadomasochism* (New York: Prometheus, 1983), 46; and Joseph Bean, *International Mr. Leather: 25 Years of Champions* (Las Vegas, NV: Nazca Plains, 2004), 15.

46 Monique Von Cleef, *House of Pain* (Secaucus, NJ: Lyle Stuart, Inc, 1973), 160–2; *Monique von Cleef v. New Jersey*, 395 U.S. 814 (89 S.Ct. 2051, 23 L.Ed.2d 728), 23 June 23, 1969; *New Jersey v. Monique von Cleef and James Albert Beard*, 102, Superior Court of New Jersey (245 A.2d 495), 2 July 1968; and *Confidential*, April 1966.

47 Bizarre Life 1, no. 1 (1966); *Monique von Cleef v. New Jersey*, 395 U.S. 814 (89 S.Ct. 2051, 23 L.Ed.2d 728), 23 June 23, 1969; and *New Jersey v. Monique von Cleef and James Albert Beard*, 102, Superior Court of New Jersey (245 A.2d 495), 2 July 1968.

48 Jordan Johnson, "'Kinky:' Britain's Perverted Set," *Bizarre Life* 1, no 1 (1966), 43–5.

49 Ian Gibson, *The Erotomaniac: The Secret Life of Herbert Spencer Ashbee* (London: Faber & Faber, 2001), 45–7 and Havelock Ellis, "Love and Pain," *Studies in the Psychology of Sex* 1 (London: William Heinemann, 1942), 131.

50 "Massage Girl Bares Strange Rites at Trial," *New York Daily News*, 18 November 1936; "Man tied to Clothes Rack, Fees of $20 per Visit Revealed," *New York American*, 21 November 1936, and Ivan Kamilov, "Cult of the Lash," *Crime Detective* 1, no. 4 (March 1939), 98, all in Sadomasochism Clipping File, Kinsey Institute.

51 Grumley, *Hard Corps: Studies in Leather and Sadomasochism* (New York: E.P. Dutton, 1977), Chapter 8.

52 Anne O. Nomis, *The History & Arts of the Dominatrix* (Basingview: Da Vinci House, 2013), 141–4.

53 Howard Becker, *Outsiders: Studies in the Sociology of Deviance* (New York: Free Press, 1963), 20–1, 31; Haining, *The Classic Era of the American Pulp Magazine*, 98; Uncle Sam's Umbrella Shop brochure, circa 1964, Sadomasochism file, Kinsey Institute; Bienvenue, "Development of Sadomasochism," 71—8, 97–9; and Von Cleef, *House of Pain*, 159.
54 "Discipline Supply," *Fantasia* 12 (undated, circa 1960), 49; The Ol' Corsetier, "On the Art and Practice of Corsetry," *Fantasia* 17 (circa 1962), 8–11, & 36; Louis Avila ad, *Fantasia* 13 (undated, circa 1961), 54; and Rubin, "Valley of Kings," 283–4.
55 David Allyn, *Make Love, Not War* (New York: Routledge, 2001), 60–2 & 243.
56 Johnson, *Buying Gay*, 131–2, 137, & 162–8 and John D'Emilio, *Sexual Politics, Sexual Communities: The Making of a Homosexual Minority in the United States, 1940–1970* (Chicago: University of Chicago Press, 1983), 136.
57 Baim and Keehnen, *Leatherman*, 258; Spring, *Secret Historian*, 316–7; Joseph W. Slade, *Pornography in America* (Denver, CO: ABC-CLIO, 2000), 71 & 152; and Johnson, *Buying Gay*, 204–5.
58 John D'Emilio and Estelle B. Freedman, *Intimate Matters: A History of Sexuality in America*, 3rd ed. (Chicago, IL: University of Chicago Press, 2012), 287–8.
59 John De St. Jorre, *Venus Bound: The Erotic Voyage of the Olympia Press* (New York: Random House), 66–7 and Toni Bentley, "The Thin End of the Whip," *Vanity Fair*, 22 January 2014 at https://www.vanityfair.com/culture/2014/02/catherine-robbe-grillet-french-dominatrix (accessed 17 May 2020).
60 John De St. Jorre, "The Unmasking of O," *New Yorker*, 1 August 1994, 42–50.
61 Eliot Fremont Smith, "The Uses of Pornography," *New York Times*, 2 March 1966, 39 quoted in David Squires, "Pornography in the Library," 78–9 in Tim Dean, et al. (eds.), *Porn Archives* (Durham, NC: Duke University Press, 2014).
62 Paul Montgomery, "Panic in Dirty Books," *New York Times*, 27 March 1966, 193.
63 William Carney, *The Real Thing* (New York: Putnam, 1968), 48–9 and Edgar Gregerson, "The Sadomasochistic Scene," Paper presented at the American Anthropological Association, New Orleans, 1969.
64 Carney, *The Real Thing*, 35 and Rodger Streitmatter, *Unspeakable: The Rise of the Gay and Lesbian Press in America* (Boston, MA & London: Faber and Faber, 1995), 104.
65 REH Bookshelf at http://www.rehupa.com/bookshelf_app2.htm (accessed 5 July 2010).
66 James Chapman, *License to Thrill: A Cultural History of the James Bond Films* (London: I.B. Tauris, 2008), 87 & 90 and Bernard Bergonzi, "The Case of Mr. Fleming," *Twentieth Century*, March 1958, 220–8.
67 Sotheby's, "Ian Fleming's Love Letters Written to his wife, Ann" at https://sothebys.gcs-web.com/static-files/41531bdc-aba3-4561-9502-3263fa02b530 (accessed 1 May 2020).
68 Eddie Muller and Daniel Faris, *Grindhouse: The Forbidden World of "Adults Only" Cinema* (New York: St. Martins, 1996), 101–2.
69 Allyn, *Make Love, Note War*, 123 and Steven Allen, *Cinema, Pain and Pleasure: Consent and the Controlled Body* (New York: Palgrave Macmillan, 2013), 29–30.
70 Anthony Carthew, "All Honor," *New York Times Magazine*, 1 March 1964, Sadomasochism Clipping File, Kinsey Institute; Patrick MacNee and Dave Rogers, *The Avengers: The Inside Story* (London: Titan, 2008), 50–1 & 69; Gloria G. Brame and William D. Brame, *Different Loving Too: Real People, Real Lives, Real BDSM* (British Columbia: Moons Grove Press, 2015), 56; and Thomas S. Weinberg and Martha S. Magill, "Sadomasochistic Themes in Mainstream Culture" in Weinberg (ed.), *S and M: Studies in Dominance and Submission* (Amherst, NY: Prometheus, 1995), 228–9.
71 Miriam G. Reumann, *American Sexual Character: Sex, Gender, and National Identity in the Kinsey Reports* (Berkeley: University of California Press, 2005), 126–7.
72 "J" [Terry Garrity], *The Sensuous Woman* (New York: Lyle Stuart, 1969), 131.

73 Erwin Goldstein and Martin Haeberle, *Sex Book: A Modern Pictorial Encyclopedia* (New York: Herder & Herder, 1971) and David R. Reuben, *Everything You Always Wanted to Know About Sex but Were Afraid to Ask* (New York: David McKay Company, 1969), 189–90.
74 Reuben, *Everything You Wanted to Know*, 134–5.
75 *People v. Samuels, Court of Appeals of California, 250 Cal. App. 2d 501. 28 April 1967.*
76 Gayle S. Rubin, "*Thinking Sex*," in Carole S. Vance (ed.), *Pleasure and Danger: Exploring Female Sexuality* (New York: HarperCollins, 1993), 305.
77 Jody Pennington, *The History of Sex in American Film* (Westport, CT: Praeger, 2007), 34.
78 Spring, *Secret Historian*, 302–3.

2

THE FIRST BDSM GROUPS, THE 1970S

In late 1970, New York's *Village Voice* rejected an ad soliciting people for a new sexual organization. Ad policies had liberalized in the 1960s, and growing numbers of publications accepted sexual personal ads, including those hinting at sadomasochism. This ad, though, went too far. So, Pat Bond, a pseudonymous New York teacher, turned to *Screw* magazine, a weekly pornographic tabloid, which ran his ad in its 28 December 1970 issue. It read:

> MASOCHIST? HAPPY? Is it curable? Does psychiatry help? Is a satisfactory lifestyle possible? There's women's lib., black lib., gay lib., etc. Isn't it time we put something together? Write PO Box . . . [1]

Shortly afterward, Bond also advertised in the *East Village Other*, an underground newspaper known for sex ads. His ads were the first public advertisements for a sadomasochistic organization in the United States. Five people responded to his first ad, three of whom met with him in his home. Over the next few weeks, more people responded. Bond arranged more meetings, and in February 1971, he and a dozen others formed The Eulenspiegel Society. Terry Kolb, the first person to answer Bond's ad, suggested the name, which referred to a medieval trickster who discovered a taste for pain. Later renamed TES, its members soon voted to open membership to all "people of SM orientation."[2]

One could join TES, the first public BDSM organization, without special invitation or introduction. It grew quickly thanks to regular advertising and meetings. Several TES members picketed the *Village Voice*, which recanted its position and accepted BDSM ads if they avoided the word "sadomasochism." A few years earlier, similar demonstrations had convinced the *Village Voice* to allow the word "gay" in personal ads. Writers in *Screw* promoted and occasionally visited TES events, but continued to deride is members as "S&M freaks." So, too, did the *Village Voice*, which announced TES's first public party, but disparaged its members as "whips-and-chains freaks." Yet, it published Kolb's essay "Masochist's Lib," demanding the right to pursue one's sexual interests without censure or harassment.[3]

In the gay community, historian John D'Emilio notes, eroticism became the basis for an identity embraced by growing numbers of people.[4] The same proved true for sadomasochists who increasingly embraced BDSM—however labeled at the time—as a sexual identity. As Bond's ads indicate, the gay community served as model for transforming erotic desire into social organization and personal identity.

The informal BDSM networks of the 1960s blossomed into dedicated organizations in the early 1970s. The more open sexual climate of the 1970s, which encouraged sexual adventurism and discussion, facilitated this, as did the proliferation of leather bars and publication of educational literature, most importantly Larry Townsend's *The Leatherman's Handbook* (1972) and Gerald and Caroline Greene's *S-M the Last Taboo* (1974). Unlike past erotica, such as Carney's *Real Thing* or *The Story of O*, a new generation of BDSM authors sought to both titillate and educate. They encouraged sadomasochists to connect with one another and make their fantasies a reality. This new literature, gay and straight, encouraged the transition from an older, secret, atomized community of BDSM enthusiasts to an open, organized community, which actively sought to reach, connect with, and educate newcomers.

Following the example of TES, other BDSM organizations formed in the 1970s. The largest, longest lived, and most influential were the Chicago Hellfire Club (1971) and San Francisco's Society of Janus (1974). Along with these organizations, dedicated spaces for BDSM activities, both commercial and private, opened in major cities, including the Mineshaft in New York and the Catacombs in San Francisco. The creation of these organizations and venues, along with growing media attention on BDSM, fueled the growth of a coherent and organized BDSM community united by sexual interest.

TES, Janus and Other Mixed BDSM Social Organizations

By mid-1972, TES had about 50 active members. Most were in their twenties or thirties. They met monthly at a local church. In 1973, TES launched a widely distributed, though infrequently published, newsletter, *Prometheus*. It incorporated in 1976, becoming a formal organization with elected officers, bylaws and increasing rules. Throughout the 1970s, it was the world's "largest organization of self-proclaimed sadomasochists." It hosted open educational demonstrations, talks and consciousness raising meetings on alternate Wednesdays, and social events and play parties restricted to members. It welcomed everyone, "experienced or new to S&M, gay, straight, or bi," and attracted out-of-town visitors. Membership grew, stimulated by continued advertising, word-of-mouth through BDSM community, and periodic press coverage, including a brief, derogatory reference on the Dick Cavett Show. Typical meetings began with a presentation by a member or guest lecturer on BDSM philosophy or technique followed by group discussions "utilizing standard consciousness-raising format." Jack Jackson, a gay African American leatherman who served a term as TES's president, was among its most popular presenters. He happily shared his expertise in BDSM technique, demonstrated it on eager volunteers and encouraged political activism among members, urging them to work for "acceptance for varying forms of 'SM' as freely chosen lifestyles."[5]

The Sexual Revolution of the 1960s and 1970s offered an unprecedented opportunity to Bond and other early BDSM activists. They hoped to capitalize on the greater sexual permissiveness of the era. Factors ranging from the birth control pill to rising wealth and consumerism, historian David Allyn suggests, encouraged sexual experimentation, which for some included BDSM. Changing perceptions of obscenity allowed sex ads, sexual publications and even movies to become more explicit, reach wider audiences and discuss previously proscribed topics.[6]

TES aimed to assure its members of the legitimacy of their sexual interests, educate them to pursue them safely, and end the stigmatization and government harassment of sadomasochists. Drafted by Bond, the TES Creed and Statement of Aims and Purposes echoed Kolb's *Village Voice* article. It rejected coercion, emphasized mutual consent and demanded the right to "pursue joy and happiness in one's own way"; to be defined by oneself and not by others; to "freely communicate and socialize with others of similar sexual orientation"; to "challenge established value systems" that repress "the sexual drives or practices of erotic minorities"; and the "right to publicize activities and views freely, without fear of occupational or professional repercussion." This would raise the "consciousness of both the public and ourselves regarding sexual minorities and sexual freedoms."[7]

As out-of-town visitors joined TES, and TES members moved to other parts of the country, TES's influence spread. Members in other cities organized small gathering of BDSM enthusiasts, which Bond encouraged. TES soon formalized this process, appointing official coordinators in several cities.

About three years after Bond's ad appeared in *Screw*, Cynthia Slater placed a similar ad in San Francisco's *Berkeley Barb*. Slater had worked as a professional dominatrix and advertised for clients in the *Barb*. Advised by Bond and assisted by her then lover, Larry Olsen, she organized the Society of Janus in the last months of 1974.[8] Slater and Olsen wanted to create an alternative to the Backdrop Club, a commercial BDSM operation, which organized itself as a private membership club to skirt prostitution and similar laws. During the day, women "worked there as professional dominants and submissives." At night and on weekends, Backdrop Club hosted social events for its members.[9]

Slater found the environment at Backdrop disheartening, both for management's focus on profit and how it treated club members. Male members paid "exorbitant registration fees" in exchange for "guaranteed sex, or whatever they came in for." Those with submissive desires were treated poorly and expected to do whatever they "were told by just anybody who came in." Expectations established by Backdrop's primary business of selling sexual services carried over into its social club. Jack Fritscher found women "pressured to put out" and "traded around like fuckable commodities on the New York Stock Exchange." It was the antithesis of what Bond, Slater and an emerging generation of BDSM activists envisioned. Bond soon criticized Backdrop for misrepresenting itself as an open, non-profit club like TES and withdrew his support. The police later raided and shut down Backdrop.[10]

Rather than an audience for commercial exploitation, Slater sought to build a community of BDSM practitioners who shared their knowledge, benefited from their mutual experience, and looked after one another. This required changing how many heterosexuals approached BDSM. Sociologist G.W. Levi Kamel noted heterosexual BDSM encounters, such as those facilitated by Backdrop, lacked many of the "self-imposed, informal social norms" common to gay leather bars.[11]

Slater built Janus's early membership from respondents to her ads, people alienated by the Backdrop, and a few professional dominants, like Slater. One of the few women welcomed in San Francisco's leather bars, Slater also attracted gay men to Janus, among them Jim Kane, who had relocated to San Francisco. By then a leading BDSM expert, Kane developed "a reputation for being the biggest 'S' in San Francisco."[12] By reaching out to the city's diverse BDSM populations, Slater began a process of acculturation across lines of sexual orientation and BDSM interests.

Like TES, Janus welcomed everyone, charged minimal fees for its programs, and attracted members of diverse sexual interests. They met regularly in Slater's home (which she rented from Kane) for BDSM discussions and demonstrations. Slater emphasized to new members that Janus was not a "cruising ground . . . therapy group . . . or sex service." It was a place to learn and share and make friends. Kane led several of Janus's first seminars. He exposed Janus members to gay BDSM practice, cruising, and the intricacies of negotiating scenes, including discussing one's limits and safety. Topics ranged from fisting to flagellation. Fakir Musafar shared his expertise on corsetry, piercing and body modification. Kaye Buckley discussed her experiences with Japan's BDSM community and businesses. Nan Borrows joined and she and other professional dominants shared their expertise. While Janus lacked much of the formal structure of TES—in part due to negative experiences with Backdrop—it boasted 50 members by 1978 and just over 100 in 1981. Its seminars attracted 50–75 attendees. Their quality was such one observer claimed: "what the Julliard School is to music education, Janus is to SM."[13]

While most heterosexuals kept their BDSM interests secret, growing numbers sought connection with fellow BDSM aficionados. Other BDSM organizations formed in the 1970s, including The Tri-State Couples Club (TCC) in New Jersey, a group for heterosexual couples founded by George Morrell, The Sadomasochist Society (TSS), an offshoot of TES founded by Dennis Rubini in Philadelphia, and Gemini, a heterosexual, male dominant club founded by Janus member Jay Wiseman in Berkeley, California in 1978. TES coordinators hosted informal meetings in cities ranging from Jacksonville, Florida to Tucson, Arizona and Vancouver, Canada. By 1979, TES had several dozen coordinators—sometimes called ambassadors—across the United States, plus three in Canada, one in Japan, and one in Germany. Janus established branch chapters in Los Angeles and other California cities. TCC established chapters in Long Island, Philadelphia and Chicago.

Other BDSM groups also formed, but few lasted long. Roissy, a California club named for *Story of O's* chateau, lasted only a few months. Esoteric Encounters, "the first and only S+M dating service," survived a few years.[14] By the end of the 1970s, perhaps a dozen heterosexual or open orientation membership BDSM groups operated in the United States. Apart from TES and Janus, their memberships were small, rarely over a dozen, and their activities generally limited to arranging parties. As psychiatrist Lawrence Mass noted, "sadomasochistic behavior among heterosexuals" was "less overtly subcultural" and "less conspicuous."[15]

BDSM in the Gay Community

BDSM became increasingly visible in gay media. A growing number of books, films and magazines celebrated leather and BDSM, most importantly *Drummer.* Founded in 1975 by John Embry, a Los Angeles gay activist, the monthly magazine chronicled gay leather culture and celebrated its outlaw image. Billed as "America's Mag for the Macho Male," it grew quickly in popularity and was soon available on newsstands and adult bookstores across the United States. Each issue included erotic stories and photographs, reviews of new clubs and bars, and a growing number of pages devoted to "Leather Fraternity" contact ads. It published the work of numerous talented artists and writers, including Chuck Arnett, Jeanne Barney, Tim Barrus, Etienne, Jack Fritscher, Robert Opel, John Preston, Cliff Raven, Samuel Steward, Tom of Finland and Jim Ward. Steward, its oldest contributor, mentored many of the younger writers.[16] Their work, epitomized by Tom of Finland's drawings of muscular, bare-chested sexually aggressive men and Preston's hard-edged erotic stories, celebrated the flourishing bar scene.

Preston's novel, *Mr. Benson*, serialized in *Drummer* in 1979 and 1980, cemented his position as *Drummer's* most popular and prolific writer. It described the sexual adventures of Jamie, a young man who learns to love and serve Aristotle Benson, an aloof, demanding BDSM master who tests Jamie's desire in a succession of painful and humiliating challenges. Jamie gives up his job and everything else in his life to keep Mr. Benson's house, worship his body, and attend to his sexual needs. He loves every minute—each humiliation, fucking and beating—as Mr. Benson, his master, instructor, confidant, torturer and lover, transforms him into the perfect slave, symbolized, as in *Story of O*, by his branding. Like O, Jamie's only options are to submit or to leave. There is no negotiation, no discussion of his limits, or his sexual desires. Jamie longed for Mr. Benson when he was away, as did *Drummer* readers who eagerly awaited each new installment of the novel. They purchased "Looking for Mr. Benson" t-shirts and wore them to cruise bars, confirming Mr. Benson's as the ideal BDSM master.[17]

Macho, anarchic figures driven by lust and sadomasochistic desire dominate *Drummer* stories, photos and illustrations. They celebrate outlaw archetypes, idealize desire and raw sexuality, and present man-to-man bonding, submissive to dominant, as the ideal path for sexual learning and BDSM acculturation. As Preston later wrote, these "one-on-one bondings spread out, forming a brotherhood" from which the leather and BDSM communities grew.[18]

Yet, formal gay leather and SM organizations emerged contemporaneously with *Drummer's* fictional outlaws. In August 1971, John Wittenkind and a dozen other men founded the first men's BDSM organization, the Chicago Hellfire Club (CHC). Wittenkind and several others were members of Second City, a motorcycle club founded two years earlier. Renslow was Second City's first president, and its members hung out at the Gold Coast. Wittenkind and his friends enjoyed Second City and the Gold Coast, but sought heavy BDSM and other sexual activities discouraged at bars or motorcycle runs. So, they founded the CHC. It hosted regular gatherings and bar nights, and became one "of the very, very few places where a network of gay men honestly into S&M can meet." Renslow's partner, Dom Orejudos, designed its logo.[19]

Pooling members' resources allowed them to secure venues for BDSM activities and to build and acquire BDSM equipment ranging from frames, crosses and similar structures for bondage and flagellation to slings for suspension and fisting. Members wanted space to swing a whip and engage in intense BDSM play without the distractions and interruptions common to bars. So, they purchased their own clubhouse for meetings, orgies and other BDSM activities, something possible because the CHC remained a small, intimate group for many years.

In contrast to TES and Janus, CHC was "shy of publicity and hard to approach." Drawing on the heritage of gay motorcycle clubs, it limited membership to gay men with significant BDSM experience sponsored by existing members. As word spread of its elaborate festivities, CHC attracted members from across the United States and Canada, growing from a dozen members to more than a hundred by 1980. Only its roughly two-dozen Chicago area members, though, received full membership and voting rights in the organization.[20]

Like leather bars, gay motorcycle clubs proliferated in the 1970s, though actually owning and riding a motorcycle became less important for membership. Exclusive and selective, these clubs required sponsorship by existing members and passing through a "pledge" period. Often small and intimate, these backpatch clubs—so called for the club logo displayed on the back of members' vests or jackets—expected a high level of participation and usually prohibited members from joining other backpatch clubs. A handful of backpatch clubs developed a reputation for intense BDSM play, but most did not. Club members occupied "a broad range of diversity in the continuum between vanilla and heavy kink."[21]

BDSM in the Media

Articles on BDSM appeared more frequently in mainstream publications in the 1970s, and BDSM themes crept into popular literature. John Norman, a pseudonymous City University of New York philosophy professor, published a series of science fiction novels set on Gor, a planet populated by muscular he-men and athletic, beautiful, submissive women—heterosexual equivalents of *Drummer* men. As Pat Califia later noted, Norman was "a sexist pig," but his books were among her "most consistently rewarding jackoff material." Norman's *Imaginative Sex* (1974) offered couples 53 BDSM scenarios to spice up their love life, including "captured by pirates" and "raped by a machine." Rolf Milonas's *Fantasex* (1975) repeated several of these. *Penthouse Forum*, famous for readers' letters chronicling their sexual adventures, regularly discussed BDSM. In 1974, it pointed to TES and announced: "many people are feeling sexually free enough to acknowledge they'd like to try some kind of leather sex." The "number of SM devotees and meeting places is growing." *Penthouse* magazine featured its first BDSM pictorial in 1976. In 1978, it launched, *Variations*, a kinky version of *Forum*, which in 1981 devoted an entire issue to BDSM. *The Joy of Sex*, the decade's best-selling sex manual, featured entries on leather, rubber and other fetishes, as well as bondage, discipline, pain and water sports. So, too, did *The Joy of Gay Sex*. Even *High Times*, a magazine devoted to legalizing marijuana, explored BDSM.[22]

Building on earlier rough trade stories, gay authors wrote novels featuring intense BDSM play. Popular titles included *The Young Master* (1970) by William Lambert III, Dick Vaden's *I Want it All* (1969), and Larry Townsend's *Leather Ad: M* (1970), *Leather Ad: S* (1970) and *Run Little Leather Boy* (1971).[23] Townsend, who was president of HELP (Homophile Effort for Legal Protection), a Los Angeles legal defense organization, developed a national network of contacts who guided him to local BDSM hot spots, shared their knowledge, and answered his detailed questionnaires. He introduced men with similar BDSM interests to one another and cultivated a host of BDSM writers whose work he published. David Reuben, it seemed, was wrong. A lot of gay men were, in fact, looking for BDSM.

Mirroring the boom in sex advice books, the first practitioner-written BDSM manuals appeared in the early 1970s: Larry Townsend's *Leatherman's Handbook* (1972) aimed at gay men and Gerald and Caroline Greene's *SM the Last Taboo* (1974), which addressed heterosexual couples. They offered advice on fantasies, role playing, meeting people, relationships, negotiating scenes, and answering contact ads, as well as buying BDSM equipment and using it safely. Both emphasized sadomasochism was not a mindless thrashing. It involved careful planning and rituals and moved through stages: negotiation, warm-up, and cycles of increasing and decreasing intensity leading to a climax followed by recovery—what later BDSM writers termed aftercare in which tops attended to the bottoms' emotional and physical well-being and scene participants renewed their bond. Heavy BDSM sessions, Townsend suggested, could provide catharsis similar to psychoanalysis.[24]

Townsend, who used short stories to illustrate his ideas, offered a particularly thorough guide to cruising leather bars for BDSM sex. An appendix identified the most promising bars and guided men to them. While admiring Carney's *Real Thing* for its literary merit, he found its approach overly rule-bound and impractical. He also, in sharp contrast to Carney, referred to BDSM activities as "play" rather than "work," emphasizing them as intense, enjoyable sexual experiences.

Normative literature, particularly Carney's *Real Thing* and Townsend's *Leatherman's Handbook*, refined the leatherman image, which Tom of Finland, Etienne and other artists popularized. Leathermen favored black over brown leather and never mixed the two. A leather jacket and boots represented a bare minimum. Adding more leather, such as chaps or pants, indicated more commitment. Fashion options narrowed and homogenized into the "Castro Clone," named for the San Francisco neighborhood famous for bars and cruising. Clones sported gym-defined bodies, blue-collar clothes—especially tight 501 jeans and boots—short haircuts, mustaches and leather jackets. As more gay men adopted the look, one could no longer be certain of someone's interests.[25]

Cruising men commonly signaled their interests with keys clipped to their belts, the left side indicating dominant (or top), the right submissive (or bottom), though in some New York bars it was the opposite. Similarly, "M" and "S" meant opposite things in different bars (either master or masochist, slave or sadist). More daring men fastened cock rings, chains or handcuffs to boots or jacket epaulets. Signals standardized as men adopted and transmuted them into a universal, periodically updated, code.[26]

By 1975, leathermen used colored handkerchiefs: black for BDSM, red for fisting, gray for bondage, dark or light blue for anal or oral sex, yellow for water sports, and orange for anything goes. People added colors over time, at least some in jest. In 1982, the Pleasure Chest offered 60 color options in "the world's most comprehensive hanky code," which included mosquito netting for outdoor sex, fuchsia for spanking, charcoal for latex fetishists, and other colors impossible to differentiate in dimly lit bars.[27] Townsend listed a more sedate ten in *Leatherman's Handbook II* (1983), which updated his classic work and offered additional and more sophisticated lessons on BDSM technique.

A nationwide leather culture and iconography developed, celebrated in art, literature, film and a growing number of beauty contests hosted by bars. Chuck Renslow and Dom Orejudos held the first "Mr. Gold Coast" contest in 1972 and developed it into the International Mr. Leather (IML) contest, launched in 1979. By the mid-1980s, IML had grown from 400 to over 1,000 attendees, making it the largest annual leather/BDSM gathering in the world. Conceived as "a male beauty contest, a parade of hunks, and an excuse to party," its winner embodied an ideal of "masculine, leather sex appeal." In 1980, it promised a host of parties at Chicago bars and bathhouses, making it "a Leather Mardi Gras, Motorcycle Run, New Year's Eve and Roman Orgy all rolled into one fantastic weekend."[28] Its winner, International Mr. Leather, accrued status and opportunities to appear in magazines and films. Orejudos created the advertising and art for the event, and his work, along with the well-muscled titleholders themselves epitomized ideal leatherman. While many winners were not sadomasochists, the overlap between leather and BDSM was such that judges expected contestants to be familiar with BDSM and "know plenty about it."[29]

In 1981, *Drummer* magazine launched its own, Mr. Drummer contest. Regional contests produced contenders who then competed to become Mr. Drummer. While IML developed out of Renslow's experience with bodybuilding and physique contests, the Mr. Drummer contests embraced the raw sexuality common to events in backroom bars, even requiring contestants to perform sex fantasy skits, which increased their entertainment value. Title contests proliferated, producing candidates who competed in local, regional and national contests.

Contact publications remained important to BDSM enthusiasts. Among the most popular was the *Rigid Bondage Roster*, a mimeographed publication by TES member Ron Bookstaff, which included erotic drawings and short stories among the personal ads. In Los Angeles in 1973, Robert Payne launched a similar contact newsletter, *The Leather Fraternity*, aimed at gay men. The newspaper *Fetish Times* also launched in 1973. It reported on heterosexual BDSM activities and organizations, but devoted most of its contents to titillating stories, often shallow sex advice, and contact ads, particularly from professional dominatrices. A successful format, it inspired better-informed competitors including *SM Express* and *S&M News*. Pornographic BDSM magazines increased in number and introduced nudity, but avoided any hint of penetration, let alone the overt sexual activity of mainstream pornography.

Leonard Burtman remained a prolific publisher, but was eclipsed by House of Milan, founded in 1964 by his cousin, Yogi Klein, and Barbara Behr. Klein and Behr first founded Futura Fashions, a mail-order fetish clothing company, but found selling photo-illustrated catalogs of women in fetish clothing more profitable than the clothing itself. For a time, they operated a fetish clothing store in Chicago, one of the first in the United States. Behr, who moved to California, transitioned to magazine publishing, anchoring the firm on *Latent Image*. Launched in 1966, it devoted many of its pages to contact ads, some accompanied by photographs.[30]

Renamed HOM and increasingly led by Behr, the firm became one of the largest fetish and BDSM publishers, issuing dozens of different magazine titles in the 1970s, including *Bound to Please, Breast Bondage, Captured, Hogtie* and *Knotty*. These followed a fairly standard format. Roughly half the pages were bondage or fetish photographs. Another quarter were contacts ads. A topical editorial by Behr, readers' letters, two or three erotic stories, and advertising filled the rest. Beginning with *Gay Bondage* magazine, launched in 1974, HOM published occasional how-to articles on BDSM technique, such as knot-tying and fancy rope-work.

HOM competitor Harmony, similarly, added educational content. *Bondage Life* 2 (1978) offered detailed instructions for safely tying wrists with rope. *Drummer's* editors recognized this demand and added educational content beginning with an article on the psychology of bondage in its twenty-fourth issue (1978). The closer a magazines' ties to the BDSM community, the more it sought to address that community's educational needs.

BDSM at the Movies

Television became more sexually daring in the mid-1970s. *The Love Boat* (1977–87), *Charlie's Angels* (1976–81) and *Three's Company* (1977–83) placed sex at the center of their plots. So, too, did many movies made for television, which "tended toward the salacious, including prostitution, white slavery, domestic violence, and rape."[31] While overt sadomasochistic imagery did not appear on American television until the 1990s, many BDSM enthusiasts celebrated Wonder Woman's 1975 television debut. Moviemakers, of course, were more daring.

Encouraged by audiences, who flocked to see *Deep Throat* (1972) and *The Devil in Miss Jones* (1973) during the short-lived "porno chic" era, directors and producers pushed sexual boundaries. Numerous films capitalized on sadomasochism's apparent popularity. Liliana Cavani's *The Night Porter* (1974), Pier Paolo Pasolini's *Salo* (1975), and Tinto Brass's *Salon Kitty* (1976) presented viewers with sadomasochistic scenes of varying explicitness and eroticism, while portraying their participants as psychologically troubled. Just Jaeckin and Radley Metzger produced soft core films based on famous BDSM novels. Jaeckin's *Story of O* (1975) added a happy ending, but otherwise followed the novel's plot, while Radley Metzger's *The Image* (1975) took more liberties with Catherine Robbe-Grillet's 1956 novel.

While less common, producers also made hardcore BDSM films. Gerard Damiano's *Story of Joanna* (1975) adapted the plot of *Story of O* and attracted considerable attention for its BDSM content and a rare male-male sex scene in a heterosexual film. It was, a recent critic notes, "the pornography film industry's only attempt to combine classy, high production value, literarily pretentious 'SM chic' with hard-core action."[32] *The Naughty Victorians* (1975) adapted from the novel *The Way of a Man with a Maid* (1908). Playful and less hard-core, it offered bondage, and flagellation, along with period costumes and high production values praised by Hugh Hefner. Unlike the novel, the film's women get their revenge by turning the tables on their male seducer. In contrast, Fred Lincoln's *Defiance of Good* (1975) was a dark and disturbing tale of a sadomasochistic man taking advantage of a troubled teenager.[33]

Short, mild BDSM scenes appeared in several mainstream pornographic films, though Metzger (credited as Henry Paris) remained the most daring. His *Opening of Misty Beethoven* (1976) ended with mild BDSM play and imagery. *Barbara Broadcast* (1977), a positively reviewed, but generally conventional pornographic film, moved through the normal progression of masturbation, oral sex, female/female and female/male scenes, but concluded with a prolonged, yet tender, BDSM scene between Jamie Gillis and Constance Money originally filmed for *Misty Beethoven*. While Gillis restrains Money with ankle and wrist cuffs and attaches clamps to her nipples, most of the scene involves cunnilingus and fellatio. He never strikes her.

Marilyn Chambers, following rave reviews for starring in *Behind the Green Door* (1972) as an unwilling woman brought to a sex club and sexually awakened in a series of escalating encounters, titillated fans with hints of her BDSM interests. The era's best-known adult star, she released two short BDSM films in 1979: *Beyond De Sade* and *Never a Tender Moment*. Both films opened and closed with Chambers briefly explaining her real-life enjoyment of bondage and pain.

A few adult theaters, particularly the Avon in New York, specialized in kinky subjects. Their films, though, were as likely to feature rape and non-consensual violence, as in Shaun Costello's *Waterpower* (1975) and Joe Davian's *Appointment with Agony* (1976), as they were consensual BDSM. Carter Stevens, who made several films for them, hewed closer to BDSM community norms, often showing consent among participants. So, too, did Annie Sprinkle who starred in several of their features.

Beginning with Fred Halsted's *L.A. Plays Itself* (1972), which featured spanking and bondage, gay hard-core filmmakers also explored BDSM. In *Sextool* (1975), Halsted and his lover, Joey Yale, engaged in intense scenes of flagellation and fucking interspersed with tenderness. These demonstrated "the true power of the M over the S even as the S overpowers the M," *Drummer* enthused, praising it, along with Richard Abel's *Nights in Black Leather* (1973) and Val Martin's *Born to Raise Hell* (1975), which offered "endless methods of sucking, fucking, stripping, whipping, shaving, slaving, eating, beating, and so forth."[34]

Sadomasochism even entered mainstream films. Barbara Streisand flirted with sadomasochistic imagery in a "Cycle Sluts" photo shoot for *The Owl and the Pussycat* (1970). The Kit Kat's performers staged a flagellation scene in *Cabaret* (1972). In Mel Brooks' *The Producers* (1967), Max Bialystock apparently engaged in BDSM games with some of his female financiers, while in *High Anxiety* (1977), villains Cloris Leachman and Harvey Korman enjoyed a dominant/submissive relationship in which Korman hoped for "more bondage" and "less discipline." In *Monty Python and the Holy Grail* (1975), Galahad is accosted by nuns who demand he tie them down and spank them. While saved from temptation by Lancelot, Galahad's plight mirrored a common complaint in the BDSM community: too many bottoms, not enough tops. Insatiably lustful, whip-wielding Dr. Frank N. Furter solves this in *The Rocky Horror Picture Show* (1975) by changing role as needed. His character embodied a polymorphous perversity that appealed to many in the BDSM community who switched between top and bottom and played with others regardless of gender or orientation.

The Night Porter, Salon Kitty and *Salo* invoked fascist or Nazi imagery, which encouraged sexploitation filmmakers to do the same, resulting, most famously, in *Ilsa, She Wolf of the SS* (1975), which reveled in torture, violence and Nazi imagery, much as certain men's magazines had a generation earlier. Most sexploitation filmmakers, though, avoided Nazis. They drew on older, oft-used themes, including women in prison and the works of de Sade, as Jess Franco did in *Eugenie de Sade* (1970); *Juliette de Sade* (1970); De Sade's *Juliette* (1974) and *Women Behind Bars* (1975). Within the BDSM community Nazi imagery was similarly rare, generally met with disapproval, and condemned by writers and editors who complained of sadomasochism's common association with "Nazi Storm troopers" and "sex murderers" like Charles Manson.[35] It bedeviled BDSM activists who sought to disentangle BDSM from rape, murder and fascism, and affirm BDSM as consensual, joyful and fun.

Movies stimulated interest in BDSM, which in turn stimulated BDSM businesses. Psychiatrists Robert E. Litman and Charles Sweringen noted "recently relaxed police attitudes" led "many book stores to add a bondage nook." Uncle Sam's Umbrella Shop expanded its offerings, and new shops, such as the Pleasure Chest, which opened in 1971, added BDSM paraphernalia. Chuck Renslow's Man's Country bathhouse catered to leathermen and opened a BDSM and leather gear shop. Specialty BDSM suppliers, which had previously operated mostly by mail, personal appointment, or inside leather bars, opened retail stores. Marquis de Suede opened near New York's leather bars and Chicago's Male Hide Leather moved from the Gold Coast's basement to its own storefront down the street. BDSM and leather clothing stores proliferated in San Francisco. Taste of Leather relocated from Febe's bar to its own storefront. Leather Forever and other new shops opened. Alan Selby relocated his Mr. S mail-order business from England to a South of Market San Francisco store in 1979. The following year, he joined Janus and added a store in Denver. The Crypt opened its first store in San Diego in 1977 and added shops in Seattle, Long Beach and other cities. Its Denver store was near The Triangle, the city's premier leather bar, which had a back room for sexual activities, strict entrance standards, and men who were "kick ass take no shit sexual leaders."[36]

Mail-order businesses also flourished, advertising their wares in the growing number of BDSM periodicals. Centurions' 100-page catalog offered enormous selections of bondage equipment, fetish clothing, paddles, whips and other BDSM paraphernalia, including rings patterned on those from *Story of O*. In theory, these would allow BDSM aficionados to identify one another.

These businesses provided a wide array of clothing, equipment and sex toys, allowing those with the means to outfit elaborate home dungeons or "play rooms," which *Drummer* periodically profiled. *SM: The Last Taboo* and *Leatherman's Handbook* offered advice on equipping them. So, too, did many BDSM periodicals, which published articles on making BDSM equipment and modifying, or "perverting," cheap, easily purchased items, which made visits to grocery and hardware stores erotic adventures and preludes to increasingly elaborate BDSM activities at home.[37]

The Great Parties

BDSM parties, usually called play parties or dungeon parties, provide safe places for attendees to engage in BDSM and other sexual activities. They flourished "as far back as the late forties." Held in private homes, they were "populated by means of informal networks of referral." Attendees were specifically invited or brought by trusted insiders, and party hosts determined the permissible limits of BDSM and sexual activity. Fueled by social networks, leather bars and new BDSM organizations, parties grew in size and number in the 1970s, gaining visibility in what anthropologist Gayle Rubin labeled "the efflorescence of the Great Parties."[38] The CHC arranged parties at its clubhouse. TES, Janus and other BDSM groups organized parties at local bars or other venues. Smaller parties took place in members' homes and provided a pleasant and intimate alternative to those arranged by commercial BDSM establishments.

Psychologist Charles Moser attended several Janus parties and noted they served "an integration and socialization function for participants." Sadomasochists meet "others like themselves, learn the rules of interaction and specific SM techniques, and most importantly are able to normalize their interests and feelings" in an atmosphere that encouraged "them to be themselves and validates their behavior" and feelings. The era's most famous parties attracted people from across the United States, as well as international visitors.[39]

Sadomasochists socialized in these sexual spaces. Clothed in their best fetish outfits, they showed off whips and other toys, which they often made themselves. BDSM play featured prominently and could be heavier, louder, more elaborate and involve more people than what couples arranged at home. Parties were a performative space in which tops and bottoms demonstrated their skills, endurance and other qualities. Tony DeBlase became famous for the elaborate webs of rope into which bound men—sometimes several at a time. At one early TES party, Sir John secured one of his slaves in stocks. A sign over her head read "Free Expert Blow Jobs. For permission, see Sir John Q." While two of his other slaves watched over her, she gave blow jobs to men to whom Sir John gave permission.[40]

For the club's fifth anniversary, CHC members organized Inferno, a one-day BDSM party in the woods. It became an annual event and expanded to a full weekend within a few years. No other club had "the equipment available, the male flesh willing," and "the expertise" of CHC's men. Invitations were "extended only to highly regarded players," and limited to about 200. Men arrived eager for action. Limits were few, and CHC offered prizes in various events and competitions, including willingness to try new things. Attendees signed disclaimers, releasing "claims for future accidents and injuries." Such accidents were rare despite the intensity of play.[41]

At Inferno X (1981), New York attendee David Stein experienced his first "SM climax," an "ecstatic mind/body release" resulting from "pain/pleasure" that "so concentrates your awareness into the here and now" that "you spin away free into no place and no time, the universe and eternity." It was "so overwhelming that mere orgasm can seem irrelevant in comparison." Men able to endure and enjoy this intense play were valued in the BDSM community, whose members thought it "highly masculine to be a superb bottom, to be able to take an enormous amount or sexual activity and pain."[42]

The CHC became famous for the equipment it provided, which its members demonstrated on Friday night, to ensure its safe use. Inferno demonstrations of BDSM technique by experienced practitioners became more detailed and elaborate over time, and attendees disseminated these lessons to their home communities. Inferno VIII (1979), for example, opened with a demonstration of fancy Japanese rope bondage on Friday night. Later demonstrations included catheters, enemas, piercing, fisting and electricity. Attendees competed for prizes in rope bondage, how much weight they could suspend from their testicles and other contests of skill or endurance, and could move among specialized venues set up around the campground, including Casa Crisco (fisting), Aqua Vita Villa (water sports), Chateau DeSade (a dungeon full of equipment), Scaffold Square (an outdoor location where men could be tied up in public view or suspended) and several others. Inferno was "a finishing school for SM."[43]

One of the most popular instructors, Tony DeBlase presented seminars on BDSM safety and technique for CHC members, as well as general audiences at Touché, the CHC's new home bar. An academic with a PhD in zoology, DeBlase organized the CHC's "Whips on Wheels" program, in which he and other CHC members gave BDSM presentations at leather bars across the country. DeBlase and Inferno popularized the use of "dungeon monitors" to supervise BDSM parties and enforce safe practices "without compromising intensity or raunchiness." In 1979, DeBlase launched *DungeonMaster*, the first educational BDSM magazine, which quickly attracted 750 subscribers.[44]

BDSM technique presented such a growing body of knowledge that "no one ever finishes learning about S/M—at least," David Stein argued, "no one who's any good at it."[45] DeBlase and others shared a wealth of practical and safety information. Check during a scene to ensure bondage does not cut off circulation. Protect delicate body parts in heavy flagellation scenes. Avoiding asparagus before water sports (it creates a foul order), and strawberries and other fruits with small seeds before anal fisting (they can puncture the rectum, leading to peritonitis). *DungeonMaster* became the primary forum for sharing new information and advancing one's BDSM technique.

Several leather bars, including the Gold Coast, Tool Box and Triangle, created backrooms for sexual activity. Dedicated establishments for BDSM play developed from these. Most enforced dress codes. Once inside, "men encountered their basest and most angelic desires." By 1970, the Manhole, Ramrod, Ramp and other bars operated in a "leather belt" south of Twenty-third Street in New York's meatpacking district where rents were cheap. At day's end, butchers, fishmongers and other merchants closed their shops and departed. Leathermen arrived, and bars and sex clubs opened. Bar names and owners changed over time, but their number grew. In many cities, the name Eagle became associated with leather, and Eagle bars sprang up across the United States including the D.C. Eagle in Washington, the Eagle in Exile in Columbus, Ohio, and Eagle 562 in Long Beach, California.[46]

In New York, the Eagle's Nest (often just called the Eagle), Stockade and Spike proved popular in the early 1970s, the latter for Sunday brunch and the meeting place for the FFA (Fist Fuckers of America) who also had parties at the Mineshaft. The Anvil opened in 1974 in the lower two levels of a building at 14th Street and 11th Avenue. Customers descended a staircase to enter and lines were always long on weekends. Go-go dancers entertained customers at the upstairs bar. It reserved one room of its "dark, dank, dirty" basement for sex. For a time, TES hosted Tuesday night parties at the Spike and arranged entry for women—who accounted for about a third of TES's membership—on those nights. Eagle's Nest enforced a "Leather and Western" dress code, and only occasionally allowed entrance to select women. On weekends, it was packed with "men in black leather with chained motorcycle caps, chains encircling shoulders or boots, handcuffs at hip, keys dangling right or left"—so many men that "it took ten minutes to snake through the crowd from the back of the first room to the back of the second."[47]

After cruising the bars, men looking for heavier scenes walked to the Mineshaft, an after-hours sex club that opened in 1976. Described in *Mr. Benson* as "New York's heaviest leather bar," it became "the preeminent ongoing leather sex establishment" of the 1970s. It was a place for "men who hunger after men and everything that's masculine."[48] One ascended a long flight of stairs to its unmarked entrance. There, doormen turned away those who failed its standards for dress and deportment, said to include Mick Jagger and Rudolf Nureyev. After passing inspection, men removed and checked as much clothing as they wished with an attendant, and entered. First time attendees purchased membership cards. Manager Wally Wallace, imitating gay bars of the past, believed this reduced his legal liability. Wallace's monthly newsletters promoted exciting future events, the details of which he kept secret, he said, to avoid provoking police raids. Regardless, rumors circulated that he paid protection money to both police and organized crime.

Sexual activity increased as one moved through the Mineshaft's upper floor and down to its lower level, which offered a "maze of rooms, stairways, toilets, closets, hallways, bathtubs, gloryholes, and sex equipment," including slings in which men could recline, legs up for fisting. Regulars, whose number included many ostensibly straight men, boasted any fantasy was available somewhere inside. For T. R. Witomski, "the Mineshaft was the fullest expression of gay sexual freedom." Whatever your scene, "wandering around the maze of rooms naked, receptive to all cocks, getting pissed on while reclining in one of the WS room's several bathtubs or taking fists—you felt accepted at the Mineshaft." No sexual behavior "was frowned on," and group sex with several men was common. Always packed, the Mineshaft became a legend, the stuff of dreams. "They'd have the mummification or electroshock parties," Lenny Waller, a fixture of New York's BDSM community, explained. "You'd have 50 guys torturing somebody in a back room at four o'clock in the morning." Yet, "there would always be a couple of guys sitting at the bar talking about opera or food." Some of these discussions became so heated Wallace posted a sign warning against loud conversation, which disturbed the sexual ambiance.[49]

Wallace staged the sexual spaces carefully, providing room for participants and voyeurs and social spaces away from centers sexual activity. Music remained low so as not to drown out "slurps, moans, whippings," and other sexual sounds. After attending Inferno, Wallace gave each staff member a copy of Townsend's *Leatherman's Handbook*, announced "S&M is more than fistfucking," and installed "bondage frames, stocks, crosses," and other dungeon furnishings, making the Mineshaft even more conducive to BDSM.[50]

BDM establishments catering to heterosexuals also opened in New York. Chateaux 19, a swingers' club, began hosting BDSM nights in 1973. By the end of the decade, Belle De Jour, The Castle, Club O and Les Scenes offered BDSM performances—usually female dominant—for paying attendees—mostly men—some of whom participated on stage. Mimicking the Mineshaft and located nearby, the Hellfire Club and The Vault offered several rooms with X-frames and other BDSM equipment on which to restrain people, bars serving non-alcoholic drinks, and a few old couches, tables and chairs at which people relaxed and socialized. Fetish magazines, including *Corporal* and *Fetish Times*, hosted parties in Los Angeles and New York. "Well-known Eastern S&M publishers" Matriarch Productions, Far Out Enterprises and Aradia Enterprises hosted an unusually large party at Plato's Retreat, New York's best-known swingers club, on 21 May 1979. It featured sadomasochism-tinged musical performances, a dance and BDSM demonstrations highlighted by Belle De Jour pounding a nail through a man's penis. Several hundred people attended, including TES president Jack Jackson and Carter Stevens, a pornographic filmmaker and publisher of *S&M News*. Afterward, Plato's hosted weekly fetish nights.[51]

Over time, New York clubs specialized. Hellfire developed a reputation for wild, "anything goes" parties, and appearances by adult film stars including Jamie Gillis and Annie Sprinkle. Professional dominants congregated at the Vault. They brought favored clients and played with them in public, demonstrating skills, which attracted new clients. In addition to its large main room, which had several X-frames along one wall with benches and other equipment in its center, the Vault's narrow, winding hallways led to smaller, intimate room and nooks. Single men wandered these passageways, searched for scenes that turned them on, and watched the activities, sometimes publicly masturbating. As a result, people often came in groups. Some played while friends policed the space around, keeping voyeurs at a distance, along with those so ill-mannered (or drunk) they tried to join in.

A scene began, a flogging perhaps, at one of the X-frames. People wandered over to watch, the crowd growing in size with the intensity of the whipping and the victim's writhing and screams. As it built to a climax, more people watched. A scene might include sexual touching, leading to intense orgasms fueled by combinations of pain, pleasure and passion. More often, they involved only carefully administered pain, with the added excitement of public display and—for those who craved it—humiliation. Tops led bottoms on leashes; bottoms kissed and licked tops' boots or high heels. Once finished, a scene's participants gathered clothes, whips and other toys, and departed. The crowd dispersed, its members moving to watch another scene, or perhaps claimed the space to begin their own scene.

These were special places to which a sexual energy clung even when crowds were sparse. They were not, though, particularly attractive. For many years Hellfire was in a dank basement with a dirt floor. Condensation dripped from exposed pipes. The Vault's floors were often sticky, and stained by bleach from repeated cleanings. Management periodically scattered sawdust to help absorb spilled fluids. Apart from the cages, bondage frames and other BDSM equipment, furnishings were old and worn. Visitors either enjoyed the ambiance, reveling in its sleaze, or worked to ignore it, focusing on the diverse people around them, their scenes and screams, and unrestrained sexuality. Watching others turned them on, as did being watched, and seeing oneself whipping or being whipped in the many mirrors.

Catacombs offered a very different environment. It began as a private sexual space in the basement of Steve McEachern's and Fred Heramb's San Francisco home. They opened it to friends who, in turn, brought even more friends to Saturday night parties. About 250 men attended its one-year anniversary party on 7 May 1975. Catacombs' reputation grew quickly. "The baaad and the beautiful hauled ass to the Mission District" to visit Catacombs. Slings hung from the ceiling and the scent of Crisco, the preferred fisting lubricant, permeated the air and coated surfaces and the floor, sometimes making walking difficult. They went through as much as 40 pounds a night. Catacombs became "a mecca for handballing. Fisters from across the western world made the pilgrimage to San Francisco to attend parties at the Catacombs," among them French historian and philosopher Michel Foucault. On alternate nights, Catacombs hosted BDSM parties, their noise contrasting with calm, quiet ambiance preferred by fisters, who needed to proceed slowly and carefully.[52]

Despite its fame, Catacombs remained an exclusive venue. Like Inferno, invitations were rare and treasured. McEachern approved guest lists and personally interviewed many men before allowing them in. It was, Jack Fritscher claimed, "easier to get into the clannish Mineshaft or the privileged Studio 54 than it was to get into the Catacombs."[53]

Like Wallace, McEachern carefully staged his sexual space, setting moods with music and lighting and raising the heat to create an ambience that encouraged sexual activity—more relaxed on fisting nights, more raucous for BDSM. He denied entry to late arrivals to avoid disrupting sexual activities. Participants described the intense sexual experiences of Catacombs parties as "empowering" and "bonding." The overall feeling "was one of family." One woman recalled,

> I was coming in a group fisting situation—lots of stimulation . . . and I was screaming, coming, and crying. And . . . I started screaming extremely

> loudly: 'I am home. I am home. I am home. . . . this was the turning point of something changing me at that moment. It was completely safe.'[54]

Cynthia Slater, who for a time dated McEachern, arranged both women-only and mixed BDSM parties at Catacombs, making it a unique environment in which men and women of various orientations shared a sexual space. The latter fostered "an attitude of respect for difference" and "created a comfortable atmosphere in which diverse populations" observed one another, appreciated "their mutual interest in kink," discovered their commonalities, and shared "experience and information." Gay, lesbian and heterosexual BDSM populations mixed and learned from one another.[55]

Catacombs, Inferno, Mineshaft and similar places and events epitomized the BDSM community of the 1970s. To varying degrees exclusive and elitist, they cultivated reputations that co-mingled sex and danger. They reflected the sexual world of *Mr. Benson*, in which sexuality was "stripped of being nice" and leather-clad demons "drove bikes through our fantasies."[56] Yet, that world was changing. The number of men who sought to realize these fantasies grew, crowding bars already packed by revelers and "tourists" who came to gawk at them. Complaints about the poor behavior of BDSM newcomers and tourists increased, as did criticisms of BDSM by outsiders.

Against Sadomasochism

More people experimented with BDSM in the 1970s, some of whom joined BDSM organizations. Their growing visibility along with increasing sadomasochistic iconography in mainstream media led *Time* magazine in 1981 to declare sadomasochism had come out of the closet "whips, chains and all."[57] The growing BDSM community presented a test of the limits of sexual expression and the sexual revolution. It was, Susan Sontag wrote, "the furthest reach of the sexual experience."[58] Was it appropriate to comingle sex and violence? How far was too far to go in BDSM play? Perhaps a little pinching, biting and spanking were alright, but what about whipping, piercing or branding? Did participant consent excuse violence? Was that consent coerced? Were women, perhaps conditioned by a patriarchal culture, actually able to consent? Was it appropriate to act out scenes of historical violence and brutality in one's sex play?

While mainstream media remained largely unaware of TES and Janus, gay leather bars and sex clubs proved hard to ignore and ignited both comment and condemnation. Psychiatrists Robert E. Litman and Charles Sweringen suggested sadomasochists were self-destructive and suicidal. "Bondage can be fatal," they warned.[59] The *Hollywood Reporter* condemned Halstead's *Sextool* as "cruel, terrorizing," and "the kind of film one can imagine Nazi concentration camp commanders commission for their jaded amusement." In 1975, Richard Goldstein presented a scathing attack in *The Village Voice*, calling "S&M" the "dark side of gay liberation." He complained about the proliferation of leather bars, the growing commonality of BDSM sex, the ease of procuring its paraphernalia at shops like the Pleasure Chest (three-quarters of whose customers, he noted, were heterosexual), and a "lashes-faire" attitude toward sadomasochism, particularly among pop psychologists. Without citing examples, Goldstein warned BDSM was "terminal sex" with "ritual shootings, stabbings, hangings, all performed with the eager consent of the victim who wants nothing more than to die with an erection." Engaging in BDSM, he warned, meant putting "your life in the hands of a dangerous person." This was the BDSM community portrayed in William Friedkin's film *Cruising* (1980), in which a serial killer stalks and murders leathermen. Goldstein presented sensationalism as reality, as did *Time* magazine, which linked the Mineshaft to murder and warned "homosexual homicides are frequent—and often gruesome." Sadomasochists, Goldstein concluded, represented the "worst in humanity." The gay rights movement should exclude them.[60]

Playboy magazine's "Advisor" was almost as harsh in its assessment. Responding to a letter writer who had seen *Story of O* and asked about crossing "the border from B/D to outright sadomasochism," *Playboy* warned this was not "a form of lovemaking." Submissives were victims, dominants did not care about their partners, and both roles were "devoid of personality." *Cosmopolitan* similarly warned readers sadomasochism represented the "dark side of love."[61]

Law enforcement agencies in the United States and Canada focused increasing attention on leather bars, sex clubs and BDSM events. As they multiplied, so too did police raids. Los Angeles police raided the Black Cat leather bar on 1 January 1967, severely beat customers, ruptured the bartender's spleen, and arrested 14 men. Larry Townsend was among those arrested in 1972, when Los Angeles police raided the Black Pipe, disrupting a fund raiser for HELP.[62]

Five minutes before midnight on 10 April 1976, 100 officers, supported by two helicopters and other vehicles, forced their way into the Mark IV Health Club in Los Angeles where *Drummer* magazine was hosting a charity "slave auction." Events like this, in which willing men "sold" themselves to the highest bidder for the night, were popular events, a BDSM equivalent of bachelor auctions. One audience member, "overcome with enthusiasm, leapt up to offer himself for sale." An undercover officer, dressed in leather, "paid $16 for him" and then signaled for the raid. Police arrested *Drummer's* publisher, staff members and several dozen others on charges including violating state laws against slavery. Those arrested were led out to waiting journalists. Several lost their jobs after names and photos appeared in local press, a tactic long used by police to harass gay bars and clubs. "Police Free Gay Slaves," announced the *Orange County Register*. *Newsweek* magazine similarly sensationalized the story.[63]

Negative media portrayals of leathermen and BDSM increased, culminating in the 1980 CBS television documentary "Gay Power/Gay Politics," which singled out sadomasochists, and claimed they were so dangerous BDSM clubs kept doctors on hand to treat injuries and "sew people up." It portrayed BDSM as an exclusively gay phenomenon, even though producers filmed most of their

BDSM footage at The Chateau, a heterosexual professional domination business. Promoting gay rights, the film suggested, would lead more people to sadomasochism, resulting in serious injuries and deaths. As Jeffrey Weeks argued, these attacks were designed to weaken "the respectability and political pull" of the gay community, question its political aspirations, and fracture its fragile unity.[64]

As historian George Chauncey notes, "the normal world constituted itself and established its boundaries by creating the gay world as a stigmatized other" before World War II. In the 1970s, many gay leaders, in turn, sought to normalize that gay world by stigmatizing BDSM. John Rechy, for example, condemned leather bars, sadomasochism, and fisting. In his novel *The Sexual Outlaw*, he repeated Goldstein's and Reuben's assertions, likening BDSM to a disease, which led to "death and permanent crippling." BDSM desires were unnatural, the result of external forces corrupting one's sexual impulses. Self-loathing and persecution by heterosexuals caused "Gay S&M." It was "the straight world's most despicable legacy."[65]

Leading feminists also condemned BDSM. Adrienne Rich called it violent and self-destructive. After attending a 1975 TES meeting, Ti-Grace Atkinson condemned BDSM for supporting patriarchal power structures. Susan Sontag noted "S-m, not swinging, is the big sexual secret of the last few years." She understood it was a theatrical performance, but found its performance troubling. The "powerful and growing currents of sexual feeling, those that generally go by the name of sadomasochism," made "playing at Nazism seem erotic." While "found among heterosexuals as well as homosexuals," Sontag claimed eroticizing Nazism was "most visible" among gay men. San Francisco Mayor Diane Feinstein declared BDSM was "something human beings shouldn't do to each other" and rebuked a city coroner for meeting with Janus members to discuss BDSM safety. Like Sontag, Susan Leigh Star, denounced BDSM as fascist and associated it with Nazism. Irene Reti went so far as to blame the Holocaust on sadomasochism. In 1980, the National Organization of Women condemned BDSM as violence. Leading feminists published *Against Sadomasochism* (1982), a collection of essays critiquing BDSM.[66]

Yet, as Alison Moore conclusively demonstrates, "the practice of describing genocide perpetrators as 'sadists' produces a conflation between private, consensual sexual pleasures and social forms of organized racial killing that is substantiated only through entirely non-empirical claims." The critics of sadomasochism had things backward. Nazi ideology was puritanical, anti-sexual and intensely intolerant. Germany's Nazi officials attacked anything that hinted at perverse sexuality. Pornographers of all types, but especially those producing fetish material, shut down their businesses or fled Nazi Germany and later Nazi-occupied western Europe. "SM fantasies of Nazism," Moore explains, were a product of "postwar historical imagination of Nazism in sexual terms," popularized by lurid magazines, pulp novels and both low-budget and art-house films. "Sexualizing the motivation of the genocidal perpetrator," Moore suggests, "provided the opportunity to shroud the ugly horror of the Holocaust in a far more inviting allure of sexual fantasy." Much to many sadomasochists' dismay, "Nazis became archetypal symbols of sexy domination."[67]

A combination of disdain and disapproval, along with the growing controversy over the legitimacy of BDSM sexuality, led most gay organizations to shun the BDSM community and discourage its visible participation in pride parades and other public events. The 1979 National March on Washington for Gay and Lesbian Rights, for example, specifically prohibited them.[68] Such bans resulted from the organizers' own concerns about BDSM, and fears organizations opposed to gay rights would use leathermen and sadomasochists to stigmatize lesbians and gay men as a whole.

Largely unaware of the feminist critique of sadomasochism, gay sadomasochists were enraged by Goldstein's attack and similar anti-BDSM polemics by gay men, which they sought to refute. Unfortunately, while most sadomasochists had little use for Nazi uniforms and symbols, a few did. Some of Tom of Finland's muscular, uniformed men resembled Nazi propaganda posters he saw in his youth. His early work depicted actual Nazis. (He later apologized and withdrew these from circulation.) For a time, *Drummer* magazine—over the objections of editor Jack Fritscher—accepted ads from the American Nazi Party. Nazi uniform caps became popular among bikers (gay and straight). Arnie Kantrowitz repeatedly complained about the appearance of swastikas in gay pornography, castigated a friend who wore a Nazi cap to the Spike bar, and worried about the "persistent Germanophilia" in leather subculture. "It is only a short step from eroticizing the swastika bearer to eroticizing the genuine fascist," he warned. Nonetheless, fascism "is in no way implicit in sadomasochism." Emphasizing the centrality of consent to BDSM play, he explained "forcing strangers to be an unwilling audience to theatrical displays of Nazism is a form of cruelty."[69]

Edmund White similarly defended gay sadomasochists. While noting "confusion arises from our double use of the word sadism to mean both criminal, brutal acts of non-sexual violence and harmless erotic games," he emphasized, like Foucault, that totalitarian regimes "have always suppressed sexual deviations of every sort, including sadomasochism." While "political oppression feeds on sexual oppression," BSDM "is too anarchic to serve the design of Fascists."[70]

Much as the gay press complained when mainstream media ignored violence against gays, leathermen complained the gay press ignored attacks on them and their bars and gathering places. The *Drummer* slave auction raid and other raids on BDSM events, Jack Fritscher complained, received little attention and no condemnation by the gay press. *The Advocate*, in fact, repeated the lurid accounts of Los Angeles Police, demonstrating "a grudge against unsavory men in leather." Tony DeBlase noted the gay and lesbian press rarely reported on the "harassment of S&M men." In November 1980, for example, a former police officer fired 40 rounds from his Uzi submachinegun at the Ramrod, killing a customer and its doorman and injuring several others. Several dozen people protested at the site the next day, and perhaps 1,500 attended a candlelight vigil for the victims. The story made the front page of the *New York Post*, but otherwise received little press coverage. Even *Advocate* consigned it to its back pages.[71]

"By ignoring and even persecuting the S&M people," Craig Hanson argued, the gay community had "done exactly what straight society has done to the rest of us." The result, Larry Townsend complained, was that a gay man new to BDSM "must first go through the trauma of accepting himself as a homosexual, and then cope with his S&M proclivities," making the coming out process "two-fold and fraught with twice the number of pitfalls."[72] Sadomasochistic leathermen were revered as symbols of gay masculinity and sexual prowess, but shunned as outlaws and fascists. Mirroring a popular poster slogan from gay pride marches, sadomasochists were the gay community's "worst fear" and "best fantasy."[73]

In general, the critique of BDSM came from two directions. The first, as Gayle Rubin noted in her groundbreaking essay "Thinking Sex" was rooted in old sex panics. BDSM was unclean, even pathological. Sadomasochists would inevitably escalate their tastes for giving and receiving pain, ultimately leading to death. While not all critics took the argument that far, they still evinced deep discomfort with BDSM sex play. As David Allyn notes, "even people who are comfortable with their own sexual desires tend to be squeamish about the desires of others."[74]

The second, the feminist critique, saw in BDSM, with its ritualized violence, pain, humiliation, and subordination, the ultimate expression of patriarchy and all its problems. They were particularly appalled by the growing visibility of women in the BDSM community and the formation of dedicated women's BDSM groups. The first of these, Samois, formed in 1978. Over the next few years, the women of Samois led the fight to legitimatize BDSM sexuality. Their aggressive efforts to push back against feminist denunciations of BDSM provoked intense debate and the publication of *Against Sadomasochism*.

Samois

Women remained a minority of the membership of both TES and Janus, but steadily increased their organizing in the 1970s. Positive articles on BDSM appeared in lesbian publications including *Hera, Lesbian Tide* and *Plexus*, which provoked substantial discussion.[75] Califia whose essay "Secret Side of Lesbian Sexuality," appeared in *The Advocate* in 1979, later explained she was "pissed off" and "tired of readings lies" about her sexuality, which either dismissed lesbian sadomasochists as nonexistent or presented them as cousins "to a rapist or chainsaw killer." She was also "tired of being alone," and "knew there would never be a leatherdyke community if somebody didn't announce that one already existed."[76] Her essay called other lesbian sadomasochists to join her.

In 1977, Janus women organized Cardea, a women's subgroup, which held separate, women-only meetings. While this helped address some of these women's concerns, particularly unwelcome male sexual advances, Cardea's uncertain place within Janus caused tension. Some lesbians refused to join Janus, since it included men. Led by Califia, several Cardea members left Janus in 1978 and formed Samois, the first women's BDSM organization.

Named after Anne-Marie's women-only estate in *Story of O*, Samois' membership increased rapidly, requiring its leaders to add officers and create six subcommittees to manage affairs. Its "Ministry of Truth" dealt with the press and spearheaded its publishing efforts. As historians Carolyn Bronstein and Alex Warner note, Samois formed partly in reaction to the feminist critique of BDSM and "the special problems of isolation and stereotyping experienced by lesbian sadomasochists." Its members sought a safe place for women to explore BDSM, but also devoted considerable energy debating anti-BDSM and anti-pornography feminists. *Off Our Backs* and other feminist publications attacked Samois members for either advancing—or being duped by—patriarchal sexual conventions. Samois' leaders confronted these charges head-on, defending women's right to engage in any sexual activities they desired. The perverse and subversive nature of BDSM, they argued undercut rather than supported patriarchy. Samois' active participation in these "Feminist Sex Wars" made it much more politically active than earlier BDSM organizations.[77]

Califia, Gayle Rubin, Carol Truscott and other Samois members wrote essays explaining, defending and teaching BDSM practices. Samois published two books: *What Color is Your Handkerchief: A Lesbian SM Sexuality Reader* (1979), a 44-page collection of previously published BDSM essays, and *Coming to Power* (1981), a diverse collection of writing by Samois members, which included poetry and short fiction. Rubin's essay, "The Leather Menace," surveyed the growing harassment of BDSM practitioners and compared them to religious heretics, "persecuted by the state, the mental health establishment, social welfare agencies, and the media." They faced "an endless stream of propaganda which rationalizes abuses against them, attempts to impair their self-esteem, and exhorts them to recant."[78]

Many women's bookstores refused to carry *Coming to Power*, and feminist publications refused ads for the book. The same businesses that refused to carry its books and flyers, also denied Samois meeting space. Samois members confronted and debated editors and bookstore owners, urging them to carry the book and promote an open marketplace for ideas. As Janet Schrim noted, "one of the basic principles of feminism is the valuing of every woman's experience. This must include women who are into SM." Were the costs of coming out as BDSM "not so excruciating," Gayle Rubin argued, "there would be groups like Samois in virtually every lesbian community in the U.S."[79]

Several scholars have recently examined Samois and the "Feminist Sex Wars." Samois members proved effective debaters and significantly shaped feminist discussions of BDSM and pornography, promoting "sex-positive feminism."[80] Debates about women's sexuality involved more than BDSM. As Lynn Comella notes, even dildos became contentious. Stores that refused to carry *Coming to Power* often refused to carry dildos, seeing them as "male-identified" and incompatible with "'women-identified' sexuality."[81] Samois members were an important force in these debates and helped shape feminist thought on sexuality. Within the BDSM community, though, their influence was even more profound. Samois' engagement with its opponents forced its members to both think deeply about BDSM and develop significant political skills, which in turn influenced the BDSM organizations that emerged in the 1980s.

Samois' active engagement in the "Sex Wars" exacerbated tensions common to BDSM groups as to the proportion of time and resources devoted to educational, political and social activities. Some members just wanted to have fun; others reveled in political battle. Some thrived in a diverse environment that included straight and bisexual women, as well as transwomen; others wanted a purely lesbian organization. Relatively few women, though, joined Samois to operate a publishing enterprise. Samois folded in 1982 as a result of these tensions. Two years later, Gayle Rubin and other former Samois members founded The Outcasts, an inclusive women's BDSM organization. While not as politically active as Samois, it, too, significantly shaped the BDSM community in the 1980s.

★★★

As Gayle Rubin explains, before 1970, people seeking "to affiliate with the leather and SM worlds" needed to overcome social barriers demarcating sexual populations, including "walls of stigma, illegality, and disreputability," and "the privacy, defensiveness, and hostility" with which sexual communities "defend themselves from unwanted tourism and harassment."[82] In the 1970s, informal BDSM networks developed into formal organizations. Leather bars grew in number. So, too, did BDSM sex clubs. Modeled on New York's Hellfire and Vault, Hellfire West opened in Detroit in 1979, as did Chicago's Leather Rose. Alongside these bars and dungeons, the first dedicated BDSM groups formed. Along with books and magazines published by BDSM experts, they eased access to their growing community and began shaping BDSM practice. They marked the emergence of a new, organizationally centered public community, which aimed to both assure members of the legitimacy of their sexual interests and educate them to pursue them safely. They transformed how people interested in sadomasochism learned about it, met people with shared interests, and engaged in BDSM activities.

Mainstream society became increasingly aware of sadomasochists in the mid-1970s, and responded to them with a mix of fear and arousal, inaugurating a short-lived era of "SM chic." This resembled "porno chic" of a few years earlier when suburbanites flocked to downtown theaters to see *Deep Throat* (1972), *Behind the Green Door* (1972) and other hard-core films. Popular magazines discussed BDSM. Musicians and fashion magazines embraced sadomasochistic imagery. Tourists went slumming in leather bars, dungeons and sex clubs. As Chad Heap notes, the VCR helped kill this new wave of slumming by allowing private home viewing of these spectacles.[83] So, too, did commentators who increasingly disparaged BDSM as fascist, reactionary, patriarchal, violent and even murderous.

As George Chauncey argues, the gay community's growing visibility in the 1920s led states to enact repressive laws, and these "growing attacks on gay men forged new bonds among them." Margot Canady makes the case even more forcefully. The state's explicit targeting of homosexuals proved a "catalyst in the formation of homosexual identity."[84] The same proved true for sadomasochists. Growing condemnation, police raids and other legal threats focused attention on sadomasochists even as society lessened restraints on sexual activity and display. This explicit targeting encouraged organizing among sadomasochists, which escalated from social events and educational activities to political activism. Increasingly, BDSM activists echoed calls for "gay liberation" by demanding "SM liberation," which to them meant self-acceptance, ending pejorative media and medical depictions of BDSM, and ending law enforcement harassment of BDSM practitioners, sex workers, publishers and sex toymakers. They sought the sexual citizenship outlined in TES's Creed: to seek out those who shared their sexual interests and engage in those interests without fear. In the 1970s, TES, Janus, Samois and other BDSM organizations laid the groundwork for the rapid growth of the BDSM community in the 1980s and 1990s.

Notes

1 *Screw*, 28 December 1970. Clipping in TES Files, Leather Archives and Museum (Hereafter LAAM).
2 TES Minutes, 7 August 1971, TES file, LAAM.
3 TES Resolution, 26 September 1971, TES file, LAAM; "Eulenspiegel—What's That," TES file, Kinsey Institute; Terry Kolb, "Masochist's Lib," *Village Voice* 16, no. 19, 13 May 1971, 4–6; Charles Kaiser, *The Gay Metropolis* (Boston, MA: Houghton Mifflin, 1997), 213; Ray Schultz, "Cruising for a Bruising" *Screw* 266 (8 April 1974), 4–7; and "Scenes," *Village Voice*, 2 December 1971, 58.
4 John D'Emilio, *Sexual Politics, Sexual Communities: The Making of a Homosexual Minority in the United States, 1940–1970* (Chicago, IL: University of Chicago Press, 1983), 10.
5 Ziva, "A Visit to Eulenspiegel," in Saul Brown, *Catalog of Sexual Consciousness* (New York: Grove Press, 1975), 107–9; Marvin X, "Prometheus Unbound: S&M Liberation Comes of Age," *Best of Fetish Times* 3 (1976); and Lawrence Mass, "Coming to Grips with Sadomasochism," in G.W. Levi Kamel and Thomas Weinberg (eds.), *S and M: Studies in Sadomasochism* (Buffalo, NY: Prometheus, 1983), 47.
6 David Allyn, *Make Love, Not War: The Sexual Revolution: An Unfettered History* (London: Routledge, 2001), 4–5.
7 TES flier, undated, circa 1972 or 1973, LAAM, TES file; and Aims and Purposes of The Eulenspiegel Society, TES file, Kinsey Institute.
8 The Society of Janus should not be confused with the similarly named Janus Society, a homophile organization founded in Philadelphia in 1962 that published *Drum* magazine.
9 Jay Wiseman, *SM 101: A Realistic Introduction* (San Francisco, CA: Greenery, 1996), 114–6.
10 Pat Bond, "Another Open Letter," *Prometheus* 6 (1975), 42; Mark Joplin, "A Chat With Cynthia Slater," *Growing Pains*, February/March 1983, 11–2; Wiseman, *SM 101*, 118; and Fritcher [as Eric van Meter], "S&M: The Last Taboo, The Janus Society," *Drummer* 27 (1978), 34.

11 G. W. Levi Kamel, "Leathersex: Meaningful Aspects of Gay Sadomasochism," in Thomas Weinberg (ed.), *S&M: Studies in Dominance and Submission* (Amherst, NY: Prometheus, 1995), 240.
12 Spring, *Secret Historian: The Life and Times of Samuel Steward, Professor, Tattoo Artist, and Sexual Renegade* (New York: Farrar, Straus and Giroux, 2010), 302–3.
13 Mark Joplin, "A Chat with Cynthia Slater," *Growing Pains*, February/March 1983, 12–7; T. Weymouth. and Society of Janus, *Society of Janus: Twenty-Five Years* (San Francisco, CA: Society of Janus, 1999), 5–10, and 16–7; and Eric Van Meter [Jack Fritscher], "The Janus Society," *Drummer* 27 (February 1979), 33.
14 Saul Brown, *Catalog of Sexual Consciousness* (New York: Grove Press, 1975), 108; James Hartwell, *Nubond* catalog (1978), 2, Kinsey Institute; Pat Bond, "Another Open Letter to Our Coordinators and Potential Coordinators," *Prometheus* 5 (1975), 40–1; "In Other Cities," *Prometheus* 11 (undated, presumably late 1970s); and Esoteric Encounters to J. Brewer, 19 December 1977, Kinsey Institute.
15 "Status Report," *SM Express*, April 1978, 2 and Mass, "Coming to Grips with Sadomasochism," 46.
16 Spring, *Secret Historian*, 359 & 370.
17 John Preston, *Mr. Benson* (San Francisco, CA: Cleis, 1983), originally serialized in *Drummer*, 1979–1980, issues 29–38, under the name Jack Prescott. The t-shirt advertisements first appeared in *Drummer* 36 (1980), 33 and *DungeonMaster* 5 (July 1980).
18 Preston in Mark Thompson, *Leatherfolk : Radical Sex, People, Politics, and Practice* (Boston, MA: Alyson Publications, 1991), 214.
19 "CHC History," *Inferno* X (1981) booklet, 27–9, Kinsey Archives; Tracy Baim and Owen Keehnen, *Leatherman: The Legend of Chuck Renslow* (Chicago, IL: Prairie Avenue Productions, 2011), 97–8; Robert Vincent Bienvenue, "The Development of Sadomasochism as a Cultural Style in the Twentieth-Century United States," PhD Diss., Indiana University, 1998, 249–50; and John Preston, "Hellfire's Inferno," *Drummer* 41 (1981), 13.
20 "CHC History," *Inferno* X, 27–9; David Stein, "S/M's Copernican Revolution" in Thompson, 146; and Michele Buchanon, "Leather Is Thicker Than Blood: Identity Formation Among Organized SM Practitioners in New York City," PhD diss., New School University, 2004, 34.
21 Ivo Dominguez, *Beneath the Skins: The New Spirit and Politics of the Kink Community* (Los Angeles, CA: Daedalus Pub. Co., 1994), 85.
22 Alex Comfort, *The Joy of Sex: A Gourmet Guide to Love Making* (New York: Fireside, 1972); Anne Riccitelli, "Sadomasochism American Style," *Penthouse Forum*, March 1974, Sadomasochism File, Kinsey Institute; John Norman, *Tarnsman of Gor* (New York: Ballentine, 1966) and *Imaginative Sex* (New York: DAW, 1974); Pat Califia, "No Fantasy Please, We're Americans," in John Norman (ed.), *Imaginative Sex* (New York: Masquerade, 1997), iii; Rolf Milonas, *Fantasex: A Book of Erotic Games for the Adult Couple* (New York: Grosset & Dunlap, 1975); Charles Silverstein, *The Joy of Gay Sex* (New York: Crown, 1977); "Leather, Sex, and Mushrooms," *High Times*, August 1976; and Ridgewell Shotwood, "Truths and Misconceptions about SM," *Taste of Latex*, Spring 1990. 4–5.
23 Allyn, *Make Love Not War*, 239.
24 Larry Townsend, *The Leatherman's Handbook* (Los Angeles, CA: LT Publications, 1972), 173; Gerald and Caroline Greene, *SM the Last Taboo* (New York: Grove Press, 1974); and Eric Chaline, "On Becoming a Gay SMer: A Sexual Scripting Perspective," in Derren Langdridge and Meg Barker (eds.), *Safe, Sane and Consensual: Contemporary Perspectives Sadomasochism* (New York: Palgrave McMillan, 2008), 155–76.
25 Rubin, "Old Guard, New Guard," *Cuir Underground* 4, no. 2 (1998); Guy Baldwin, *Ties That Bind: The SM/Leather/Fetish Erotic Style* (San Francisco, CA: Daedalus, 1993), 111; and Mark P. Levine, *Gay Macho: The Life and Death of the Homosexual Clone* (New York: NYU Press, 1998), 7.

26 W. Charles Clark, "Stonewall and the SM-Leather Lifestyle 3: The Brambles, the Baths, the Bars, and the Trucks," *Checkmate* 15 (May 1996), 8–9 & 18 and Gayle S. Rubin, "The Valley of the Kings: Leathermen in San Francisco, 1960–1990," PhD diss., University of Michigan, 1994, 294–5.
27 "Color Your Own Handkerchief," *The Advocate* 163 (7 May 1975), 4; Joe Parisi, "Stereotyping," *The Advocate* (27 August 1975), 26–7; and "Pleasure Chest Introduces the Most Complete Hanky Guide," *DungeonMaster* 16 (1982), 7.
28 Rubin, "Valley of the Kings," 416 and Joseph Bean, *International Mr. Leather: 25 Years of Champions* (Las Vegas, NV: Nazca Plains, 2004), 15.
29 Baim and Keehnen, *Leatherman*, 333–8; Joseph Bean, *International Mr. Leather: 25 Years of Champions* (Las Vegas: Nazca Plains Corp., 2004), 6–13; and Guy Baldwin, *The Leather Contest Guide* (Los Angeles, CA: Daedalus, 1993), 78.
30 Bienvenue, "Development of Sadomasochism," 207–10.
31 Elana Levine, *Wallowing in Sex: The New Sexual Culture of 1970s American Television* (Durham, NC: Duke University Press, 2007), 83–4.
32 Connie Shortes, "'Cleaning up a Sewer:' The Containment of SM Pornography," *Journal of Popular Film and Television*, 26, no. 2 (Summer 1998), 72–9.
33 The Naughty Victorians, Podcast 9, *The Rialto Report*, 5 May 2013, https://www.therialtoreport.com/2013/05/ (accessed 6 June 2019).
34 Harold Fairbanks, "Peter, Peter, Peter," *The Advocate* 11 (September 1974), 30; Sidney Charles, "Sextool," *Drummer* 1 (1975), 34–5; and Sidney Charles, "Born to Raise Hell," *Drummer* 4 (December 1975–January 1976), 15.
35 Jack Fritscher, *Gay San Francisco: Eyewitness Drummer Vol. 1* (San Francisco, CA: Palm Drive, 2008), 416; Arnie Kantrowitz, "Swastika Toys," in Mark Thompson, *Leatherfolk: Radical Sex, People, Politics, and Practice* (Boston, MA: Alyson Publications, 1991), 193–209; Marcus Grumley, *Hard Corps: Studies in Leather and Sadomasochism* (E P Dutton, 1977), chapter 6; and "The Binding Pain," *Bound* 5 (1975), 5.
36 Robert E. Litman and Charles Sweringen, "Bondage and Suicide," *Archives of General Psychiatry* 27 (July 1972), 82; Joe Parisi, "Chicago's Renslow," *The Advocate* (2 June 1976), 41–3; W. Charles Clark, "Stonewall and the SM-Leather Lifestyle 3: The Brambles, the Baths, the Bars, and the Trucks," *Checkmate* 15 (May 1996), 8–9 & 18; Rubin, "Valley of the Kings," 194, 283–7; and Peter Fiske, "A Profile of Mr. S: Alan Selby," *Drummer* 135 (1989), 7–10.
37 Joe Cook, "Famous Dungeons of San Francisco," *Drummer* 17 (1977), 8–11 and "The Dungeon Workshop," *DungeonMaster* 5 (1980), 5.
38 Rubin in Thompson, *Leatherfolk*, 121.
39 Peggy J. Kleinplatz and Charles Moser, *Sadomasochism: Powerful Pleasures* (New York: Harrington Park, 2006), 29; Charles Moser, "SM (Sadomasochistic) Interactions in Semi-Public Settings," *Journal of Homosexuality* 36, no. 2 (1998), 25; and Rubin in Thompson, *Leatherfolk*, 120–1.
40 Sir John, *The Q Letters* (Buffalo, NY: Prometheus, 1993), 153.
41 John Preston and Anthony DeBlase, "Hellfire Inferno," *Drummer* 35 (1980), 14–20.
42 David Stein, "Inferno X: A Bottom's First Time Impression," *DungeonMaster* 14 (1982), 1–2 and Levine, *Gay Macho*, 97–8.
43 Rubin in Thompson, *Leatherfolk*, 120–1 and Geoff Ferguson, "SM Networking: A Beginning," *GMSMA News* 2, no 3 (June 1984), 8.
44 David Lewis, "A Top's View," *DungeonMaster* 6 (September 1980), 1–2 and DeBlase to Pleasure Chest, 4 November 1981, LAAM, DeBlase Papers, Box 29.
45 Stein, "Inferno X," 1.
46 Califia, "Tribal Rights: Gentle Warriors," *The Advocate* (15 August 1989), 67 and Levine, *Gay Macho*, 52–3 & 64.
47 Edmund White, *City Boy: My Life in New York During the 1960s and '70s* (New York: Bloomsbury, 2009), 232–4; Charles Kaiser, *The Gay Metropolis*, 243–4; Ray Schultz, "Cruising for a Bruising," *Screw* 266 (8 April 1974), 4–7; Mister Marcus, "Academy

Awards, Leather Style," *The Advocate* (29 March 1972), 18; Grumely, *Hard Core*, Chapter 1; and Arnie Kantrowitz, "Christopher Street," *The Advocate* (18 June 1975), 36.

48 John Preston, *Mr. Benson* (New York: Masquerade, 1992), 45; Rubin, "Catacombs" in Thompson, *Leatherfolk*, 121; and Leo Cardini, *Mineshaft Nights* (STARbooks Press, 2007), 52.

49 T.R. Witomski, "Requiem for the Mineshaft," *Drummer* 96 (1985), 81 and Peter Blauner, "A Walk on the Wild Side," *New York*, 14 May 1990, 36.

50 Jack Fritscher, "Mineshaft," *Drummer* 19 (1977), 82–3; Joel I. Brodsky, "The Mineshaft: A Retrospective Ethnography," in Thomas Weinberg (ed.), *S and M: Studies in Sadomasochism* (Amherst, NY: Prometheus, 1995), 205; W. Charles Clark, "Stonewall and the SM-Leather Lifestyle, Part 3: The Brambles, the Baths, the Bars, and the Trucks," *Checkmate* 15 (May 1996), 8–9 & 18; and Fledermaus [Tony DeBlase], "The Mineshaft, 1976–1985," *DungeonMaster* 30 (undated, 1985 or 1986), 14–5.

51 Grand Matriarch, "SM Party at Plato's Retreat," *Best of Fetish Times* 8 (1980), 13–5.

52 Rubin in Thompson, *Leatherfolk*, 121; Bill Brent, "Remembering the Catacombs," *Black Sheets* 12 (undated, 1996 or 1997), 40–5; and Jack Fritscher, "The Catacombs," *Drummer* 23 (1978), 8–11.

53 Fritscher, *Gay San Francisco*, 105.

54 Carla, quoted in Bill Brent, "Remembering the Catacombs," *Black Sheets* 12 (undated, 1996 or 1997), 44.

55 Geoff Mains, *Urban Aboriginals* (Los Angeles, CA: Daedalus Publishing, 2002), 178; Rubin in Thompson, *Leatherfolk*, 131; Weymouth, *Society of Janus: Twenty-Five Years* (San Francisco, CA: Society of Janus, 1999), 11–5; and Guy Baldwin, "A Second Coming Out," in Thompson, *Leatherfolk*, 178.

56 John Preston, "What Happened?" in Thompson, *Leatherfolk*, 212–3, and 214.

57 John Leo, "Stomping and Whomping Galore," *Time*, 4 May 1981, 74.

58 Sontag, "Fascinating Fascism," *New York Review of Books*, 6 February 1975.

59 Robert E. Litman and Charles Sweringen, "Bondage and Suicide," *Archives of General Psychiatry* 27 (July 1972), 80–5.

60 Richard Goldstein, "S&M: The Dark Side of Gay Liberation," *Village Voice*, 7 July 1975, 1 and 10–3 and "The Gay World's Leather Fringe," *Time* 115 (24 March 1980), 74–5.

61 TES to *Playboy*, June 1976, Lesbian Herstory Archive, SM file; and Natalie Gittelson, "The Dark Side of Love," *Cosmopolitan*, March 1983, 221–3.

62 "Revisiting the Black Cat," *The Advocate*, 17 February 2012, at https://www.advocate.com/arts-entertainment/features/2012/02/17/revisiting-black-cat (accessed 18 December 2018).

63 Fritscher, *Eyewitness Drummer*, 626; Susan Fraker and John Barnes, "Of Human Bondage," *Newsweek*, 26 April 1976, 35; Judy Wilmore, "The Great Slave Market Bust," *The Advocate*, May 1976; Edward Alwood, *Straight News: Gays, Lesbians, and the News* Media (New York: Columbia University Press, 1996), 5–7; and Bernardo Alexander Attias, "'Police Free Gay Slaves': Consent, Sexuality, and the Law," *Left History* 10, no. 1 (Fall/Winter 2004), 55–83.

64 Edward Alwood, *Straight News: Gays, Lesbians, and the News Media* (New York: Columbia University Press, 1996), 185–6; Jeffrey Weeks, *Sexuality and Its Discontents: Meanings, Myths, and Modern Sexualities* (London: Routledge, 1990), 48; and Skip A. [Aiken], "Don't Close the Closet Door Just Because There's Leather Inside" in *What Color Is Your Handkerchief* (San Francisco, CA: Samois, 1979), 26–7.

65 George Chauncey, *Gay New York: Gender, Urban Culture, and the Making of the Gay Male World, 1890–1940* (New York: Basic Books, 1995), 26; Larry Townsend, "We, the People." *The Advocate* 160 (26 March 1975), 42–3; and John Rechy, *The Sexual Outlaw: A Documentary* (New York: Grove, 1977), 260 and 262.

66 Adrienne Rich, "The Meaning of Our Love for Women Is What We Have Constantly to Expand" in *On Lies, Secrets and Silence: Selected Prose, 1966–1978*

(New York: Norton, 1979), 225; Ti-Grace Atkinson, "Why I'm Against SM Liberation," in Robin Ruth Linden, et al. (eds.), *Against Sadomasochism* (San Francisco, CA: Frog in the Well), 90–2; Susan Sontag, "Fascinating Fascism." *The New York Review of Books*, 6 February 1975; Susan Leigh Star, "Swastikas: The Street and the University," in *Against Sadomasochism*, 131–6; Irene Reti, *Remember the Fire: Lesbian Sadomasochism in a Post Nazi-Holocaust World* (Santa Cruz, CA: HerBooks, 1986); and Alex Warner "'Where Angels Fear to Tread': Feminism, Sex and the Problem of SM, 1969–1993," PhD diss., Rutgers, 2011, 29–31, 112–3, and 128–9.

67 Alison Moore, *Sexual Myths of Modernity: Sadism, Masochism, and Historical Teleology* (Lanham, MD: Lexington, 2016), 162 & 167–8.

68 Weeks, *Sexuality and Its Discontents*, 48.

69 Arnie Kantrowitz, "Swastika Toys," in Thompson, *Leatherfolk*, 193–4 & 207.

70 Edmund White, "Sado Machismo," in *The Burning Library: Essays* (New York: Vintage, 1995), 66.

71 Jim Downs, *Stand by Me: The Forgotten History of Gay Liberation* (New York: Basic, 2016), 30; Fritscher, *Eyewitness Drummer*, 117; Tony DeBlase, "Safety Valve," *DungeonMaster* 6 (September 1980); and Alwood, *Straight News*, 197–9.

72 Craig Hanson, "S&M and the Gay World," *Gay News*, 1 September 1972, 8–9 and Townsend, "We, the People," 42–3.

73 Michael Bronski, *A Queer History of the United States* (Boston, MA: Beacon Press, 2011), 220.

74 Gayle Rubin, "Thinking Sex: Notes for a Radical Theory of the Politics of Sexuality," in Carole Vance (ed.), *Pleasure and Danger* (New York: Routledge, 1984) and Allyn, *Make Love, Not War*, 52.

75 Barbara Ruth, "Cathexis (on the nature of S&M)," *Hera*, December 1975 (reprinted in *Lesbian Tide,* May/June 1977, 10–1); Karla Jay, "The Spirit Is Feminist but the Flesh Is?" *Lesbian Tide*, October 1974, 15; Jeanne Cordova, "Towards a Feminist Expression of Sado-Masochism," *Lesbian Tide*, November/December 1976, 14–7; and Janet Schrim, "SM: Is It Oppression?," *Plexus*, March 1979.

76 Pat Califia, *Public Sex: The Culture of Radical Sex* (San Francisco, CA: Cleis, 1994), 12.

77 Gayle Rubin, "Samois," *Leather Times* 21 (Spring 2004), 3–7; ["Organizational Structure of Samois," Lesbian Herstory Archive, SM File; Carolyn Bronstein, *Battling Pornography: The American Feminist Anti-Pornography Movement, 1976–1986* (Cambridge: Cambridge University Press, 2011), 286; and Warner, "'Where Angels Fear to Tread': Feminism, Sex and the Problem of SM, 1969–1993," PhD diss., Rutgers, The State University of New Jersey, 2011 49–52.

78 Rubin, "The Leather Menace," 225–6.

79 Rubin, "The Leather Menace," 222 and Janet Schrim, "SM for Feminists," *Gay Community News*, 9 May 1981, 8–9.

80 Bronstein, *Battling Pornography* and Warner, "Where Angels Fear To Tread".

81 Lynn Comella, *Vibrator Nation: How Feminist Sex-Toy Stores Changed the Business of Pleasure* (Durham, NC: Duke University Press, 2007), 54.

82 Rubin, "Valley of the Kings," 221.

83 Chad Heap, *Slumming: Sexual and Racial Encounters in American Nightlife, 1885–1940* (Chicago, IL: University of Chicago Press, 2009), 282.

84 Chauncey, *Gay New York*, 355–6 & 360 and Margot Canaday, *The Straight State: Sexuality and Citizenship in Twentieth-Century America* (Princeton, NJ: Princeton University Press, 2009), 4.

3

"SOMEWHERE TO GO"

BDSM Groups Proliferate, 1980–86

Between 1980 and 1986, the number of BDSM organizations in the United States grew from less than a dozen to about 200. By 1986, one existed in almost every state of the union. Several BDSM organizations focused as much on politics and influencing mainstream society as they did their members' social and educational needs. Supported by growing numbers of magazines, newsletters and zines, they began codifying BDSM practice, including negotiating informed consent, the course of a BDSM scene and the organization of parties. This increasing organization, though, eroded BDSM's outlaw image—an image leaders of many BDSM organizations rejected. Growing numbers of sadomasochists embraced formal organizations and the standards of conduct they—and the burgeoning BDSM literature—promoted.

The leaders of these organizations, buoyed by their rapid growth, believed hundreds of thousands—if not millions—of Americans shared their BDSM interests, a belief reinforced by sex surveys and anthologies of sexual fantasies, such as the two *Hite Reports* (1981) and Nancy Friday's *My Secret Garden* (1973) and *Men in Love* (1980), which indicated interest in bondage, spanking and related activities. *Playboy* magazine reversed its negative portrayal of BDSM and dispatched a reporter to tour New York's BDSM clubs. So, too, did *Cosmopolitan*, whose surveys indicated 18 percent of women had experimented with bondage, 16 percent with spanking and 13 percent with verbal humiliation. About 12 percent had acted out forced sex fantasies. The attraction of BDSM for "certain women" was "undeniable." Society of Janus leaders believed 20,000 sadomasochists lived in San Francisco, though they were mostly "closeted married couples." Despite members' worries about the Reagan administration's anti-sex policies and anti-BDSM articles in the media, Janus's Don Miesen declared "SM liberation is a war that could be successfully fought." They simply needed to reach out to closeted sadomasochists and better explain BDSM to the general public.[1]

While explaining BDSM to outsiders proved problematic, BDSM organizations attracted people previously hesitant to explore their fantasies. Growing numbers of sadomasochists affiliated with local organizations, subscribed to BDSM publications and participated in BDSM events outside their homes. BDSM organizations displaced bars and sex clubs as the primary centers of BDSM socialization and education and provided a base for political action.

The Problem with Leather Bars

Encouraged by *Drummer* and other publications, gay sadomasochists explored leather bars in greater numbers. While some reveled in their sexually charged atmosphere, others found them disappointing or intimidating. Part of the problem was that dressing in leather did not necessarily indicate BDSM interests. Rick Leathers synopsized the problem. Both self-identified leathermen and sadomasochists, patronized the same bars. While "alike in their symbols," they were "radically different in their goals." Despite their "macho image" and enjoyment of wearing "leather, denim, or uniforms," the "in-bed sexuality" of most leathermen was "fairly conventional." They might enjoy a bit of rough sex and dirty talk, but had no interest in bondage, flagellation or other BDSM activities. Yet, they displayed its symbols, causing confusion and frustration. Only a handful of men at "Eagle's Nest, Spike, and other so-called S&M bars were actually into sexual sadism or masochism," one New Yorker complained. They just liked the "macho atmosphere."[2]

Even worse, leather bars had become "something of a tourist adventure" for men with no interest BDSM. The movie *Police Academy* (1984) and its sequels made light of this with unsuspecting characters lured into the Blue Oyster leather bar and forced to tango with its macho—but harmless—inhabitants. For Marcus Grumley, "hardcore leather sensibility," which used "leather in both sexual display and sadomasochistic ritual," provided "a common vocabulary . . . of stance and attitude, . . . which the desired partner will decipher and respond to." Men paired up "more by signal than conversation."[3] This vocabulary broke down when men, like Al Pacino's character in *Cruising*, used symbols without understanding or intention to follow through with the activities they promised. The bars, a *DungeonMaster* reader complained, were full of "campy ladies in leather." They dressed, but did not act, the part.[4]

As Mark Levine notes, the prevailing "masculine erotic script" encouraged gay men to experiment with leather and BDSM, which many "homosexuals regarded as archetypically masculine," due to its "stereotypical male role performances (dominance, control, endurance) and symbols (whips, chains, leather)." Most avoided anything involving pain, though a few, in order to "butch sex up," experimented with light bondage, water sports and fisting. So-called clones used the "signifiers, the props of S/M," without actually engaging in the practice. They wore the same black leather, but made sure "no one got the wrong idea."[5] Except, of course, men did.

Many motorcycle clubs, in turn, resented being confused with sadomasochists. The Leatheriders complained people misinterpreted their logo as "indicating Leatheriders B.C. is a heavy S&M, macho or leather club." They changed it, hoping this "dismissed our unwanted, sadistic and masochistic ghosts to the darkness of their own thoughts."[6] Confusion reigned as the symbols and styles of presentation promoted by Carney, Townsend and others lost their certainty.

In the bars themselves, David Stein found "leather, leather everywhere, but hardly any SM in sight." Even at the Mineshaft, he found activities mild, just "some ass slapping and titwork." TES members similarly complained most men at the Spike and Eagle's Nest came for "the macho atmosphere," rather than "S&M." For most bar patrons, they joked, S&M meant "stand and model" their tight leather outfits or uniforms. Most BDSM play remained private and secret, Stein discovered. "Plenty was going on, but you had to be invited to the party." Those invitations went mostly to "the young, the beautiful, and the reckless." Newcomers like him found it difficult to connect with experienced practitioners and learn about BDSM. You could not talk your way into an invitation "because bar etiquette stipulated that no one talked to anyone unless they were already friends or else cruising each other." The latter "called for detached, objectified, and phallocentric, sexual conduct." Men sought "recreational sex for orgasmic release with partners selected for physical attractiveness." They were not there to talk.[7]

Similarly, newcomers did not ask questions, since doing so hurt their status. Men at the Ramrod, Tony DeBlase observed, "dress up and look pretty, or 'macho,' for each other." At clubs like the Mineshaft, "they do interesting things to each other," but "at none of these places do they actually TALK to each other!" Sadomasochists met in bars, and perhaps engaged in light play. Heavy BDSM activity, discussed only in "whispers or code," took place in private, "behind closed doors." Newcomers found it difficult to locate and connect with this secret world. Stein wanted not just heavier, but more sophisticated, BDSM play, the sorts of activities he experienced after attending CHC's annual Inferno weekend in 1981.[8]

The limited clientele of leather bars and sex clubs like the Mineshaft—gay men who met their standards and a few, select others—left a large, unserved population with BDSM interests. Newcomers felt shunned, lesbians and heterosexuals excluded. TES abandoned its bar nights due to the mutual discomfort between TES members and the Spike's regular clientele, as well as TES members' desire for heavier BDSM activities than bars offered or allowed—desires shared by many others. BDSM newcomers increasingly turned to organizations like TES and Janus, or founded new organizations, which encouraged egalitarian patterns of BDSM education and socialization.

"Safe and Sane SM"

While desperate to learn about BDSM, many newcomers worried about potential dangers. DeBlase provided safety information in his hands-on demonstrations and regularly warned people to keep their activities "safe and sane," to hurt their lovers in ways they found pleasurable while causing no lasting harm. After he founded Sandmutopia Supply Company, a mail-order company selling simple BDSM toys, DeBlase distilled practical advice and common questions into short, two- to four-page "Tech Notes." Enclosed with orders, they taught customers to safely use nipple clamps, rope and other toys, and weave elaborate rope harnesses around their partners.

Hosts of private parties or intimate clubs like the Catacombs similarly worked to keep guests safe. Gay men learned from older, more experienced men "how to dress, how to behave, and the practical technologies of SM play or fist fucking."[9] As Gayle Rubin notes, "S&M functioned through the 'old boy' network of knowledgeable Tops and bottoms." They "kept out the kooks" and "passed on information about 'good matches' and people to avoid." Warnings about people who behaved recklessly were passed through the community. Reputations within this "small, gossip-ridden community" were fragile. So, this provided "a good deal of social control over patterns of play." It became a "point of competition among tops, sadists, dominants, Mistresses, and Masters" as to "who is the safest (as well as the hottest, the most imaginative, and the most proficient)." This emphasis on "skill and accomplishment, rather than looks or popularity," Ivo Dominguez pointed out, allowed people overlooked in leather bars "to shine."[10]

Rubin and Dominguez, though, describe ideal situations, which proved difficult to maintain as the BDSM community grew. Instead of encouraging safety, one Samois member complained, competition for status actually encouraged people to push scenes beyond comfort zones—a problem exacerbated by the increasingly performative nature of public scenes at BDSM parties. A constant tension existed between the erotic appeal of "pushing limits," and the need for safety. TES, Pat Bond explained, had already grown too large to police by word-of-mouth.

> Years ago, we were proud to say that people in Eulenspiegel knew one another and if anyone ever did anything gross or laid a trip on anyone against their will, that person would be immediately ostracized . . . Today, however, our constituency is sufficiently large that not everyone knows everyone else

or "the nasty tricks that some people pull."[11]

Similarly, complaints about the alienating nature of leather bars increased, as did reports of miscommunication, violations of consent, and similar problems as men of different backgrounds, regions, experience and BDSM interests mingled in increasingly crowded bars. In 1985, the apparent murder of a BDSM partner by New York art gallery owner Andrew Crispos, which local BDSM groups discussed repeatedly, heightened safety concerns.[12]

Despite the Crispos case, which remained a rare exception, leather bars and sex clubs were far from the dangerous denizens portrayed in *Cruising*. Yet, they served BDSM newcomers poorly and proved inadequate to socialize, integrate and educate their growing numbers. The Mineshaft inaugurated demonstrations of safe technique, but these remained rare and the practice did not spread widely. Jockstrap contests and similar raucous events attracted more customers than educational seminars. The Mineshaft's newsletter offered occasional advice on "how to keep Mr. Goodbar out of the Mineshaft and out of your life," as well as warnings about youth gangs that attacked single gay men strolling from nearby leather bars to the Mineshaft, but these, too, proved rare. Safety discussions dampened the sexual atmosphere on which these venues thrived.[13]

The influx of people new to BDSM overwhelmed old patterns of person-to-person acculturation and education and encouraged the development of new educational and social systems. DeBlase first addressed this need in hands-on demonstrations and seminars. In November 1979, he launched *DungeonMaster* magazine to reach a larger audience. Envisioned as "a *Popular Mechanics* of S&M," it focused on practical matters. Successive issues described and illustrated safe ways to restrain men, where (and how) to beat them, and the construction (and concealment) of home BDSM equipment. More specialized topics included fisting, electricity and using music in BDSM scenes. As DeBlase boasted, *DungeonMaster* was the first "publication to concentrate on S&M as a safe, sane, enjoyable activity, rather than a collection of dangerous or impossible fantasies."[14]

DeBlase organized *DungeonMaster* columnists, who represented some of the most experienced sadomasochists in the country, into "Sandmutopia University" (S and M utopia), an informal group of speakers who visited bars and BDSM organizations demonstrating BDSM technique. "Student IDs," good for six classes, were $15. By 1984, courses included: bondage, catheters, CBT (cock and ball torture), clamps, electrotorture, fisting, flogging, master/slave roles, mummification, needles, shaving, enemas and watersports. Across the United States, other people offered introduction to BDSM seminars, including Laura Goodwin in Denver and Jan Hall in Ohio.[15]

DungeonMaster's "Safety Valve" column, Sandmutopia University, and DeBlase's promotion of "safe and sane SM," which by the mid-1980s included a trilogy of educational videos, encouraged other publications to address safety. Magazines ranging from *Drummer* to the numerous titles produced by Harmony and HOM, the leading producers of heterosexual BDSM pornography in the United States, added safety warnings and instructions. So, too, did *Penthouse* magazine, which offered practical instruction and safety information for BDSM beginners.[16] BDSM—at least organized BDSM—was no longer just about getting laid.

AIDS, Fear and BDSM

In the 1970s and 1980s, many outsiders viewed BDSM as both an arousing erotic spectacle and something dark and dangerous, an intersection highlighted the night of 10 July 1981 when a fire swept through San Francisco's Folsom neighborhood, home to leather bars, BDSM clubs and many men who patronized them. The fire damaged or destroyed 25 buildings, including the Barracks bathhouse, and left about 100 people homeless. Firefighters claimed they smelled "burning meat," and broke into homes, expecting to find BDSM "slaves" chained to beds or trapped in dungeons. They found no such victims. Firefighters, police and local government officials toured the charred clubs and homes, including the apartment of Mark Chester, a famed BDSM photographer whose mostly intact home boasted a well-equipped BDSM play space, pictures of which appeared in local papers. When Chester returned home, he found it looted. Most of his whips and BDSM gear, clearly visible in newspaper photos, were gone. Other men reported similar thefts. While local officials regularly condemned BDSM, some of these officials were attracted enough by its paraphernalia to abscond with it.[17]

The HIV-AIDS crisis heightened fears of BDSM. In the *New York Native*, Craig Johnson resurrected old canards linking fascism, murder and sadomasochism. "SM and safe sex are incompatible," he declared, claiming BDSM spread AIDS. Officials in numerous cities exploited AIDs fears to close sex clubs and bathhouses. Leather bars and BDSM clubs became favorite targets. In 1983, undercover police raided the Gold Coast and arrested seven men for their activities in its downstairs dungeon, "the Pit," along with its bartender. The following year, New York police raided Club O. Canadian police used vaguely worded "Bawdy House" laws to raid leather bars, bathhouses and private homes in Toronto. In Edmonton, "Operation Soap," targeted bars and small businesses, including Robert Montgomery, who made "custom leather gear and sex toys" in his home.[18]

In 1985, encouraged by the *New York Post*, which vilified gay sex clubs, New York City officials closed the Mineshaft in November, the "legendary St. Marks Baths" in December, and Plato's Retreat on New Year's Eve. Mayor Ed Koch praised city health inspectors for daring to witness Mineshaft's "horrendous" sexual activities. Increasing harassment from city officials, who focused most of their attention on gay businesses, forced the Anvil, Asstrick and Hellfire to close. The same proved true in other cities, including San Francisco where city officials pressured the Catacombs, Cauldron and Slot to close. All told, more than 250 of the United States' roughly 400 sex clubs and bathhouses closed. Facing similar pressure, several BDSM publications also shut down, including SMads, a contact newsletter launched in 1973. The era of "great parties" ended.[19]

Negative media portrayals increased, which existing BDSM institutions proved unable to counter. David Cronenberg's film *Videodrome* (1983) dramatized Johnson's claims, presenting masochists as suicidal men excited by their own deaths. Censors ended Hollywood's flirtation with BDSM, demanding the removal of a BDSM scene from *Crimes of Passion* (1984), starring Kathleen Turner.

Members of the BDSM community were outraged by these attacks, which Ivo Dominguez labeled "leatherphobia," the "assertion that SM/Leather/Fetish people are depraved, deviant, degenerate, diseased, debauched, and without a shred of moral fiber." Particularly painful was the association of BDSM with AIDs, which had already claimed several of the community's leading members. As historian Michael Bronski points out, "many of the lists of 'dangerous' sexual activities found in early HIV prevention guidelines included activities, such as S/M, that were socially frowned on but not able to transmit HIV." Whipping did not spread AIDS.[20]

BDSM activists pointed out that rates of AIDS infection were no higher among sadomasochists than the general gay population and that bathhouses and sex clubs were actually the best places to disseminate safe sex information. Their protests fell on deaf ears. Many in the BDSM community feared increasing government repression—fears reflected in Samuel R. Delany's 1984 novel *Stars in My Pocket Like Grains of Sand*, in which "all sadomasochism was hunted out and punished with barbaric single-mindedness." As DeBlase pointed out, authorities attacked BDSM venues because they were easy targets. No one would "come to their aid because of the taint of S&M."[21]

The same proved true of obscenity prosecutions. Warren Burger's 1969 ascension to chief justice of the Supreme Court reversed the court's stance. Several new rulings undid previous lenient obscenity rulings. *Miller v. California* (1973) eliminated the "utterly without redeeming social value" standard. Instead, it required a "work taken as a whole" to lack "serious literary, artistic, political, or scientific value," and left this to be interpreted by local community standards. The ruling, partly a response to the growing popularity of adult films, encouraged new pornography prosecutions. Prosecutors first targeted major filmmakers, including *Hustler* publisher Larry Flynt, and the producers and stars of *Deep Throat* (1972), the era's highest grossing adult film. The trials were prolonged, costly and mostly inconclusive. Seeking easier targets and encouraged by US Attorney General Edwin Meese, prosecutors in the 1980s returned their attention to sadomasochistic and violent pornography.

The 1986 report of Meese's Commission on Pornography confirmed DeBlase's expectation by focusing most of its attention on homosexual, sadomasochistic and violent pornography. From its outset, the Meese Commission aimed to refute the conclusions of the 1972 President's Commission on Obscenity and Pornography, which recommended decriminalizing pornography, having found no links between it and crime. The 12-member Meese Commission included several leading social conservatives, among them James Dobson and Alan Sears who were outspoken opponents of pornography and the LGBT rights movement. Its chair, Henry Hudson, was a Virginia prosecutor famous for closing adult bookstores. The committee sponsored no original research, instead personally reviewing pornographic materials, a 100-page list of which appeared in its report. It held public hearings in Chicago, Houston, Los Angeles, Miami, New York and Washington at which 208 people testified. Most were law enforcement officials or anti-pornography activists. The 1,960-page report focused on gay and BDSM material even though these constituted a small percentage of the pornography market. Commission members likened BDSM to rape, rejected the idea that BDSM activities could ever be consensual, and highlighted BDSM material to condemn pornography in general.[22]

It was, Gayle Rubin pointed out, a well-rehearsed narrative. Viewing pornography led one to view BDSM or other "extreme" pornography, which corrupted the viewer into committing rape and other crimes. It was a "just-so story that revitalizes the notion that sex perverts commit sex crimes, not normal people." The Meese Commission scapegoated "an unpopular sexual minority and its reading material" and blamed them for a host of social problems. Speaking at Living in Leather I (October 1986), Rubin warned attendees the Meese Report was just the beginning. They should expect increasing legal harassment.[23]

As Meese intended, many municipalities passed new laws restricting pornography, despite widespread condemnation of the Report as inaccurate and misleading. Obscenity prosecutions increased, many of which targeted BDSM filmmakers for whom the Report had an unintended effect. By singling out BDSM activities, it helped establish BDSM films as a distinct genre.[24]

In the past, some mainstream pornographic films, such as *Barbara Broadcast* (1977), included a BDSM scene along with the expected oral sex, masturbation and copulation. Already diminishing in mainstream pornographic films, BDSM activities disappeared from them entirely following the Meese Report.

BDSM filmmakers, who mostly avoided intercourse, eliminated it entirely. Producers and distributors came to believe any film with both BDSM and sexual penetration would be prosecuted, and did not cross that line. For the next decade, BDSM films focused exclusively on bondage, flagellation, fetish costume and role play without any genital activity or penetration. The first episode of the long-running *Dresden Diary* series (1986), for example, kept genitals covered or off-camera, hinting at off-camera sexual activity (fellatio) only once.

Anti-pornography organizations and law enforcement agencies also targeted BDSM magazines, as did customs officials. Canadian customs inspectors seized BDSM magazines, as well as issues of *Drummer* and *On Our Backs*. British customs officials seized *DungeonMaster*. Virginia prosecutors successfully convicted an adult bookstore for obscenity by focusing jurors' attention on a handful of sadomasochistic titles in the store. Following similar cases, which included the seizure of BDSM magazines and videos and the prosecution of several distributors, *Drummer* announced a reduction of "bondage and S/M in photos to avoid legal problems."[25]

Police also targeted BDSM organizations, which often met in members' homes. Beaver Falls, Pennsylvania police raided a TCC play party on April 5, 1986 and charged homeowners (and TCC founders) George and Marie Morrell, with prostitution along with 25 of their guests. Many of the women were strip-searched while male officers watched. As the editor of *Growing Pains* noted, the Meese Report had made it simply "a question of when and in what form the first raid on a private [BDSM] organization's activities would take place."[26]

Janus raised funds for TCC's defense, and warned more raids would likely follow, which they did. Raids on professional dominants, such as Cheri Benton and

Pamela Gitthens, Sacramento high school teachers who moonlighted as "mistresses of sadomasochism," remained common. Both lost their jobs, as did Benton's husband, also a teacher. Grand Rapids, Michigan police raided the home of Faye Marie Bond, a professional dominatrix and BDSM author who operated as Marquise Marie. They arrested her and her husband for obscenity and keeping a house of ill fame. In 1987, Los Angeles Police raided a commercial BDSM club where the Los Angeles chapter of Janus met. Shortly afterward, they charged the largest local distributor of "S&M videos" with obscenity despite its effort to avoid carrying films with "certain prohibited sexual acts" (urolagnia and fisting) or that included both penetrative sex and BDSM. The following year, Los Angeles police launched a series of raids on leather bars. The FBI raided Steven Toushin, a Chicago theater owner and BDSM film distributor whose catalog included titles featuring heavy BDSM, fisting and water sports. *Growing Pains* concluded the BDSM community faced "growing official intolerance for our chosen lifestyle."[27]

"Somewhere to Go"

Legal harassment and a rapidly expanding BDSM population encouraged the formation of new BDSM organizations, which multiplied rapidly in the 1980s. As New York BDSM organizer Gerrie Blum wrote, BDSM newcomers needed "somewhere to go" and "someone to tell." They needed "local support networks" and places "to be 'out,'" accepted and 'validated;' places to relax and be themselves "with no defenses and no deception."[28] Generally conceived as safe places to meet like-minded people, the next generation of BDSM organizations proved more welcoming than bars and focused significant attention on safe BDSM education. Older members of the BDSM community, displaced when the Mineshaft and similar clubs closed, joined newcomers there and shared their skills.

Through the 1970s and 1980s, TES and Janus attracted members outside their immediate locales, and established a presence in other cities. Terry Kolb, who moved to California, led a short-lived TES chapter in Los Angeles before joining Janus. When its outreach effort peaked, TES had coordinators—also called ambassadors—organizing gatherings in 40 cities, though only "Chicago, Cleveland, Jacksonville, Philadelphia, Toronto, and Vancouver were consistently represented" at TES meetings. Janus had members in more than a dozen cities across the United States. Neither organization's members, though, wholeheartedly supported operating beyond their immediate locales. Janus never formalized its approach to members outside California. TES's ambassadors represented a compromise between those favoring and opposing expansion. They gave TES a presence in other cities, but without formal mission or authority.[29]

Gay men played vital roles in TES's growth and accounted for half its membership in the mid-1970s. Despite living in California, Larry Townsend joined TES, believing it would build "bridges of understanding" among diverse BDSM populations. Articles in the *East Village Other* and *The Advocate* echoed his sentiments and encouraged cooperation among gay and straight sadomasochists. Yet, TES's heterosexual membership grew quickly. By the early 1980s, its gay members had become a distinct minority.[30] Janus experienced a similar change as heterosexual members came to outnumber the gay leathermen who helped establish it.[31]

As TES and Janus grew, both became more bureaucratic and less welcoming to newcomers, particularly women. Several of them decried the open misogyny of too many TES men who expected all women to submit to them. Gay and lesbian members felt increasingly alienated. Several women in Janus wanted an organization that focused more directly on their distinct needs. This resulted in the creation of Cardea, a women's group within Janus, which developed into Samois in 1978. Two years later, TES experienced a similar exodus as many of its gay and lesbian members left, joining either Gay Male SM Activists (GMSMA) or Lesbian Sex Mafia (LSM), which formed within a few months of each other.[32]

GMSMA

GMSMA formed much like TES. In August 1980, Brian O'Dell placed ads in *Gay Community News* for men interested in BDSM. He met with David Stein and six other respondents who formed GMSMA, which held its first official meeting early in 1981. Stein reached out to Tony DeBlase, whom he met at the CHC's 1981 Inferno. Happy to help, DeBlase promoted GMSMA in *DungeonMaster*, put New York area CHC members in touch with GMSMA, and presented educational workshops at GMSMA meetings.

Rather than a small, closed, intimate group like motorcycle clubs or the CHC, GMSMA's leaders formed an open, politically active organization. They worked to grow it quickly, disprove "prevailing stereotypes and misconceptions about SM," and win a visible place for kinky men in the gay and lesbian rights movement. In addition to TES-like consciousness raising meetings and BDSM educational presentations, GMSMA members supported local gay and lesbian causes. Despite initial opposition, they won acceptance of a GMSMA contingent in the city's gay pride march. Afterward GMSMA participated in other marches and demonstrations, organized political actions of its own, and raised funds for them.

In 1983, GMSMA secured a meeting place at the newly opened New York Lesbian and Gay Community Services Center, which it helped fund. Much like the pride parade's leaders, the center's board members reversed their initially negative decision after GMSMA leaders rallied their supporters and made their case at an open meeting. The board allowed GMSMA to meet in a room, which GMSMA members cleaned and upgraded with new lighting. Over time, GMSMA became vital to the center's finances—in many years its largest contributor. Similarly, GMSMA became one of the largest financial contributors to the Christopher Street Liberation Day Committee, which coordinated New York's pride march. By 1984, three GMSMA members held seats on its board, including O'Dell who was its male co-coordinator.[33]

GMSMA arranged BDSM demonstrations at the Mineshaft, attracting men who found "SM experiences, fantasies, and questions," which were "accepted and respected" by men like themselves. This was "no small thing in a world which does not value and does not even understand what we want." GMSMA welcomed men "just coming out into SM" and those of "long experience." By 1984, it had 70 active members. Biweekly educational presentations attracted crowds of 200. Over the next three years, membership rose to 350, making it by far the world's largest men's BDSM organization. Of the 210 men who attended Inferno XVII (1988), 40 were GMSMA members. GMSMA remained the largest men's organization through the 1990s. Its Speakers' Bureau worked with the Gay Officers Action League to educate police about BDSM and sent members to speak about BDSM at local colleges and various community and social organizations to "demonstrate that people into kinky sex are normal."[34]

LSM

Women with BDSM interests faced similar problems, plus two others. First, they were excluded from most leather bars and BDSM clubs, which were male-only preserves. While a few bars allowed select women, the environment was often unwelcoming, with women shunned or avoided by men complaining about smelling "fish." Second, the members of many local women's political organizations associated BDSM with patriarchal oppression and violence and excluded—and sometimes harassed—BDSM-identified women.

Inspired by Samois, Dorothy Allison and Jo Arnone founded LSM contemporaneously with GMSMA. It was "a support group for women, primarily lesbians, who practice, advocate or have fantasies which involve 'politically incorrect sex,'" including "SM, fetishism, cross dressing, butch/femme roles, public and recreational sex." They organized LSM's first official meeting in October 1981 and pledged members to uphold four tenets: "confidentiality, consensuality, safety, and the right of women to use their sexual bodies as they choose." Samois supported its formation, referred New York women on its mailing list to LSM, and sent Califia and Rubin to speak at LSM meetings. Samois encouraged the formation of women's BDSM groups across the United States, such as Briar Rose in Ohio, as well as the first women's BDSM group in Europe, Werkgroep Vrouwen en SM (Women's SM Working Group), which formed in the Netherlands in 1979.[35]

LSM gained national attention in 1982 when members of Women Against Pornography (WAP) protested Barnard College's ninth annual Feminist and Scholar Conference, which focused on women's sexuality. Carole Vance, its organizer, sought to address hotly controversial issues and attracted leading scholars and writers as presenters, some of whom were associated with BDSM, including Dorothy Allison, Amber Hollibaugh, Joan Nestle and Gayle Rubin, one of Samois' leading voices. Nestle may have inflamed matters when she told reporters the "conference was about pleasure and sexuality and WAP has nothing to say on this."

WAP's leaders saw connections between pornography and sadomasochism. As historian Carla Freccero points out, "if pornography sexualizes the subordination of women, then sadomasochism, by reenacting relations of domination and submission, celebrates that sexualization."[36] Increasing complaints by WAP and similar organizations, who claimed the conference would promote pornography and sadomasochism, convinced several conference participants to drop out. College administrators seized many of the conference's handouts.

Yet, the conference took place while WAP picketed its meetings and distributed flyers condemning participants' sexual interests. Vance edited and published the presentations as *Sex and Danger: Exploring Female Sexuality* (1983), a landmark work. The Sunday of the conference, LSM arranged a speak-out on "politically incorrect sexuality," which attracted 400 women who discussed "all the ways we are labeled 'sexual outlaws.'" Hollibaugh spoke for many of them when she praised

> all the women who don't come gently and don't want to; don't know yet what they like but intend to find out; are the lovers of butch or femme women; who like fucking men; practice consensual SM; feel more like faggots than dykes; love dildoes, penetration, costumes; like to sweat, talk dirty, see expressions of need sweep across their lovers' faces; are confused and need to experiment with their own tentative ideas of passion; think gay male porn is hot; are into power.[37]

Hollibaugh implied women at the speak-out felt more connected sexually to rough sex, sadomasochism, and gay leathermen than to mainstream lesbianism. Pat Califia declared it explicitly: "If I had a choice between being shipwrecked on a desert island with a vanilla lesbian and a hot male masochist, I'd pick the boy."[38] Samois, in particular, was influenced by leathermen. Its members even adopted the common practice of motorcycle clubs of wearing jean vests with the club logo on the back. Many of the women who attended Catacombs parties engaged in BDSM with men, despite primarily identifying as lesbians. Some, like Cynthia Slater, even participated in the men's fisting parties. These women enjoyed what later writers called "cross-orientation play," engaging in BDSM and related activities with people outside their primary sexual orientation. They found it enriching.

The publicity surrounding the Barnard conference, despite its acrimony, fueled LSM's growth, which it showcased a few months later with a large contingent in the Gay and Lesbian Pride Parade. A year later, Debi Sundahl launched *On Our Backs* magazine, marketed to "lustful lesbians," and offering "explorations of body image, sex toys, identity, s/m, butch/femme, relationships, sensuality and raw lust"—a magazine aimed at women exploring BDSM and "politically incorrect sexuality."[39]

While all BDSM groups of the 1970s and 1980s, emphasized the safety and privacy of their members, none did so more than LSM, perhaps as a result of the

Barnard Conference. LSM required all new members to attend a workshop on safe BDSM. It hosted these, along with more specialized workshops and demonstrations, in members' homes and later at the Lesbian Herstory Archives, which occupied much of member Joan Nestle's Upper West Side apartment. Members hosted BDSM play parties in their homes, and several LSM members, who also belonged to TES, worked with TES to arrange women-only events at Club O, Hellfire and similar venues. As LSM grew, its members benefitted from New York's rich selection of bars and clubs. Jo Arnone arranged monthly women-only play parties at Asstrick, a "men's fistfucking bar," renamed "Ms. Trick" for these nights. Les Scenes, a woman-owned bar with BDSM play space, opened in January 1983.[40]

Following the Barnard conference, feminist debates on sex, sadomasochism and pornography attracted attention throughout the BDSM community. Attacks on BDSM practitioners encouraged cooperation—political and social—between "feminist sexual radicals" and male BDSM organizations, which previous feminist attacks on Samois had not.[41] LSM leaders Allison and Arnone met repeatedly with O'Dell and Stein as GMSMA and LSM formed and grew. They found common ground on their perceptions of the BDSM community's needs, the role the BDSM community could play in the gay and lesbian civil rights struggle, and even the importance to clearly identify themselves as BDSM organizations. Both participated in local gay and lesbian events and sought alliances with BDSM and gay and lesbian organizations. In June 1982, they jointly hosted "Power Play: SM and the Liberation of Gay & Lesbian Sexuality," a seminar at which men and women discussed how coming out as sadomasochists affected their lives.[42]

The following year, encouraged by GMSMA's David Weinbaum, they jointly hosted a fundraiser for New York's pride march. Later named Leather Pride Night, the event became New York's premier annual BDSM event. TES and two motorcycle clubs, Defenders and Pocono Warriors, joined to support the event, which included parties at various bars, seminars, demonstrations, contests and a charity auction over which Arnone presided. It became one of the primary fundraising events for New York's Lesbian and Gay Pride March—in some years its single largest contributor.[43]

A BDSM Group for Everyone

As Gerrie Blum noted, people with BDSM interests across the United States needed "somewhere to go" and "someone to tell." More than sexual partners, they wanted to make significant and deep connections with people who shared their interests, be part of a community, and learn about and engage in BDSM activities in a safe environment.[44]

The success and rapid growth of GMSMA, LSM and Samois inspired new BDSM organizations to form. People advertised in *DungeonMaster* and other venues to organize GMSMA-like groups. Dozens of new BDSM organizations formed in the early 1980s: Avatar, Leathermasters, and Leather and Lace in Los

Angeles; Briar Rose in Ohio; Disciples of de Sade in Dallas; Bound & Determined, Dreizehn, and Urania in Boston; Shelix in Northampton, Massachusetts; 15 Association and The Outcasts in San Francisco; SigMa in Washington, DC; Atlanta SM Solidarity (ASS), Chicagoland Discussion Group (CDG); Denver Area Dominants and Submissives (DADS); Portland Power and Trust; Vancouver Alliance for SM (VASM); and many others. *DungeonMaster* listed new groups as they formed and pointed new men's groups to experienced BDSM practitioners—often Inferno veterans—who led workshops at their meetings. More than half of these new organizations were for gay men, and like GMSMA, benefited from gay gathering places, including bars, community centers and gay-friendly churches, at which they hosted meetings.

As new BDSM organizations formed, TES and Janus curtailed their geographical outreach, much to the relief of members worried about policing "far-flung organizations." TES reduced its ambassadorships, officially ended them in 1985. Leaders of Janus found coordinating and managing 900 members and a half dozen chapters across California difficult. Tensions among chapters increased, and Janus's large Los Angeles chapter split off in 1987, becoming Threshold. Its other local chapters—all fairly small—dissolved shortly afterward, leaving only the original Society of Janus in San Francisco.[45]

By 1986, more than 100 BDSM organizations operated in cities across the United States and Canada. Practically every major city had one. New York, Chicago and other metropolises had several. Most organizations restricted membership by gender and orientation. Roughly a quarter, including DADS and CDG, emulated TES and Janus and welcomed everyone. Women-only groups, such as Briar Rose, LSM, Portland Power and Trust, and The Outcasts, were the least numerous and accounted for perhaps 10 or 15 percent of new BDSM organizations.[46] With only a few exceptions, these new organizations advertised their existence. Unlike entering the Mineshaft or joining a motorcycle club, people need not prove themselves by dress, behavior or personal references. Anyone could join regardless of their level of experience, depth of leather wardrobe or number of toys. GMSMA members were "not required to wear leather, . . . a patch, an emblem, or a uniform . . . attend a certain number of meetings or go through a 'pledge' period [or] prove SM preferences or proficiencies." All men were welcome.[47]

The 15 Association was among the few exceptions. Founded by Peter Fiske and several other men from Janus, several of whom attended CHC's Inferno, the 15 Association emulated the CHC's exclusive, fraternal organization, emphasized heavy BDSM activities, and outfitted its own clubhouse for parties. Referencing the frictions between sadomasochists and leathermen, 15 Association ads explained: "Not every man wearing leather is into S&M. . . In San Francisco the two 'communities' have blended into an indistinguishable one. We're changing that." The 15 Association was "for gay men into S&M." It was "not for novices," nor "a 'training school' for men who think they might be interested in S&M." It was for men who had already "made those major decisions." Like the CHC, its exclusiveness and emphasis on heavy play made it a distinct, prestigious and influential organization. After Tony DeBlase attended one of its dungeon parties and published the photos in *Drummer*, requests for 15 Association membership poured in.[48]

The National Leather Association

The establishment of so many BDSM organizations led to discussions to form a national organization, which would help BDSM activists network with one another, coordinate the growing number of events, and lead their community's efforts to win social acceptance, inclusion in the gay and lesbian rights movement, and end government harassment of its members, events and gathering places. In 1984, CHC and GMSMA discussed forming a Council of SM Organizations (COSMOS) to share resources and experience with each other and new BDSM groups as they formed. Leaders of neither organization, though, followed through.[49] Instead, Steve Maidhof led a group of relative newcomers to form the National Leather Association (NLA) in Seattle.

Maidhof, a registered nurse and Catacombs regular, moved from San Francisco to Seattle following his partner's death from AIDS-related illness in 1985. There, he became active in the BDSM community, won the Washington State Mr. Leather contest, and competed for 1986 International Mr. Leather (IML). Maidhof hoped to use IML to raise AIDS awareness and promote political activism, but IML's organizers at the time still discouraged distractions from the event's promotion of raw sexuality and masculine beauty. That disappointment led him to organize a conference focused specifically on education and political action.

Influenced by his time in San Francisco, Maidhof recruited three men, Billy Jefferson, George Nelson and Wayne Gloege, and three women, Cookie Andrews-Hunt, Jan Lyon and Vik Stump, for the conference committee. They settled on the name Living in Leather (LIL) for the conference and National Leather Association (NLA) as the sponsoring organization. George Nelson suggested the names. The others accepted them with little thought to their implications, either the claim of national membership or describing themselves as a leather rather than BDSM organization. The NLA was the first BDSM organization aimed at both gay men and lesbians. It consistently emphasized—and often required—gender parity in its leadership.

In Seattle on October 10–12, 1986, the NLA hosted Living in Leather (LIL), the first national BDSM conference. Billed as the "National Conference for Lesbians and Gays of the Leather Lifestyle," it attracted 99 attendees who included many of the BDSM community's leading figures: Tony DeBlase; Gayle Rubin; *Urban Aboriginals* author Geoff Mains; Mr. S founder Alan Selby; sex activist and *On Our Backs* editor Susie Bright, who hosted a "hands-on lesbian fist fucking workshop"; and Pat Califia, the keynote speaker.

Some found the notion of "gay leathermen and lesbian leatherwomen sitting in the same room while we discussed our sexuality quite far out," but conference presenters worked to unite them. Califia had repeatedly advocated this for a decade and encouraged LIL attendees to look beyond divisions of gender and orientation in the realms of both personal pleasure and political activism. Gays, lesbians and heterosexuals had "mutual ground to get together" and should do so both to oppose threats to sexual freedom and to expand their own sexual horizons.[50] Maidhof similarly encouraged attendees to "take time to embrace our similarities," "celebrate our differences" and unite the BDSM community's disparate constituencies.[51]

At Living in Leather, daytime educational and political seminars were followed by evening entertainments at local leather bars, including skits, erotic readings and play parties at the recently formed Seattle Dungeon Guild's clubhouse. Its leader, Dean Dunlap, wrote a column on electrical devices for *DungeonMaster.* Many seminars addressed BDSM technique, such as Geoff Mains' "Flowers of Pain," but almost half were political. The panel on "Leather and the Press," discussed countering the media's negative portrayals of BDSM. In "The Gathering Shit Storm," Gayle Rubin placed the Meese Report in the context of past sexual panics and warned attendees the government would increase harassment of BDSM as part of continuing efforts to suppress sexual expression. She urged attendees to organize and fight back. Presenters on other panels echoed these calls for unity and activism. Geoff Mains and Corona urged LIL's diverse attendees to claim their shared "leather experience" and embrace it "as a culture."[52]

DeBlase, who became a central figure in the NLA, described this first Living in Leather conference as revolutionary. In contrast to his demonstrations at Inferno and the Mineshaft, "we were in the Seattle conference center using real conference rooms to talk about everything from censorship to pornography to fisting techniques. This was not a dimly lit backroom; there was nothing sleazy about it." Ten years later, he recalled, "it was one of the most OUT, Up Front, liberating leather experiences I have had." Janus member Frank Jur declared the world "will never be the same." Never before, Susie Bright observed, had there "been an organization that embraced every member of SM lifestyle: men, women, professionals, weekend swingers, political activists, contest queens and media fiends." Men and women of all orientations and interests mixed freely. The "comradeship and genuine sexiness that graced such a mixed gathering was the most moving aspect of the convention." The assumption "that girls don't like raw sex and boys don't like anything but, found itself whipped right out of the convention."[53]

For Maidhof, LIL's success demonstrated the BDSM community's unity of purpose and desire for organizational growth. Continuing efforts, he promised, would produce "an outpouring of love, support, respect" and recognition of the BDSM community's burgeoning "political and social power."[54] The NLA, which began founding chapters in other cities, presented its statement of purpose shortly afterwards. It called for:

1 The Promotion of the Gay and Lesbian Leather lifestyle;
2 Establishment of increased communication between men and womyn in leather;

3 Fundraising for charities that have given direct service to men and womyn of the leather community;
4 Establishment of a support network for brothers and sisters in leather;
5 The provision of social and recreational activities for its members;
6 Activism to destroy stereotypes and misconceptions regarding the members of the leather family in the community at large.

The last of these was of personal importance to many of the NLA's founders. Not only did the *Seattle Gay News* and other gay publications regularly publish denunciations of sadomasochism, but members of the NLA were harassed for their BDSM interests. Its leaders received death threats. Maidhof, in particular, was singled out. He was threatened and his apartment vandalized. As he noted, attacks on the BDSM community increased as the AIDS epidemic spread. "The Gay community, needing someone to blame for this horrible disease." Lacking a "more tangible target, they direct their fear at us." Often, "our own [gay] brothers and sisters are more judgmental than the straight community."[55]

To counter these negative perceptions, Maidhof advocated expanding the NLA's educational and political activities. "It is more important than ever that we band together, present a united front, and take our place as leatherpeople in the gay political process." Much as members of the BDSM community needed to be educated about safe technique, mainstream society—and the gay community—needed to be taught BDSM activities were safe. BDSM, he argued, needed to be made socially acceptable.[56]

Stimulated by Living in Leather and Maidhof's calls for action, the NLA grew to 100 members by December and kept growing as Maidhof reached beyond Seattle. The NLA was, he announced, the "largest co-sexual leather/SM organization in the country."[57] It added another annual event, May Day, a two-day event focused on fun, with fewer political workshops, more parties. It was a "delightful combination of celebration and practical information" that included the newly inaugurated Mr. and Ms. NLA contest, the first coed leather title.

While Living in Leather provided separate play spaces for men and women, May Day featured a mixed gender dungeon on the upper floor and separate male and female dungeons in the basement below. Attendees from San Francisco, Gayle Rubin noted, "are not only comfortable with such parties; we treasure them as special occasions to share our mutual interests, learn from one another, and experience the feelings expressed in the old saying, 'leather is thicker than blood.'" For most lesbians and gay men, though, mixed parties were "a novel idea." Some found them "downright distressing."[58]

The shared May Day play space symbolized the NLA's effort to unite the BDSM community. Tony DeBlase did scenes there most of the night, many featuring "intricate rope suspension bondage." He tied and suspended one man, attaching an "electrical device" to his genitals, eliciting "low moans of appreciation that let everyone know he was having a good time." The energy "was intense, erotic, and somehow uplifting." The feeling in the room, as men and women gathered to watch, "was positively reverential." The shared appreciation of DeBlase's finesse "became a form of communion" as the watchers realized how much they had in common with one another.[59] Meanwhile, cries of pain and pleasure drifted in from the downstairs dungeons, along with the rhythmic thudding of whipping and the scents of leather, sex and sweat. The evening's heaviest flagellation scenes took place there, particularly in the women's dungeon, shocking some men who never realized women played that hard—the evidence of which people confirmed the next day when they showed off their welts and bruises.

Jan Brown, who won the Ms. NLA contest and helped found NLA's Vancouver chapter, called on May Day attendees to unite against those who compared them "to Nazis and fascists," who censored their publications, reviled them in public and blamed them for AIDS. They needed to take the courage they deployed in their BDSM scenes, "the sweet bravery of submission and surrender" and "the sweaty courage of the top, taking control in a scene," and mobilize them for politics. It was time to "say no to this shit" and fight back.[60]

Planning for May Day and Living in Leather II, scheduled for August 1987, encouraged the NLA's leaders to both clarify their organization's policy on non-gay members, and consider whether its focus was specifically "SM" or the broader category of "leather." They agreed the name National Leather Association was poorly chosen and confusing, but preferred it to narrower terms to advertise their openness to a broadly defined "Leather/SM/Fetish" community.[61]

Heterosexuals posed a larger dilemma and provoked heated debate. While the NLA formed as an explicitly gay and lesbian organization, at least one heterosexual couple attended LIL. More heterosexuals joined over the next year, leading one member to worry how the NLA would ensure "straight men kept their hands off the lesbians." Other members worried heterosexuals would "take over" the NLA. Yet, there was no practical way to exclude them—or reason to—if they behaved. After all, part of the NLA's mission was "to recruit puppies and novices of any gender" and provide them educational and social opportunities.[62]

Concluding the NLA was "too small at this time to be diluted with a large influx of straight people," its leaders compromised. They decided to welcome heterosexual members, but not specifically invite them. Those who found the NLA presumably knew how to behave. The NLA included mixed and heterosexual BDSM organizations in its mailings, but did not advertise in straight publications, even when offered free ad space in magazines catering to professional dominatrices.[63] The decisions to retain "leather" in the NLA name and tentatively reach out to heterosexuals affirmed Maidhof's desire to unite the BDSM community, but reflected discomfort with how that united community would look and behave.

Tony DeBlase similarly promoted a broad definition of "leather" within which BDSM resided. As he wrote a *Drummer* reader, "For want of a better term, we use 'leather' to include a great variety of masculine images including black leather, cowboy, police, military, fireman, construction worker, athletic, trucker, logger, gangster, gladiator, mountain man, redneck, etc." *Drummer* advocated "broadening" rather than narrowing definitions. Leathermen were "not a uniform homogenous sea of black leather." They varied dramatically over "preferred style of dress, sexual fetish, preferred activities, tolerances, etc." The CHC similarly explained "S&M means different things to different people." There was no "real S&M," only "different areas of interest, different levels of experience, and different personal desires." Rather than narrowing acceptable boundaries of dress and conduct, DeBlase urged readers to broaden their outlook. Tolerance within a broadly defined community would help them grow, win acceptance from gay organizations, and tolerance by mainstream society.[64]

Contemporaneously with the NLA, Nancy Ava Miller began organizing People Exchanging Power (PEP). She attended several TES meetings in the early 1980s and explored her BDSM interests, first as submissive and then as dominant. In 1985, she placed ads seeking a submissive man and received 170 responses. Inspired by anthropologist Gini Graham Scott's book on the Service of Mankind Church, a San Francisco female dominant BDSM, Miller organized PEP in Phoenix, Arizona. She travelled regularly, and over the next few years founded PEP chapters in Albuquerque, Denver, Houston, Nashville, Washington and other cities. Unlike Janus or NLA, PEP chapters operated independently of one another. Miller exercised no control over them, nor did chapters consult with one another. Over time, some dropped the PEP name entirely. The Phoenix chapter became APEX (Arizona Power Exchange), while PEP-DC, whose members worried Miller's activism would bring them undue attention, changed their name to Black Rose in 1989. Miller, in turn, entered the phone sex business in 1991, which further encouraged some PEP chapters to distance themselves.[65]

The rapid formation of PEP chapters provides another indication of the significant demand for local BDSM organizations, though PEP's decentralized nature and the predominance of heterosexuals in most PEP chapters, limited its influence on the BDSM community. So, too, did their lower level of political activism, especially when compared to GMSMA, LSM and the NLA.

Members of the BDSM community became more politically aware in the 1980s, influencing their organizations and even title contests where contestants, like Maidhof, encouraged activism. Title contests grew in size and number, showcasing the BDSM community's greater organization, their members' desire to fight back against pejorative depictions, and their efforts to grapple with the AIDS crisis. While IML remained a macho beauty pageant, contestants' speeches became more political. IML 1985 Patrick Toner raised funds for AIDS charities—the first IML winner to do so. Scott Tucker, the 1986 winner, proved even more outspoken. A gay liberation activist prior to winning IML, he encouraged other title holders to become politically active, fighting for gay rights and against AIDS. This trend accelerated over time, influenced by title contests like the NLA's, which aimed specifically to produce political activists.

The organizers of the International Ms. Leather (IMsL) contest, launched their event in 1987 with the expectation contestants were already politically active. Its winner would be a "spokesperson for leatherwomen." Their activism further encouraged male contests to move in that direction. In 1989, Jim Kane protégé Guy Baldwin, a psychotherapist, early member of Janus, and frequent Inferno attendee, won both the Mr. NLA contest and IML. Well-known for his monthly column on relationships in *Drummer*, he emphasized political action throughout his title year, speaking at more than 70 events. No longer "just hunks and sex symbols," by the early 1990s people expected leather titleholders, particularly Mr. Drummer, International Mr. Leather and International Ms. Leather, to be activists. Speaking at local and regional title contests, they disseminated political information and encouraged activism and fundraising for social and political causes, working to secure a "rightful place among other erotic minorities." While John Preston resented the change, complaining politics had intruded on a private, sexual space, most welcomed it.[66]

Somewhere to Shop

While BDSM organizations encouraged members to make their own fetish clothes and toys, BDSM became increasingly commercial in the 1980s. The proliferation of organizations, publications and events facilitated the growth of old BDSM businesses and fueled the emergence of new businesses and craftspeople who derived their primary income from sales to the BDSM community. San Francisco's Mr. S and Chicago's Paul C Leather developed national reputations for their goods and pioneered new designs for sturdier and more comfortable bondage gear, such as wrist cuffs designed to spread pressure under load so as not to cut off circulation. BDSM cognoscenti benefitted from improvements in the quality, quantity, variety, versatility and safety of BDSM equipment, which became increasingly specialized as new craftspeople entered the marketplace and older ones diversified their catalogs.

Whips, in particular, went through a dramatic transformation, from "poorly designed and badly made" to "exquisitely designed, beautifully crafted" instruments, which enhanced "the sensate experience." A skilled craft, whipmaking required time and practice to master. Jay Marston, a member of several women's BDSM groups in San Francisco, became the first person to derive her primary income from BDSM whipmaking. She launched Hedonic Engineering in 1984 and revolutionized whips for BDSM play, improving their balance to make them more accurate and easier to handle and employ in long scenes without wearing out one's wrist. She also introduced new styles, which came to be called "floggers"—whips composed of a solid handle, covered by braided leather, from which numerous leather tails or tresses emerged. These ranged from soft deerskin for sensual play to bull hide, bison and other thicker leathers for heavier scenes. She made long floggers for flashy, twirling displays of a top's prowess and short ones "for fucking and whipping at the same time." Soft, wide tails produced a thudding sensation like a vigorous massage, which many people enjoyed. Narrower, denser leather—especially if braided—produced a stinging sensation and were more likely to leave welts and bruises. People referred to these as "cats" or "braided cats," terms derived from the nautical "cat o' nine-tails," which sailors made from rope.

BDSM cognoscenti debated the relative merits of whips, types of leather, and thud v. sting for various situations and tastes. Owning one whip was no longer enough. For people who wanted to play heavy, Marston made a protective harness to protect the spine and kidneys. She carefully designed and padded her ankle and wrist cuffs to prevent nerve compression and made them in smaller sizes, which better fit women. In flagellation scenes, tops generally began with light whips, warming up the bottom and then used a variety of whips to achieve different sensations at different times on different parts of the body, increasing and decreasing the intensity of pain and pleasure they inflicted while building to a climax.[67]

Marston's design innovations and success inspired other BDSM craftspeople, including Jeanette Heartwood, who in 1989 began offering sensual floggers in a dizzying variety of colors. In 1994, she made the whips for the movie *Exit to Eden*. "Adam and Gillian" (Mitch Kessler and Gerrie Blum) who launched Adam's Whips and Gillian's Toys in 1987, followed a typical progression of first making BDSM implements for themselves and then for their friends before launching their business fulltime. They created several dozen styles of whips "to suit the preferences and tolerances of a variety of play partners," ranging from soft deerskin to harsh bull hide, and were among the first to offer a variety of colors other than black. "You can't play with just one whip," they suggested, comparing BDSM to the many clubs required for golf. Joe Wheeler apprenticed under one of the last traditional bullwhip makers and brought those skills to the BDSM community, sparking interest in playing with single tail whips ranging from short, four-foot signal whips to bullwhips of ten feet and longer, which required exceptional care and skill to wield.[68]

Businesses became increasingly important in supporting the growth of the BDSM community. Earlier BDSM business people, such as Alan Selby, who raised enormous funds for AIDS research and care, established a tradition of giving back to the BDSM community and supporting its endeavors. New businesses did the same, which encouraged members of the BDSM community to shop within the community. The trend spread to pornographic films where community members made films with BDSM people for BDSM people. Among the first was JimEd Thompson (working as Russell Budd). Unlike many contemporary BDSM films, in which the flogging was simulated and the skin reddened with make-up, Thompson promised *Journey into Pain* (1984) featured "real scene people" and "unsimulated SM action." There was "no substitute for the real thing."[69]

By the early 1990s, more than 15 BDSM businesses operated in Chicago alone, including Male Hide, Paul C Leather and Taboo Tabou. Denver boasted at least half a dozen, including The Crypt and UZI. Seattle featured several BDSM and fetish businesses along Pike Street, though San Francisco's Folsom Street featured the highest density of BDSM, leather and fetish shops, bars and clubs—so many they launched their own street fair in 1984. Over the next decade, the Folsom Street Fair grew to become the world's largest BDSM/leather/fetish event.[70]

Not surprisingly, several dozen BDSM businesses operated in New York. These ranged from more than a dozen storefront shops, including Purple Passion, owned by former TES president Hilton Flax, and new clubs devoted to BDSM play, such as Paddles, which catered to heterosexual couples and presented a friendly, welcoming and clean environment, which contrasted sharply with the Vault. While some people were turned on by the sleaze of the old clubs, most women, as Lynn Comella noted in her study of sex shops, favor "a more sanitized and wholesome version of sexuality." Growing numbers of BDSM businesses catered to their tastes, offering clean, well-lit stores, educated staffs, and a wide, colorful selection of clothing, gear and implements.[71]

Like the woman-owned sex shops Comella studied, specialty BDSM shops provided important educational information to their customers, not just about the products themselves, but also general information about BDSM. In the film *Exit to Eden*, a helpful store clerk explains the use of safe words to stars Dan Aykroyd and Rosie O'Donnell. Usually active members of the BDSM community themselves, BDSM shop owners and their employees helped customers explore their interests and connected them with local BDSM organizations and events.

The ready availability of BDSM education encouraged more sophisticated BDSM play, which was enabled by access to better and more diverse whips, restraints and other equipment. Articles in *DungeonMaster* and its pansexual companion, *Sandmutopia Guardian and Dungeon Journal*, which DeBlase launched in 1987, offered increasingly detailed and narrowly focused discussions of topics ranging from how to conduct a realistic strip search to instruction on devices ranging from whips and canes to electrical devices like TENS units, which encouraged people to buy them. So, too, did title contestants who performed fantasy scenes showing off hot clothes and cool toys, and glorified flashy BDSM play.

BDSM became a crossroads of consumerism and sexuality. Its dual requirements of drama and paraphernalia, sociologist Barbara Ehrenreich suggested, accounted for some of its appeal and made it "the ultimately commercial form of sex." From "a strictly capitalist viewpoint," it is "the ideal sexual practice." The whips, restraints, costumes and other gear are "not just an optional enhancement," but essential to the very imagining of a BDSM scene, necessitating "a sexual marketplace, impersonally promoting the 'objects' of desire."[72] The synergy among BDSM organizations, publications and businesses fueled that marketplace.

Becoming an effective and popular BDSM top, though, required more than a lot of toys. It required skills gained through education and experience. Tops needed to operate within their scenario-defined roles and effectively apply their whips and other accoutrements. In flagellation scenes, they use a variety of instruments and adjust their intensity as the scene ebbs and flows. Control is vital. Nothing, Outcasts member and whip expert Quartermaster, explained is "less erotic than pain resulting from ignorance or pain of which the Top is unaware." A skilled "Top can use a whip to seduce a bottom into intense sexual excitement, into extremities of pain, or into a trancelike state of grace." For a long flagellation scene, she suggested, "turn down the lights, turn up the heat, put on some music, and tie the person down." Sexual arousal increases pain tolerance, and striking the "sweet spot," the "inner most half circle" of the buttocks stimulated sexual arousal.[73] A successful scene modulated pain, pleasure and other sensations, increasing or decreasing as needed while building to a climax.

Whipping, of course, was just one of the skills expected of tops. Some bottoms enjoyed hot wax, which required skill to employ, both in accuracy and in judging distance so that it hit the body at just the right temperature. When dropped from a candle held close to the body, hot wax is painful and causes mild burns. When held farther away, the wax cools quickly on impact, conveying a brief moment of pain followed by a pleasant warmth as it cooled. Beeswax, which burns too hot, was avoided. Other bottoms expected detailed role play, exotic toys like TENS electrical units, piercing with needles, or elaborate rope bondage, which might take an hour to weave and tie. "A good top," bottoms complained "is hard to find."[74]

Bottoms, too, had much to learn, particularly those attracted to heavier scenes, which required processing pain "into a tide of pleasure." Joseph Bean suggested a number of techniques from breathing, visualizing and internalizing the scene's scenario that would reduce "the experience of pain as pain," and "encourage the experience of joy" through intense sensation. Communication was vital. "SM bottoms learn very quickly what kinds of stimulation and sensation they do and don't want" and "how to encourage Tops to give them the stimulation they want" while avoiding anything unpleasant.[75] The growing number of BDSM events allowed bottoms and tops to refine and show off their skills.

***

The organized BDSM community experienced tremendous growth in the 1980s. "S&M," psychologist Robert Stoller notes, became "a trendy thing." Barbara Ehrenreich suggests "it was the sexual marketplace, more than anything else, that brought S/M into the mainstream of sexual options" because "the market demands novelty." People were looking for something new.[76] Novelties, though, wear off. The organized BDSM community—that is the people who joined BDSM organizations, read *DungeonMaster*, *Sandmutopia Guardian*, and other educational BDSM magazines, and attended conferences like Living in Leather—kept growing. People found these organizations welcoming. For their members, BDSM was more than the latest sexual novelty. It was—or at least was becoming—an important part of their sexual identities.

Many of these people found leather bars and sex clubs alienating. Rather than the perfect leather daddy embodied by "Mr. Benson" and sexually focused bar culture, many newcomers wanted "somewhere to go and someone to tell."

They sought a relaxed environment that encouraged discussion and learning, as well as socializing and sex.[77] Their search for alternatives fueled the formation of GMSMA, LSM and dozens of other BDSM organizations across the United States, a process accelerated by the AIDS crisis, and the closing of backroom bars, bathhouses and sex clubs. By the end of the decade, most American cities boasted a BDSM organization, often several, which appealed to different, genders, BDSM interests and sexual orientations.

Unlike bars and sex clubs, which served to facilitate sexual encounters, the central ethos of BDSM organizations became education, marked by regular meetings featuring demonstrations and/or discussion. Nourished by an expanding BDSM press, BDSM organizations and businesses described, defined and codified BDSM activity, making information on safety and technique readily available and reshaping the BDSM community. Newcomers no longer needed to learn at the feet of old masters.

Tony DeBlase emerged as the BDSM community's central figure, a leading educator and opinion leader who promoted and diffused new techniques, safety advice and other information through his magazines, public demonstrations and personal contacts. Even before its 1986 purchase by DeBlase, *Drummer* magazine reflected this change, transitioning from "do it" literature and pictorials aimed at "1970s sex vets" to "how do I do it?" articles and practical discussions of "how to run a safe-sex and a consensual S&M scene." DeBlase completed this transformation, stressing "safe/sane sex" in its articles and adding columns to answer "questions about safe/sane S/M," and "sex in general."[78] *DungeonMaster* and *Sandmutopia Guardian* attracted subscribers by focusing almost entirely on BDSM skills.

Bars and other older BDSM institutions also proved unable to counter increased harassment of sadomasochists by local and national government officials. They proved an inadequate foundation from which to fight for political and social rights. New BDSM organizations, particularly Samois, GMSMA, LSM and the NLA embraced these challenges. Their proliferation encouraged political activism and discussion to create a national BDSM organization. As Ivo Dominguez wrote, no "existing non-SM/Leather/Fetish-identified national organizations will be willing or able to address satisfactorily the needs of the Kink community." Sadomasochists needed to fight for their rights themselves and combat "specific incidents of censorship or legal outrage." To do that, they needed a national organization.[79]

Notes

1 Shere Hite, *The Hite Report: A Nationwide Study of Female Sexuality* (New York: Dell, 1981) and *The Hite Report on Male Sexuality* (New York: Dell, 1981); Nancy Friday, *My Secret Garden: Women's Sexual Fantasies* (New York: Simon & Schuster, 1973), and *Men in Love, Men's Sexual Fantasies: The Triumph of Love Over Rage* (New York: Dell, 1980); John R. Petersen, "A Walk on the Wild Side," *Playboy*, August 1983, 88; Teresa Carpenter, "Women and Erotica," *Cosmopolitan*, January 1984, 248; Dianne Grosskopf,

"Sexual Practices—a Sizzling Update," *Cosmopolitan*, September 1983, 196; Society of Janus, "Letter to San Francisco Chronicle and the Mayor," *Growing Pains*, April 1981, 4; and Don Miesen, "An Editorial," *Growing Pains*, February 1981, 4.

2 Rick Leathers, "Two Nations--One Territory: S&M vs. Leather," *DungeonMaster* 5 (July 1980), 1 and "All You Ever Wanted to Know about S&M and Then Some," *Gay*, October 1973, Sadomasochism Clipping File, Kinsey Institute.

3 Michael Grumley, *Hard Corps: Studies in Leather and Sadomasochism* (E P Dutton, 1977), chapter 1.

4 "Letter from Bill L.," *DungeonMaster* 10 (May 1981), 4 and Gayle S. Rubin, "The Valley of the Kings: Leathermen in San Francisco, 1960–1990," PhD diss., University of Michigan, 1994, 43.

5 Mark P. Levine, *Gay Macho: The Life and Death of the Homosexual Clone* (New York: NYU Press, 1998), 95.

6 "Leatheriders," *Chains* 6 (1980), 10.

7 David Stein, "SM's Copernican Revolution: From a Closed World to an Infinite Universe," in Mark Thompson (ed.), *Leatherfolk : Radical Sex, People, Politics, and Practice* (Boston, MA: Alyson Publications, 1991), 142 and Levine, *Gay Macho*, 79.

8 Fledermaus [Tony DeBlase] "On the Go," *DungeonMaster* 13 (1982), 6 and "All You Ever Wanted to Know About S&M and Then Some," October 1973, clipping, Sadomasochism file, Kinsey Institute.

9 Rubin, "Valley of the Kings," 313.

10 Anthony F. DeBlase, "A Word from the Top: Human Bondage Requires a Human," *DungeonMaster* 37 (1987), 4 & 17; Gayle Rubin, "The Leather Menace," in Samois (ed.), *Coming to Power: Writing and Graphics on Lesbian S/M 3rd Edition, Revised and Updated* (Boston, MA: Alyson, 1982), 205; and Ivo Dominguez, *Beneath the Skins: The New Spirit and Politics of the Kink Community* (Los Angeles, CA: Daedalus Pub. Co., 1994), 87–8.

11 Pat Bond, "Perverse Perspectives: The Name of the Game," *Prometheus* 10 (undated, probably late 1977 or early 1978), 34 and Alex Warner, "'Where Angels Fear to Tread:' Feminism, Sex and the Problem of SM, 1969–1993," PhD diss., Rutgers, The State University of New Jersey, 2011, 88.

12 Joel Brodsky, "The Mineshaft: A Retrospective Ethnography," 213 in Thomas Weinberg (ed.), *S and M: Studies in Sadomasochism* (Amherst, NY: Prometheus, 1995), 195–218; Jack Fritscher, *Gay San Francisco: Eyewitness Drummer Vol. 1* (San Francisco: Palm Drive, 2008), 536–7; Bruce Marcus, "The Crispo Case, Consent, and S/M Reality," *Drummer* 126 (1989); and David France, *Bag of Toys: Sex, Scandal, and the Death Mask Murder* (New York: Warner Books, 1992).

13 Jack Fritscher, "Mineshaft," *Drummer* 19 (1977), 82–3; Ray M., "Mineshaft's School for Lower Education," *DungeonMaster* 12 (September 1981), 1–3; Brodsky, "The Mineshaft: A Retrospective Ethnography," 205; and Mineshaft newsletters, undated, DeBlase Papers, Box 41, LAAM.

14 Fledermaus [Tony DeBlase], "Up Front," *Sandmutopia Guardian & Dungeon Journal* 1 (January 1988), 4; *DungeonMaster Yearbook* 1 (1983), 1; and DeBlase, "What Is S&M," *DungeonMaster* 4 (May 1980), 1–2.

15 Sandmutopia University flyers and brochures in LAAM, DeBlase Papers, Box 28.

16 V.K. McCarthy, "S&M for Beginners," *Penthouse*, August 1982, 132–6 & 150–4.

17 Mark Chester, "The Folsom Street Fire--A Personal View" *Growing Pains*, August 1981, 13–4; Fritscher, *Eyewitness Drummer*, 467; and "SM Is Something Human Beings Shouldn't Do to Each Other," Janus Flyer, 1982, Lesbian Herstory Archive, SM File.

18 A.B. Heilbrun and David T. Seif, "Erotic Value of Female Distress in Sexually Explicit Photographs," *Journal of Sexual Health* 24 (1988), 47–57; Craig Johnson, "SM and the Myth of Mutual Consent," *New York Native*, 29 July 1985; Tracy Baim and Owen Keehnen, *Leatherman: The Legend of Chuck Renslow* (Chicago, IL: Prairie Avenue Productions, 2011), 122; Jay Blotcher, "Sex Club Owners: The Fuck Suck Buck

Stops Here," 25, in Dangerous Bedfellows (eds.), *Policing Public Sex* (Boston, MA: South End Press, 1996); and Rubin, "The Leather Menace," in Gayle S. Rubin, *Deviations: A Gayle Rubin Reader* (Duke University Press Books, 2011), 200–1.

19 David Stein, "Shafted," *GMSMA Newslink* (January 1986), 2; T.R. Witomski, "Requiem for the Mineshaft," *Drummer* 96 (1985), 81; Joyce Purnick, "City Closes Bar Frequented by Homosexuals, Citing Sexual Activity Linked to Aids, *New York Times*, 8 November 1985, B3; Tucker, "Rawhide: The Mystery and Power of Leather," *The Advocate* 472 (12 May 1987), 42; and "Report," *Drummer* 102 (1986), 55.

20 Michael Bronski, *A Queer History of the United States* (Boston, MA: Beacon Press, 2011), 227.

21 Dominguez, *Beneath the Skins*, 33; Delany, *Stars in My Pocket Like Grains of Sand* (1984), quoted in Call, *BDSM in American Science Fiction*, 63; and Fledermaus [Tony DeBlase], "The Mineshaft, 1976–1985," *DungeonMaster* 30 (undated, 1985 or 1986), 14–5.

22 Attorney General's Commission on Pornography, *Final Report*. (Washington: GPO, 1986) at https://catalog.hathitrust.org/Record/000824987 (accessed 6 February 2017).

23 Gayle S. Rubin, "Thinking Sex," in Carole S. Vance (ed.), *Pleasure and Danger: Exploring Female Sexuality* (New York: HarperCollins, 1993), 298 and Rubin, "The Coming Shit Storm," presentation at Living in Leather I, 10–12 October 1986.

24 Pat Califia, "The Obscene, Disgusting, and Vile Meese Commission Report," in *Public Sex: The Culture of Radical Sex* (Pittsburgh: Cleis Press, 1994), 95–104; Hendrik Hertzberg, "Ed Meese and His Pornography Commission: Big Boobs," *New Republic*, July 1986, 14, 21–4; and Philip Nobile and Eric Nadler, *United States of America vs. Sex: How the Meese Commission Lied about Pornography* (New York: Minotaur: 1986).

25 Carolyn Shortes, "'Cleaning Up a Sewer': The Containment of SM Pornography," *Journal of Popular Film and Television* 26 (1998), 72–80; Robert J. Stoller, *Pain & Passion: A Psychoanalyst Explores the World of S & M* (New York: Plenum Press, 1991), 243; "Leather/SM Censorship," *Chain Link* 2 (Spring, 1987), 5; Pagan, "SM Porn Conviction in Seattle," *First Link* 4, no. 6 (June 1990), 9; Anthony F. DeBlase, "Editorial," *Drummer* 99 (1986), 4–5; and Jube Shiver Jr., "Va. Firm Guilty in Obscenity Case," *Washington Post*, 10 March 1982, C7.

26 "TES/TCC Party Raided in Western Pennsylvania," *Growing Pains*, May 1986, 3.

27 Ira, "L.A. SM Report," *Growing Pains*, August 1987, 1; Diana Vera, "Late News Flash" *Growing Pains*, August 1987, 7; "SM in Court," *Growing Pains*, July 1983, 2; Fledermaus [DeBlase], "Off the Top," *Drummer* 113 (1988); Steven Touschin, *The Destruction of the Moral Fabric of America* (Chicago, IL: Wells Street Publishing, 2006); and "Justice for Pamela Gitthens," *Growing Pains*, August 1983, 2.

28 Gerrie Blum, "Somewhere to Go, and Someone to Tell," in Laura Antoniou (ed.), *Some Women* (New York: Masquerade, 1995), 212.

29 0069 [Pat Bond], "Open Letter to Coordinators," *Prometheus* 4 (1975), 42–4; Pat Bond, "Another Open Letter to Our Coordinators and Potential Coordinators," *Prometheus* 5 (1975); "TES History," *Prometheus*, April/May/June 1993, 31; and "Officers Report," *Growing Pains*, June 1984, 19.

30 Larry Townsend, "The Compatibility of Contrasts," *Prometheus* 3 (1974), 16; Randy Wicker, "Love Is a Leather Strap (Ouch!)," *The Advocate*, undated 1972 clipping, TES file, Kinsey Institute; and David Stein, "SM's Copernican Revolution" in Thompson, *Leatherfolk*, 145–6.

31 T. Weymouth, *Society of Janus: Twenty-Five Years* (San Francisco: Society of Janus, 1999), 18–9.

32 Lolita, "Pat Bond Goes to LIL VII," *Prometheus*, July/August 1992, 10; John Strap, "Early Eulenspiegel" Prometheus, April/May/June 1993, 30–1; Grumley, *Hardcore*, Chapter 3; and Judith Coburn, "S&M," *New Times*, 4 February 1977, 50.

33 "March with Pride!" *GMSMA News* 1, no. 5 (June 1983), 1; "Washington Coverage," *GMSMA News*, Winter 1988, 6; David Stein, "The Road Ahead: Time for Decision," GMSMA *Newslink*, Summer 1989, 25; "Gay Male S&M Activists," *DungeonMaster* 6

(1981), 5; Arnie Kantrowitz, "Minority's Minority Steps from the Shadows: Gay Male S/M Activists," *The Advocate*, 29 May 1984, 22–3 & 30–1; and David Stein, "Tony DeBlase (1942–2000): A Personal Reminiscence," *GMSMA Newslink* 48, Fall 200, 26–7.

34 "Coming Of Age In SM," *GMSMA Newslink*, Spring 1986; "These Boots Are Made for Marching," *GMSMA News* 2, no. 3 (June 1984), 1; "Pride," GMSMA *Newslink*, Summer 1988, 6; and "GMSMA a Big Part of Inferno XVII," *GMSMA Newslink*, Fall 1988, 11.

35 LSM 20th Anniversary Booklet; LSM Flyer, Fall 1981; LSM Flyer, Winter 1981, Lesbian Herstory Archive, SM File; and Robin Bauer, *Queer BDSM Intimacies: Critical Consent and Pushing Boundaries* (Basingstoke: Palgrave Macmillan), 18.

36 Carla Freccero, "Notes of a Post-Sex Wars Theorizer," 313 in Marianne Hirsch (ed.), *Conflicts in Feminism* (New York: Routledge, 1990), 306–25.

37 Amber Hollibaugh, "Desire for the Future: Radical Hope in Passion and Pleasure," in Carole S. Vance (ed.), *Pleasure and Danger: Exploring Female Sexuality* (Boston, MA: Routledge, 1984), 403.

38 Califia, "A Secret Side of Lesbian Sexuality," *The Advocate*, 27 December 1979, 19.

39 Bronstein, *Battling Pornography*, 298–304; LSM 20th Anniversary Booklet; and LSM Summer 1982 Flyer, Lesbian Herstory Archive, SM File.

40 LSM, 20th Anniversary Booklet.

41 Freccero, "Notes of a Post-Sex Wars Theorizer," 312.

42 LSM Summer Schedule, 1982, Lesbian Herstory Archive, SM File.

43 "These Boots Are Made for Marching," *GMSMA News* 2, no. 3 (June 1984), 1 and Michael Musto, "Gay Leather Scene Tones Down from Hard-Core to Dress-Up," *New York Times*, 22 December 2015 at https://www.nytimes.com/2015/12/24/fashion/gay-leather-scene-tones-down-from-hardcore-to-dress-up.html (accessed 12 February 2020).

44 Gerrie Blum, "Somewhere to Go, and Someone to Tell" in Laura Antoniou (ed.), *Some Women* (New York: Masquerade, 1995), 203–15.

45 "TES History," *Prometheus*, April/May/June 1993, 31; Frank J., "What Is to Be Done?," *Growing Pains*, January 1987, 4–6; and Weymouth, *Society of Janus: 25 Years*, 21–6.

46 Gayle Rubin, "Samois," *Leather Times* 21 (Spring 2004), 3–6; David Stein, "SM's Copernican Revolution," in Thompson, *Leatherfolk*, 145–6; and Steve Stein, *Twenty-Five Years of Living in Leather: The National Leather Association, 1986–2011* (Palm Coast, FL: Adynaton, 2012), 12–4.

47 Richard Canter, "From the President," *GMSMA Newslink*, Spring 1994, 2.

48 Fifteen Association advertisement, *DungeonMaster* 5 (July 1980), 3 and 15 Association to DeBlase, 18 April 1988, LAAM, DeBlase Papers, Box 39.

49 Geoff Ferguson, "SM Networking: A Beginning," *GMSMA News* 2, no 3 (June 1984), 9 and "COSMOS," *DungeonMaster* 27 (1984).

50 *Living in Leather Souvenir Program*, NLA Files, LAAM; Frank Jur, "'Living in Leather' Conference," *Growing Pains*, November 1986, 9–11; "Fisting Two," *On Our Backs* 4, no. 3 (Winter 1988), 6–7; Pat Califia, "LIL 1 Keynote Address," DVD, NLA Archives; and Califia, "A Secret Side to Lesbian Sexuality," *The Advocate*, 27 December 1979.

51 Anthony F. DeBlase, "Letter to the Editor," *The Inquisitor* 2, no. 11 (March/April 1992), 5–6 and Steve Maidhof, LIL 1 Welcome Address, NLA Archives.

52 *Living in Leather Souvenir Program*, NLA Files, LAAM; Susie Bright, "Living in Leather," *On Our Backs* 3, no. 3 (Winter 1987), 14; and Frank Jur, "'Living in Leather' Conference," *Growing Pains*, November 1986, 9–11.

53 Tony DeBlase, "LIL 10 Keynote Address," NLA files, LAAM; *Living in Leather Souvenir Program*, NLA Files, LAAM; Susie Bright, "Living in Leather," *On Our Backs* 3, no. 3 (Winter 1987), 14; and Frank Jur, "'Living in Leather' Conference," *Growing Pains*, November 1986, 9–11.

54 *Living in Leather Souvenir Program*, NLA Files, LAAM and LIL 1 Opening Ceremonies, DVD, NLA Archives.
55 Steve Maidhof, "Leatherphobia," *Chain Link* 1 (Spring 1987), 2 and Maidhof, "Top Priority," *Chain Link* 1 (Spring 1987), 2.
56 Steve Maidhof, "Leatherphobia," *Chain Link* 1 (Spring 1987), 2.
57 "Help," *First Link* 1, no. 2 (undated 1987), 2.
58 Gayle Rubin, "May Day," *DungeonMaster* 33 (September 1987), 36–7.
59 Gayle Rubin, "May Day," *DungeonMaster* 33 (September 1987), 36–7.
60 Jan Brown, "Contestant Speech, May 3rd, 1987," *Chain Link 2* (Summer 1987), 14.
61 Rubin, "Valley of the Kings," 44.
62 Staffing and Membership Committee Report, 6 June 1987, NLA Archives.
63 Staffing and Membership Committee Report, 6 June 1987; Minutes, Board Meeting, 9 June 1987; Retreat Agenda, 16 January 1988, and Board of Directors Meeting, 16 January 1988; all in Board Meetings file, NLA Archives.
64 Fledermaus [DeBlase] to JD, *Drummer* 103 (1987), 4 & 29 and *Inferno X* (1981), 7.
65 Nancy Ava Miller, *Pervert: Notes from the Sexual Underground* (Albuquerque: PepLove Press, 2009), 99–117, and 294–305; Bakos, *Kink*, 163; Dan Rider, "Interview with Nancy Ava Miller of PEP," *Growing Pains*, February 1988, 10–2; and Frederick S. Lane, *Obscene Profits: The Entrepreneurs of Pornography in the Cyber Age* (New York: Routledge), 1601–13.
66 Rubin, "Elegy for the Valley of the Kings," 126–8; Preston, "What Happened" in Thompson, *Leatherfolk*, 211–4; and Guy Baldwin, *The Leather Contest Guide* (Los Angeles, CA: Daedalus, 1993), 119–20.
67 Gayle Rubin, "Milestones in Modern Whipmaking," *DungeonMaster* 48 (1994), 22–3; Carol Truscott, "Interview with Jay Marston," *Sandmutopia Guardian* 7 (1990), 13–9; and Hedonic Engineering Catalog.
68 "B&D Hits the Big Screen," *Bizarre* 7 (1995), 17–21; Heartwood Whips of Passion catalog, circa 1994; Gerrie & Mitch, "Message from the Publishers," *Sandmutopian Guardian* 18 (1995), 4; "About Adam and Gillian," at https://www.aswgt.com/biography.html (accessed 20 May 2019); and "Joe Wheeler: Master Whipmaker," *Skin Two* 15 (1994), 18.
69 Carol Truscott, "Pain Suite" *Sandmutopia Guardian* 2 (1988), 40 and Journey into Pain ad, *Strict* 1, no. 6 (HOM, 1984), 46.
70 "Chicago: The Tough Go Shopping," *Skin Two* 15 (1994), 21; Jack Fritscher, "Leather's Burning Man," *Bay Area Reporter*, August 2011; and Fritscher, "First for Folsom," *Drummer* 79 (1984), 90.
71 "New York Bound," *Skin Two* 13 (1993), 57–77 and Lynn Comella, *Vibrator Nation: How Feminist Sex-Toy Stores Changed the Business of Pleasure* (Durham, NC: Duke University Press, 2007), 100–1.
72 Barbara Ehrenreich, Elizabeth Hess, and Gloria Jacobs, *Re-Making Love: The Feminization of Sex* (New York: Doubleday, 1986), 125–6.
73 Quartermaster, "Fundamentals of Flagellation," *Sandmutopia Guardian* 5 (1989), 28–41.
74 Levine, *Gay Macho*, 96–8.
75 Joseph W. Bean, "Pleasure Not Panic: The Art of Welcoming Pain," *Sandmutopia Guardian* 11 (1993), 7 & 9–11.
76 Stoller, *Pain & Passion*, 283. Barbara Ehrenreich, *Re-Making Love: The Feminization of Sex* (New York: Doubleday, 1986), 122.
77 Gerrie Blum, "Somewhere to Go, and Someone to Tell," in Antoniou, *Some Women*, 212.
78 Fritscher, *Eyewitness Drummer*, 202 and 482 and Anthony F. DeBlase, "Publisher," *Drummer* 99 (1986), 4.
79 Dominguez, *Beneath the Skins*, 106–7.

4

CREATING A NATIONAL BDSM ORGANIZATION, 1987–89

In examining lesbian and gay political activism, historian Michael Bronski suggests "the emergence of political action from within a community predicated on finding sexual partners was not only logical but vital."[1] While not necessarily vital for the BDSM community, increasing political activism was certainly a logical development, particularly following the Supreme Court's 1986 decision in *Bowers V. Hardwick* upholding the right of states to criminalize sexual activities occurring in the privacy of one's home, the Meese Report's focus on sadomasochistic pornography, and increasing government harassment of BDSM businesses, publications and practitioners.

In the mid-1980s, Samois, GMSMA and other BDSM organizations claimed more visible roles in the gay/lesbian rights movement. They worked to expand their influence and coordinate their efforts with one another, often using the collective term SM/leather/fetish to attract more people to their efforts. As more and more BDSM organizations formed across the United States, their leaders discussed working together on issues ranging from AIDS fundraising and legal defense to campaigns against censorship and the stigmatization of BDSM by both the gay community and mainstream society. Pat Califia urged them to embrace a "common identity as sadomasochists." Individual organizations were too small to influence even local politics. They needed to create a national BDSM organization.[2]

Creating that organization, though, proved difficult, often straining the unity its leaders advocated. They needed to work past differences of gender, sexual orientation, BDSM interest, geography, social class and race, and agree on the proposed organization's missions, suggestions for which included coordinating local BDSM groups, educating people on safe BDSM technique, promoting BDSM as a safe sexual practice to the general public, fighting back against government harassment of BDSM businesses, individuals and organizations, and winning the BDSM community a prominent role in the movement for lesbian and gay rights.

Marching to Unity

Unifying the BDSM community required its diverse populations to look past gender, orientation and other divisions to focus on their shared interests as sadomasochists. Creating a national organization required them to determine its structure and membership. Would it be specifically BDSM, or would it include motorcycle clubs and other leather groups? How would it be organized? Who would be allowed to join? Would it be a loose affiliation of existing BDSM organizations or a formal, hierarchal organization like CHC or GMSMA, which followed detailed bylaws and Roberts Rules of Order?

In October 1980, leaders of several San Francisco BDSM organizations, including Janus, Gemini (a male-dominant heterosexual group), Service of Mankind Church, and several professional dominance businesses and bar owners met to form a coalition. It proved impossible, though, to work across lines of gender, class and sexual orientation. "Gay male bar owners couldn't envision working with heterosexual female dominants, lesbians didn't want to work with male dominants," and all three of these constituencies "distrusted professional dominants." Continued efforts, though, resulted in success several years later when San Francisco BDSM organizations appointed representatives who met with one another to share information. These "informal diplomatic relations" focused almost entirely on winning inclusion for BDSM organizations in local gay and lesbian pride events. They did not spread beyond the Bay Area, even as Janus established chapters outside San Francisco.[3]

TES, GMSMA, LSM and other New York area BDSM organizations similarly worked together on local events, such as Leather Pride Night, but efforts to reach beyond New York failed. TES appointed ambassadors in other cities, but these efforts proved problematic. Members preferred to focus on local issues, and neither TES nor Janus successfully adapted its governing structure to operate beyond its immediate region. The leaders of CHC and GMSMA periodically discussed creating a federation of gay BDSM organizations, tentatively named COSMOS (Council of SM Organizations). People liked the idea, but no one stepped forward to lead COSMOS's creation.[4]

Announced for 1987, planning for the Second National March on Washington for Lesbian and Gay Rights refocused BDSM activists on uniting their community. The march presented an opportunity for them to operate on a national level, win clear and recognized inclusion in the struggle for gay and lesbian rights, and fight back against their stigmatization. This required explaining BDSM and presenting it positively to outsiders, which required crafting a useful definition of BDSM.

Safe, Sane, Consensual: Developing a Useful Definition of BDSM

As BDSM groups formed, their members struggled to define BDSM, develop a vocabulary to discuss their desires, and explain their sexual activities, both to outsiders and potential sex partners. Friedken's film *Cruising* presented the fears of mainstream society, depicting sadomasochists as deranged killers. Adriane Lyne's *9 1/2 Weeks* (1986), in contrast, presented what troubled many sadomasochists: out of control tops and abusive relationships. In the film, mysterious, wealthy John (Mickey Rourke) engages art dealer Elizabeth (Kim Basinger) in escalating BDSM scenes, showcased the opposite. Without discussion or negotiation, Rourke's character pushes Basinger's character until she breaks. During filming, the director similarly worked to make Basinger feel afraid.[5] To prevent this, BDSM activists developed and taught a nuanced understanding of consent, and searched for ways and terminology to explain what they did.

Because of its association with serial killings and violent crime, most BDSM activists preferred the initials S&M, SM or S/M, which could mean sadism and masochism, slave and master, or even, according to *Drummer* editor Jack Fritscher, "sensuality and mutuality." To escape association with crime—or the works of de Sade, who had few admirers in the BDSM community—people suggested alternative terms. The most popular were dominance and submission (D&S or D/S) and bondage and discipline (B&D), terms frequently used in classified ads. Members of Janus debated terminology in the early 1980s, frustrating several members who suggested compromising on the joint term DS/SM. Instead, Janus leaders settled on D/S, which its *Growing Pains* newsletter used for several years before editors reverted to SM.[6]

Whatever term(s) they used, early BDSM organizations emphasized the importance of consent, which had deep roots in BDSM literature. In 1961, a writer in *Fantasia*, a quarterly magazine reminiscent of *Bizarre*, called de Sade "sickening" and explained there was nothing wrong with a "whipping between consenting adults." The following year, Carlson Wade similarly emphasized the importance of "freely-given consent" in *Exotica*.[7] A 1973 New York gay men's forum insisted BDSM required mutual consent and "the production of pleasure for both parties." If an activity was consensual, sadomasochists argued, it was not assault and therefore not a crime. Several women made this argument in the "Healthy Questions about Sado-Masochism" workshop at the Women's Health and Healing Conference in Los Angeles in 1976. TES founder Pat Bond explained how sadomasochists negotiated consent to a psychotherapists' conference the following year. Barbara Ruth insisted "the S&M bond is built on consent, while Jack Fritscher described the Catacombs as "a handball court for consenting adults." As Michael J. Mitchell noted, the "issue of force versus consent" was the "biggest single hurdle that S&M had to clear to achieve knowledgeable public acceptance."[8]

Members of BDSM organizations constructed definitions of BDSM, which relied on consent and safety as their foundations. LSM members "united in the principles of confidentiality, consensuality, and safety." The 15 Association insisted on "consensual, safe, and responsible SM." Samois' Statement of Purpose declared "SM must be consensual, mutual, and safe," a position its members articulated in their newsletter, two books and articles by several members, including Califia, Rubin, Victoria Baker and Carol Truscott. All participants in a BDSM scene needed to discuss and negotiate activities ahead of time, respect one another's limits, and be able to halt activity if something went wrong. Safe words—single words called out to immediately stop a scene—became the norm in the 1980s as most BDSM organizations and venues adopted them.[9]

Janus members defined SM or D/S as "an exchange of power between mutually consenting persons." It was, they wrote Mayor Dianne Feinstein, "mutual, loving, safe, moral, and healthy." By the early 1980s, Janus members settled on the simple declaration that "all SM activities can and should be consensual, non-exploitative and safe" and developed etiquette guidelines requiring ongoing consent.[10] Jack Fritscher echoed this in *Drummer*, explaining "both men" in a scene needed to "consent to a definite energy exchange." So, too, did BDSM businesses, such as the Chateau, a professional dominance business in Los Angeles and San Francisco, whose owners explained to a television talk show audience that "S&M is consensual, totally consensual between the two parties."[11]

DeBlase favored "safe and sane," a phrase used in the past to promote the safe use of fireworks in Independence Day celebrations. The CHC adopted the phrase and in 1981 described its purpose as providing "education and opportunities for participation in S&M sex among consenting adult men . . . striving always to educate and promote safe and sane enjoyment of men by men."[12]

Writing for *Drummer*, Don Miesen sought to capture and explain the variety and allure of "erotic play based on deliberate roles of domination and submission." "SM," he said, "is hurting the one you love, just exactly right." It is "putting up with a picky, uncertain submissive," a novice "who doesn't know how to say what he wants to say; but finally says it, and takes your breath away with the magnificent totality of his submission." It is "fun play," but "also serious play, because we consciously choose our roles" and "act out, fulfill, and make real our erotic fantasies." All "SM games" are "variable and negotiable," involve "fantasy sharing," and can "only be consensual."[13]

Harmony and HOM, the leading publishers of heterosexual BDSM pornographic magazines, similarly encouraged negotiation and safe play. HOM's "Rules of the Game" explained everyone involved needed to "willingly consent" to all activities. "B&D is a harmless fantasy and can be a highly imaginative form of foreplay… as long as all participants perform as consenting adults," and "special care is taken to insure the safety of all parties involved."[14]

Consent, Pat Califia declared, is the "only factor that determines whether or not a sexual act is moral or ethical." Freely given consent changed power dynamics. This marked the BDSM community's "true importance" as "probably the first group of people in all of human history who have said power doesn't have to be an evil thing." In fact, it was the BDSM community's "dedication to the concept of consent," Califia thought, which made it "so fucking dangerous." Sadomasochists threatened the status quo by insisting "people are entitled to decide what they want to do with own bodies, and do it," which is "why they hate our guts."[15]

Influenced by these discussions, GMSMA members merged "consent," articulated by TES, Janus, Samois, LSM and others, and DeBlase's "safe and sane" phrase, adopted by CHC and popularized in *DungeonMaster*, to form "safe, sane, consensual." People engaging in BDSM, they argued, were sane, consenting adults who ensured the safety of their partners. GMSMA members formally adopted the phrase in 1983, and its leaders, particularly Barry Douglas, who spearheaded many GMSMA initiatives, increasingly used the phrase.[16]

The 1987 March on Washington for Lesbian and Gay Rights

Throughout the 1970s, BDSM organizations sought visible places in the Gay Liberation Movement. San Francisco's Gay Freedom Parade and other local pride events banned their participation, as did the 1979 National March on Washington for Lesbian and Gay Rights. It was not just mainstream society that feared BDSM, Pat Califia complained. "Conservative gay liberationists and orthodox feminists are also embarrassed by kinky sexual subcultures," even, she added "if that's where they do their tricking." These assimilationists hoped, as Daniel Harris argues, "to present a rosy-cheeked, choirboy image of the homosexual to mainstream America." Visibly kinky marchers were not welcome.[17]

A prolonged fight won Society of Janus inclusion in the 1978 San Francisco's Gay Freedom Parade. Yet when they arrived, parade monitors tried to exclude them due to overt displays of BDSM paraphernalia, mostly chains and collars. When Califia and several Janus officers refused to back down, officials relented. The Janus contingent, which included a few members of Samois, marched, but were met with boos, hisses and shouts of "Nazis" and "fascists" along the route. They, in turn, passed out copies of Skip Aiken's article "Don't Close the Closet Door Just Because There's Leather Inside," which explained "SM is by definition consensual" and is "antithetical to rape, violence, and murder." Aiken had made these points before, such as the 1981 conference of the International Gay Association in Italy, where organizers told him the issue was not participation by BDSM people, per se, but rather their visible participation in leather, uniforms and BDSM accoutrements. A BDSM presence would give people the wrong idea about the gay and lesbian rights movement, particularly if sadomasochists wore leather, led submissives on leashes, or flogged them, which some wished to do.[18]

In 1979, the San Francisco parade again refused participation to BDSM organizations. Aiken urged members of the BDSM community to push back. While others marched "militantly out of their closets," sadomasochists "were urged to keep a low profile, leave our leather at home, and keep quiet." That needed to change. Over the next half dozen years, San Francisco BDSM organizations faced periodic bans from parade officials, which they challenged at parade organizing meetings. In 1984, San Francisco BDSM organizations and businesses organized the first Folsom Street Fair to celebrate the neighborhood's leather bars and BDSM shops. It grew in size each succeeding year, attracting ever larger crowds, and this success helped convince march officials to allow BDSM organizations.

In 1986, they allowed an officially designated "SM contingent." The following year, it included a "precision whip drill team," which won the Cable Car Award for "Most Outrageous" contingent.[19]

Similar disputes occurred in other cites as new BDSM organizations pressed for inclusion, winning some fights, but losing others. In Albuquerque, the local gay community center banned PEP from meeting there.[20] Many people, David Stein complained, associated BDSM with "with sleaze, drug abuse, and promiscuity."[21] Even those unopposed to BDSM often argued its visible presence at pride events hurt the cause. Members of the BDSM community encountered such consistent opposition; one member of Urania, a women's BDSM group, asked: "Am I paranoid or are they really out to get me?" How should "SM women relate to the non-SM world?" To whom, she asked, was it safe to come out? How much—if any—of one's BDSM sexuality was it safe to exhibit?[22]

In New York, GMSMA's leaders made "establishing a positive presence in the gay community" a priority, and successfully lobbied New York lesbian and gay organizations to allow BDSM organizations to participate in pride events and use facilities, such as the Lesbian and Gay Community Services Center, where GMSMA hosted BDSM presentations and discussions. Its effort, though, required constantly pushing back against its detractors and making substantial financial contributions to gay causes, which GMSMA proved adept at raising through beer busts, raffles and BDSM demonstrations at local bars and clubs.[23]

TES marched in New York pride parades in the 1970s, and was joined by GMSMA and LSM in the early 1980s despite some opposition. "The gay establishment," GMSMA's leaders complained, "would rather we just disappeared. We know why we're having trouble relocating our meeting space. We know why we're having trouble getting credit for our achievements." GMSMA had to work harder and raise more money than similarly sized organizations to win acceptance. Yet, it rose to the challenge, encouraging members in 1984 to march "with boots polished, keys and chains sparkling in the sun, buttons and pins in place on leather vests or lapels."[24] Over the next few years, GMSMA raised funds for numerous causes, establishing a national reputation for activism. It made itself too large to ignore.

The organizers of the 1987 March on Washington for Lesbian and Gay Rights hoped to field an unprecedentedly large number of marchers and reached out to BDSM, leather and drag queen organizations and others excluded from the 1979 march. GMSMA members attended early planning meetings and convinced organizers to include a designated "SM-Leather Contingent."[25] GMSMA chairman Barry Douglas received a seat on the march's steering committee, as did a representative of drag queen organizations. March organizers "jokingly referred to them as the 'butch' and 'fem' seats." Brenda Howard, a member of LSM and TES, agreed to co-chair the SM-leather Contingent, and she and Douglas appointed ten regional coordinators in November 1986 to recruit marchers. It was, DeBlase proclaimed, a major achievement. For "the first time, a gay/

lesbian political activist group specifically designated leather as a recognized subset whose input is specifically included in planning and activities."[26]

Other BDSM community members, such as Cookie Andrews-Hunt, served on the march's regional committees. George Nelson, the NLA's Secretary and newsletter editor, was ecstatic. Members of the BDSM community were "no longer willing" to let others "make our decisions for us." They were finally unifying, letting

> the rest of our homophile family know that we are going to be recognized as a living part of that family, to be heard and take an active part in the activities, decisions, and plans of our local and national communities.[27]

At the March on Washington, about 700 people marched behind the "SM-Leather Contingent" banner. Hundreds of other members of leather and BDSM organizations, such as Briar Rose founder Jan Hall, marched with their local lesbian and gay organizations or other parade contingents. Participants observed "safe, sane, consensual" t-shirts scattered among marchers, along with lots of leather, but no chains, whips or other overt indications of BDSM. While they represented just a fraction of the 200,000 marches, the Leather Contingent nonetheless demonstrated the growing size and cohesion of the BDSM community. Barry Douglas proclaimed the weekend "an overwhelming affirmation or our rights, freedoms, values, and joys." Sadomasochists should "no longer be ashamed." They had assumed their "rightful position at the forefront of the gay movement."[28]

A Second Coming Out

The stigmatization of BDSM encouraged many people to conceal their BDSM interests. "As the rest of the Gay/Lesbian community was bursting out of its closet doors," Steve Maidhof noted, many remained behind "that secret closet marked Leather/SM." Told their visible presence at pride marches "would only hinder the movement," they revealed themselves as gay, but kept their BDSM secret in a "closet within a closet." That needed to change.[29]

Douglas presented the SM-Leather Contingent's participation in the March as the tipping point in that change. Many agreed. DeBlase launched *The Sandmutopia Guardian* magazine, the pansexual counterpart of *DungeonMaster*, on the eve of the march. Its early issues covered the march and encouraged BDSM practitioners to unite socially and politically. So, too, did Dave Rhodes' recently launched magazine, *Leather Journal*, chronicled leather and BDSM events around the country, particularly the formation of new clubs and title contests to which Rhodes added his own Pantheon of Leather Awards in 1991. Both magazines facilitated the formation and growth of BDSM organizations, and encouraged individuals to reveal their BDSM identities—what many gay and lesbian sadomasochists termed a "second coming out."[30]

Many people, particularly women, lost friends and were shunned for revealing BDSM interests. Juicy Lucy "had friends scream insults at me, tell me I'm to be pitied, like a man, oppressive to womyn, disgusting, not welcome in their home, untrustworthy, etc." Of the 539 women who responded to a survey sponsored by Female Trouble, a Philadelphia women's BDSM group, over half reported incidents of harassment and discrimination by fellow lesbians. Just over a quarter suffered physical assault because of their BDSM identification. One woman was severely beaten at the Michigan Womyn's Music Festival for wearing a leather jacket. Others, among them Jay Marston, who sold her leatherwork at the festival, reported routine harassment, including spitting, insults and verbal threats. While other attendees enjoyed the festival's "erotic lesbian paradise," BDSM women traveled in groups and arranged their own security patrols to keep themselves safe.[31] The festival presented in microcosm both the feminist debates on sadomasochism and the routine problems sadomasochistic women faced.

Susie Shepherd, who won the International Ms. Leather contest in 1989, found coming out as a lesbian "much easier" than coming out BDSM. She first attended a dungeon party in 1980, but remained ambivalent about her desires. Only several years later did her friends Judy Tallwing McCarthy and Sashie Hyatt "blow open" her "leather closet door." Gayle Rubin suggested there would be BDSM organizations like Samois "in virtually every lesbian community in the U.S. if the costs of coming out were not so excruciating."[32] *Drummer* columnist Guy Baldwin complained about "kink-o-phobia." Like "lesbians and gay men, we kinky people are seen by most of the world as sick and dangerous." Like gays and lesbians, kinky people were "only supposed to *do it* in secret, in private, in shame, in fear, in self-loathing, and most of all, in silence." He urged *Drummer* readers to come out as sadomasochists.[33]

Like coming out as gay, Geoff Mains explained, coming out as BDSM required "an experience of intense personal discovery and acceptance." Ivo Dominguez described it as seven-step process, beginning with "stirrings" and "denial" and escalating through "whole hog" explorations of kinky sex, development of a "leather persona," and finally "homecoming" in which people accepted the "authenticity of their identity as a SM/Leather/Fetish person" and "develop a sense of responsibility towards the Kink community." [34]

Whatever the process, more and more sadomasochists responded to calls to come out. Many did so at the March on Washington. Among them was Peri Jude Radecic, executive director of the National Gay and Lesbian Task Force (NGLTF) from 1987 to 1994. During her tenure, she ensured the inclusion of panels addressing the BDSM community at the NGLTF's annual Creating Change conferences, which GMSMA and the NLA staffed. A few months after the march, she was the keynote speaker at Living in Leather VIII in Houston.[35]

The March on Washington popularized the phrase, "safe, sane, consensual." Alan Long, a close friend of Barry Douglas, designed its logo, which appeared on promotional literature for the BDSM contingent and its t-shirts. Douglas used it in all the Leather Contingent's correspondence, and others adopted it, particularly the NLA's leaders. So, too, did Tony DeBlase, and the phrase appeared increasingly in NLA newsletters, *Drummer, DungeonMaster* and other publications.[36]

The afternoon before the March on Washington, Saturday, 10 October, the NLA organized a BDSM conference. Several hundred people attended, including many prominent BDSM activists, some of whom met one another for the first time. Many stayed in the same hotel, which provided additional opportunities to socialize and organize, as did a post-conference party hosted by PEP's Washington chapter and SigMa, Washington's largest men's BDSM organization.[37]

Apart from a workshop on relationships, the conference's seminars focused on political activism and media relations, such as "Increasing SM/Leather Presence in Gay and Lesbian Politics," "SM/Leather and the Women's Movement" and "S/M and the Law." Presenters addressed reaching out to new and isolated sadomasochists, educating the gay community about BDSM, and countering myths and stereotypes about BDSM. In her keynote address, Judy Tallwing McCarthy, winner of the recently launched International Ms. Leather (IMsL) contest, stressed the need to unite "leather/SM/fetish folks," forming "a true community." Dave Rhodes saw "women sharing with men," and "men willing to accept women," and declared the conference a good beginning. New friendships formed and rivals buried hatchets. It was time for the BDSM community to mobilize and demand legislators and law enforcement BDSM involved "mutual consent and pleasure," not "uncontrolled brutality, rape, and violence." Several pointed out the BDSM community was "the first to engage in safe sex, because of the potential dangers inherent in SM." They were not "sex-crazed and whip-wielding maniacs." No one thought more and more deeply about safe sex than they did.[38]

Barry Douglas, too, saw the event as the "beginning of our coming together." Sadomasochists were "no longer alone." Over 300 organizations supported the Leather Contingent: "support groups, social groups, educational groups, sex groups, political groups," gay, straight and "bi groups, and innumerable combinations of them all." Attending the conference and marching together made them a community, a community with its own demands, including "the right to love whom we please," and the "right to express that love in the privacy of our own homes, in any manner that is safe, sane, and consensual."[39]

Samuel R. Delany suggests we live in a system that places pleasure and responsibility in opposition. "Good people" accepted this contractual system. "Anyone who rebelled was a prostitute or pervert, or both." Sadomasochists clearly fell into the latter category and they increasingly resented being labeled perverse. Their desire for inclusion, though, encouraged them to hide their BDSM interests. Delany argues "tolerance—not assimilation—is the democratic litmus test for social equality."[40] In the aftermath of their success at the March on Washington, BDSM activists faced the choice between assimilating to win inclusion by hiding their BDSM practices or insisting on toleration by displaying all their leather, whips and chains.

Going National

The SM-Leather Contingent conference ended with a belatedly organized discussion to form a national BDSM organization chaired by GMSMA's Ray Matienzo. Was it time to go national? Most attendees had already left for parties arranged at local leather bars, but about 60 people attended. Most agreed the growing BDSM community needed some nation-wide structure to mobilize and coordinate its events, fundraising and political action. Among them was Gayle Rubin who in the most recent issue of *DungeonMaster* suggested the NLA was "uniquely qualified" to lead the BDSM community. It had just hosted its second Living in Leather conference, formed chapters in Vancouver and Portland, Oregon, and was growing rapidly.[41]

While some agreed with Rubin's assessment, most expressed skepticism. A few found the NLA's name, with its premature declaration of national status, offensive. GMSMA, TES and other older BDSM organizations all had more members than the NLA. Many people from the West Coast who had attended Living in Leather favored uniting behind the NLA. Most of those from the East favored forming a new national organization. Regardless, this small gathering lacked the authority to either anoint the NLA or create something else.

Douglas, who arrived late, suggested a dedicated meeting to form a national organization, which people suggested should maintain a directory of BDSM, leather and fetish organizations; coordinate their efforts; publish a newsletter; monitor mainstream media portrayals of sadomasochism; sponsoring a national BDSM conferences; and liaise with lesbian, gay and other organizations promoting sexual freedom.[42]

Jim Richards arranged for the Disciples of De Sade to host the meeting in Dallas. Richards, who had his first BDSM encounter as a street hustler in the 1960s, joined Avatar while living in Los Angeles, and later the CHC, which connected him with a dozen other Dallas-area members who joined him to form Disciples of De Sade.[43]

The Dallas Conference

A few months later, BDSM leaders gathered in over the weekend of 12–14 February 1988. That conference went by several names, none of them official: Beyond Vanilla, the Dallas Follow-Up Meeting, the Washington Continuation Conference, or simply the Dallas Conference. It attracted the community's most prominent activists and educators, including Califia, DeBlase, Douglas, Maidhof, Renslow, Rubin and Stein. Members of Janus, TES, CHC, GMSMA, NLA, Outcasts and 47 other organizations attended, as did several businesses owners, and about two-dozen people unaffiliated with any organization. Several of the latter, all men, listed themselves on registration forms as "goddamn independent" or GDI. Members of the fraternal leather "backpatch" clubs often used the phrase with derision, but these men valued their independence.

Most of the 129 attendees were gay men, one of whom traveled from Puerto Rico. The rest were from the United States. Almost all were white. Many belonged to several BDSM organizations, making precise determination of some attendees' organizational affiliations difficult. Texans and Oklahomans accounted for roughly a quarter of the attendees. David Stein, Barry Douglas and 12 other New York-area members of GMSMA attended, making it the largest delegation. CHC's delegation, with eight Chicago-area members, was second. The Outcasts, Society of Janus, SigMa, Atlanta SM Solidarity, and PEP each sent three or four members. Pat Bond and Nancy Ava Miller were among a handful of heterosexuals. Only one-sixth of the attendees were women, reflecting both the smaller number and smaller membership of women's groups, many of which lacked the funds to send representatives. Instead, they gave instructions and proxies to women able to attend.[44]

Maidhof's health was failing, so Cookie Andrews-Hunt, the NLA's photographer and publicist, and David Meador, a Virginia travel agent who handled the Leather Contingent's travel arrangements, officially represented the NLA. Many other attendees were NLA members, but this was because the NLA awarded membership to everyone who attended Living in Leather II, not due to any close affiliation with the NLA. Several of the NLA's most vocal critics were NLA members.[45]

Attendees' demographics reflected the BDSM community of the mid-1980s. They were overwhelmingly white, middle class, college educated and urban. Several had graduate degrees; a few had doctorates. Men's organizations predominated at the conference. Even if one ignored the backpatch clubs, only some of which affiliated closely with the BDSM community, men's organizations accounted for at least two-thirds of the nation's BDSM organizations. Women's groups remained rare, accounting for between 5 and 10 percent of the nation's BDSM groups, though about 15 percent of Dallas delegates. In contrast, heterosexual or mixed groups accounted for perhaps a quarter of the nation's BDSM groups. No exclusively heterosexual organization sent delegates to Dallas. Only a handful of the mixed groups did, including DADS, Janus, PEP and TES.

These demographics were changing, which DeBlase recognized by launching *The Sandmutopia Guardian* magazine, a multi-gender and orientation companion to the male-oriented *DungeonMaster.* Its first issue, which appeared shortly after the Dallas Conference, listed 24 BDSM clubs that accepted men and women, 23 for men only, and 17 for women only. While hardly a complete listing, the ratios reflected both the magazine's audience and how growing numbers of women's and mixed BDSM groups were changing the community. Edited by Carol Truscott, a veteran of Samois and other San Francisco BDSM groups, it became one of the leading voices encouraging cross-orientation play and advocating pansexuality—that people move past narrow divisions of gender and orientation and embrace and participate in a diverse, sexual community.[46]

DeBlase encouraged people to arrive in Dallas with open minds and work toward consensus. Unity was imperative. They needed to set aside "petty bickering and 'them against us' attitudes—whether they be east vs. west, big vs. small, male vs. female, homo vs. bi vs. hetero, old established vs. new upstart, highly structured vs. loosely affiliated." No one would be "totally satisfied," but everyone "interested in Safe-Sane-Consensual Leather/SM sexuality" should support whatever national organization resulted.[47]

Instead, the conference erupted in acrimonious argument and intense politicking along exactly those lines. Disputes erupted before the event and continued afterward, leaving many participants embittered. Recriminations lasted years. Some friendships never recovered. Ivo Dominguez declared the conference "horrific," a gathering "so acrimonious there should have been a psychic smog alert and so filled with intrigue that it should have been raided by the karma police." Others complained about an "inordinate amount of political back-stabbing and childish name-calling. One man found it so "nauseating" he wanted to "crawl into the arms of the biggest, furriest, protective Leather Daddy there and just cry."[48]

Before the conference, the Outcasts consulted other women's BDSM groups, developed a series of proposals and circulated them. They advocated a politically active national organization that hosted an annual convention, published a broadly distributed newsletter and promoted education on safe technique. It would serve as a liaison between local clubs, spearhead legal defense and anti-defamation efforts, and include women in prominent positions. Proxy instructions from several women's groups reflected the Outcasts' position, which advocated a national organization similar to the NLA. The critical issues for LSM were representation of women and gender parity. Southern Kink, an Atlanta-area women's group, opposed the inclusion of any exclusively heterosexual BDSM organization. Most of the female delegates met Friday evening before the conference's official start, and agreed to demand "equal representation of women."[49]

Other delegates also politicked before the conference. GMSMA's leaders corresponded with several men's groups and met in person with New York–area clubs. GMSMA's leaders, who were the most persistent advocates for creating an alternative to the NLA, hoped to create an "organization of organizations," composed of representatives from BDSM groups across the United States. They arrived in Dallas with a block of supporters, which included members of CHC and SigMa.[50]

Less formal coalitions of attendees, generally based on region or sexual interest, formed during the conference. The occasional gatherings of these and other factions or perceived factions, particularly the women's caucus, fueled rumors they intended to "hijack" the conference and force through their agenda.[51]

On Friday night, Barry Douglas met with about two-dozen prominent attendees. They drew up a preliminary agenda, designated an ad hoc steering committee, and chose 12 people to lead small group discussions Saturday morning. Over lunch, the steering committee would use their input to draft the agenda for the rest of the conference. The small groups considered:

1 Should a new organization be created or can an existing organization serve our needs?
2 Why do we need a national or international SM-leather network?

3 The purpose and goals of the organization.
4 Would membership of this group be restricted to gay/lesbian or SM groups? What about heterosexuals? What about leather, uniform and similar groups? What about businesses or groups outside the U.S.?
5 What status would individuals have in the organization?
6 Representation of women.
7 The structure of the organization.
8 Outreach to people of color.[52]

Attendees agreed they faced "a growing threat from the Right and waning support from the larger gay and lesbian community." They needed to unify. Almost everyone agreed the BDSM community needed a national organization, so discussion quickly shifted to its membership, structure and mission. What would it do? Who would be allowed to join? How would its members be represented? Would it seek to grow the BDSM community, or would that be left to local BDSM organizations? Would it be an "organization of organizations," or could individuals join on their own? BDSM organizations varied dramatically in size and structure, so how would voting in the new organization work? If they opened the organization to everyone, would heterosexuals become its majority, as they had in TES and Janus?

Informal discussions continued over lunch, while the steering committee finalized the afternoon agenda. These discussions exposed divisions among attendees and also the lack of preparation by conference organizers. No one had considered voting procedures. Would it be by organization or by individual delegate? Voting as individuals clearly favored the large men's organizations, which arrived with numerous delegates. Yet, voting by organization would exclude the two-dozen independent delegates and still marginalize women, though it would allow Dorothy Allison, Pat Califia and Cookie Andrews-Hunt to vote the proxies they brought from other women's organizations. Either choice would offend some people and itself depended on agreement on how votes would be counted.[53]

Barry Douglas and Gil Kessler of GMSMA opened the afternoon discussion by advocating a national organization composed of existing BDSM organizations. Stacy Dennen from the Society of Janus responded by advocating equality for women, outreach to people of color and forming alliances with other sexual advocacy groups. Robert Key, representing SigMa, generally echoed Douglas and Kessler, but warned the funding required for any large organization would prove difficult to raise. Could the BDSM community finance a national organization?[54]

Cookie Andrews-Hunt, representing the NLA, spoke next. The NLA's leaders recognized they faced substantial opposition from GMSMA and other eastern BDSM organizations. So, Andrews-Hunt did not press their case. Instead, she explained the NLA needed more time to consider the opportunities presented by the meetings in Washington and Dallas and discuss them with its members. Nonetheless, the NLA would support whatever organization and decisions emerged from Dallas.

With the NLA off the table, delegates agreed to form a new organization. It would be open to all members of a broadly defined BDSM, leather and fetish community, including heterosexuals, gays and lesbians. Dennen was particularly pleased to know the new organization would be "pan-sexual and pan-genderal." Throughout the conference Dennen repeatedly defended "placement of bisexuals and heterosexuals in the directing body of the organization" against accusations—mostly from gay men—that heterosexuals did not care enough about national organizing to "to speak up" and were happy to have others "represent them." [55]

Many—probably most—heterosexuals in the BDSM community, continued to use pseudonyms or "scene names," while more and more gay and lesbian sadomasochists used their real names. DeBlase, for example, abandoned his Fledermaus *nom de plum*. While a minor source of irritation, it underlined a significant difference between gay and straight sadomasochists. The latter were often reluctant to publicly reveal their sexual interests and "come out." In contrast, gay and lesbian sadomasochists increasingly declared BDSM a central part of their sexual identity and declared it publicly.

Other issues proved more contentious, and efforts to vote on them erupted into arguments on voting procedure—both for the conference itself and the organization the delegates hoped to create. Most members of GMSMA and other large, older, men's organizations, including CHC, SigMa and Dreizehn, favored what they called an "organization of organizations"—an umbrella organization composed of representatives from established BDSM groups around the country. So, too, did Pat Bond of TES.

Other delegates, particularly women and unaffiliated men, favored a less formal organization, one that anyone could join, which would welcome newcomers to BDSM, particularly women and people of color who were underrepresented in existing organizations. Allison, Califia and others spoke forcefully for individual membership—a position diametrically opposed to GMSMA's.[56] Large, local BDSM organizations like GMSMA, they suggested, should serve in an advisory capacity. Suggestions for gender parity in leadership positions, a precedent established by the NLA and March on Washington SM-Leather Contingent, further complicated the debate. Tempers became so heated the "conference nearly dissolved" when factions "could not even manage to obey parliamentary procedure as they wrangled." Speakers on both sides indicated "they would walk out and boycott any organization created" if their demands were not met.[57]

Tempers flared and several people voiced their distrust of the proceedings. To settle the impasse, Tony DeBlase agreed to chair the proceedings, with Chuck Renslow serving as parliamentarian, and a two-thirds majority required to pass any measures. DeBlase sought compromise, suggesting an organization of organizations specifically tasked to reach out to individuals, but without success. After several hours of argument, he tabled the agenda, formed a committee composed of himself, Califia, Dennen, Douglas, Key, Maidhof, Richards, Rubin and Stein to develop the new organization's statement of purpose, and adjourned the meeting until Sunday morning. Most attendees went to the Trestle leather bar for the conference's Saturday night "Fetish and Fantasy Party." There, tempers cooled, but politicking continued as DeBlase and others sought a workable compromise.[58]

The Saturday debates underlined divisions among three of the BDSM community's constituent populations: members of backpatch clubs, members of the new, open BDSM organizations, and GDIs. Backpatchers criticized BDSM organizations for their "lack of camaraderie," while GDIs sneered that Backpatch clubs were cliques "for people who can't make it on their own." Leaders of open BDSM organizations, in turn, viewed many backpatch clubs as "just leather dress-up with no real kink." Like the backpatch leaders, though, they often portrayed GDIs as a drain on their resources—people who benefitted from the BDSM community's new institutions, but gave little back. Attendee John Ramsey spoke for many GDIs when he rebutted these accusations, emphasized the importance of GDIs, their participation in numerous events including the March on Washington, and argued for their full inclusion: "We worked in D.C. and now you [GMSMA] are telling us thanks but no thanks."[59]

The views of Dallas attendees generally reflected their personal experiences, the organizations to which they belonged, and their comfort with the existing status quo. GMSMA's "organization of organizations" proposal would preserve the existing status quo with the organized BDSM community dominated by gay men, their clubs and bars. In contrast, BDSM women, who had suffered determined attacks on their sexuality, were barred from many BDSM organizations, events, bars and clubs. Women's and mixed groups were "smaller and fewer." Many women lacked local organizations to join. As Ice Camins-Bretts, who represented two women's groups, Urania and Bound and Determined, pointed out, an "organization of organizations" was "obviously in the best interest of men's clubs . . . as men have many clubs available to them."[60] Reaching out to women and others underrepresented in the BDSM community would change the status quo.

Douglas and other GMSMA members thought a national organization should focus on winning the BDSM community inclusion in the larger gay and lesbian community and fighting back against government harassment. Allison, Califia, Rubin and other women suggested the new organization should also help resolve problems within the BDSM community. A national organization with open membership offered the opportunity to re-shape its demographics by attracting new members, particularly from traditionally underserved areas of the nation and underrepresented constituencies, particularly women and people of color, as well as promoting a shared system of values to all sadomasochists. The model promoted by GMSMA offered little to people living in places where the potential BDSM community was too small to form local organizations. Why not reach out to these isolated sadomasochists?[61]

On the other hand, everyone at the conference recognized the majority of BDSM people were heterosexual. Several worried heterosexual men would inevitably come to dominate any open membership group. The "organizations of organizations" model would prevent this.

Most of those who favored GMSMA's "organization of organizations" were members of rigidly structured Midwest and East Coast men's groups. Most of those in opposition hailed from the West Coast where Catacombs parties, Janus and the NLA provided successful examples of mixed gender and orientation events and organizations. A centralized, hierarchal "organization of organizations" was the antithesis of the informal, free-spirited groups common to the West Coast.

Debate resumed Sunday morning, becoming increasingly strained as tempers flared and proposals for compromise became increasingly convoluted. An "organization of organizations" would not address the needs of those living outside major metropolitan areas, nor were its advocates able to explain the criteria for judging organizations for admission. As DeBlase pointed out, "club," like BDSM, was hard to define. BDSM organizations varied from those with a "rigorous application policy with pledge periods, membership votes, etc." to those with an "open membership policy, welcoming virtually anyone who is willing to pay dues" to clubs "without formal memberships at all." Some elect officers and file paperwork to become legal corporate entities, but many did not. Which clubs would be judged worthy of joining the "organization of organizations?"[62]

Debate paused for lunch while DeBlase and the Steering Committee met at a nearby restaurant to work out a series of compromises. They agreed on a rough statement of purpose for the organization and to work for gender parity in its leadership. At David Stein's suggestion, they divided voting power between individuals, who received one-third, and organizations, which received two-thirds voting power. That afternoon, attendees accepted that voting system, agreed GMSMA's phrase "safe, sane, and consensual" best exemplified BDSM activity, and accepted the name Safe, Sane, Consensual Adults (SSCA) for the new organization. With little time remaining and tempers still hot, they elected four women and five men to be the SSCA's interim steering committee (ISC): Ice Camins-Bretts, Ty Clements (Dreizehn, Boston), Tony DeBlase, Stacy Dennen, John Ferrari (Avatar, Los Angeles), Jan Hall (Briar Rose, Ohio), Shannon Kennedy (unaffiliated, Detroit), Jim Richards and Silas McGowan (Atlanta SM Solidarity), one of the few African Americans at the conference. As Jan Hall later noted, the majority voted for voices of moderation rather than the vocal, and somewhat volatile, faction leaders. Barry Douglas, Pat Califia and other well-known BDSM activists lost the election. With the exception of DeBlase, no one on the ISC was well-known nationally.[63]

Attendees agreed on the importance of educating mainstream society about BDSM and political lobbying, but not educating members of the BDSM community. GMSMA and its supporters saw this as a local issue and did not want a national organization stomping around in their backyard. The contentious debates on voting procedure and electing the ISC consumed so much time, attendees never finalized and voted on the SSCA's statement of purpose, a draft version of which circulated after the conference. It drew from suggestions made at the Leather Contingent's meeting in Washington, the NLA's statement of purpose, and the proposal circulated by the Outcasts. It called for the SSCA to "help build, strengthen and defend the SM, leather, and other fetish communities," "promote the rights of adults to engage in all safe, sane, consensual erotic activities," educate "about safe, sane, consensual behavior," present "a more accurate, positive image" of BDSM, and oppose threats to sexual freedom. It would reach out to people of color and ensure women occupied "visible positions of leadership." Its duties would include:

1 Communication: newsletter, directory, calendar, national media watch;
2 Networking (national conferences, helping to establish new local organizations, facilitate interaction of established organizations;
3 Education (hotline, speakers' bureau, exchange of program ideas and materials);
4 Political activity (legal defense fund; decriminalization of all safe, sane, consensual sexual behavior among adults, anti-defamation, liaison with other groups supporting sexual civil rights, alert membership regarding potentially repressive legislation);
5 Archive/library;
6 AIDS action, education and fundraising.

The contentious conference ended with most attendees unhappy. The draft Statement of Purpose reflected the superior organization and planning of the Outcasts and other women's groups, as well as a general desire to diversify and educate the BDSM community. Yet, numerous issues remained unresolved or unclear. No one knew how local BDSM organizations would qualify to join the SSCA or how much it would cost. Efforts to produce stronger statements on gender parity, race and outreach failed due to lack of time and consensus. A few delegates, in fact, groused that several of the ISC's newly elected leaders were chosen due to issues of race or gender rather than their leadership experience.

The "organization of organizations" advocates were disappointed by the dilution of the SSCA with individual members. Pat Bond complained the ISC did not include any of the first generation of BDSM organizers like himself. "New York was totally frozen out," Stein complained, "despite having three of the largest, oldest, and most visible SM organizations in the country." While denouncing the conference's "backbiting and rumor-mongering," he chronicled GMSMA's grievances in letters to *Drummer* and other publications. GMSMA's hopes

> nearly died as factionalism and mistrust undermined what had been accomplished in October [at the March on Washington]. The dream of a network created by and for independent organizations, each representing and directly serving its own individual members was shattered.

He demanded the ISC add representatives from "excluded regions and major organizations," adopt a more rational voting system, and not squander resources "on a quixotic effort to recruit 'GDIs,'" [64]

GMSMA's Ray Matienzo declared SSCA "a deformed child" for which he blamed the machinations of "a handful of women" led by Pat Califia. She and "her bevy of sycophants" were determined to have their own way "at any and all costs" and "neuter every male" in Dallas. Claiming they had "publicly defamed the reputation of GMSMA," enraged GMSMA members publicly revoked the honorary memberships previously awarded to Allison and Califia, GMSMA's only female honorees. [65]

The acrimony continued in the BDSM press. *Sandmutopian Guardian* editor Carol Truscott denounced Stein for continuing the rancor of Dallas. Joe Bridwell condemned GMSMA for "throwing a tantrum" and "rumor-mongering and undermining" the SSCA. Leaders of the Chicago Hellfire Club, in turn, shared GMSMA's disgruntlement and groused over not having a seat on the ISC. Like GMSMA's leaders, CHC's president opposed a national organization with individual members, writing the ISC: "I feel for the person in East Bumfuck, Iowa, who has no group," but "when I felt the need for a larger organization strongly enough, I found one." There was no reason to believe people who had "assiduously spurned association with any organization to date will now all of a sudden 'see the light,'" and join SSCA.[66]

Yet, these isolated sadomasochists were starting to reach out. One lonely Alaskan sadomasochist wrote the *Advocate* seeking connection. The few leathermen he knew were "so far back in the S/M closet" they were in danger of becoming "leather-lined garment bags." Where could he meet men who shared his interests?[67]

The conference's most lasting legacy was not the SSCA, but establishing "safe, sane, consensual" as the defining criteria of BDSM. It marked the culmination of 20 years of discussions seeking a positive and succinct definition of these activities. As Victoria Baker noted, people made lots of suggestions at the conference, but they all boiled down to "safe, sane, consensual." The phrase articulated "that which binds us together, that which we all understand about our activities, that which helps us to do the work of becoming understood in the world."[68]

Attendees of the Dallas Conference introduced the phrase to their friends, and BDSM organizations adopted it. Within a few years, virtually every leading member of the BDSM community used the phrase to separate BDSM activities from criminal violence. Discussing what exactly constituted "safe, sane, and consensual" behavior became a regular topic of BDSM discussion groups. CDG, for example, presented demonstrations of transgressive scenes, which members discussed. Local NLA chapters and the NLA's LIL conferences regularly featured spirited discussions of consent, safety and "edge play."[69]

The SSCA

The members of the SSCA's Interim Steering Committee (ISC) elected John Ferrari and Stacy Dennen its co-chairs and arranged to meet at major BDSM/

leather events, including the upcoming International Mr. Leather contest (May) and Living in Leather III (October). They mailed surveys to BDSM organizations to solicit their advice and over the next few months worked to garner support. Several dozen organizations responded. Janus member Frank Jur urged the SSCA to "protect my rights as a citizen of the US who is also an S/M person," encourage "the interchange of ideas between organizations," and reach out to isolated "'lone wolf' individuals" who lacked local organizations. SHELIX founder Bet Powers urged the SSCA to get "S/M de-criminalized" and "sex laws off the books."[70]

To resolve lingering acrimony and complaints about non-representation from large organizations and certain regions, the SSCA's leaders offered to add representatives from New York, Washington DC, the Southwest and the Pacific Northwest. In a special meeting, about 30 members of GMSMA, LSM and TES elected Barry Douglas to represent New York. Judy Tallwing McCarthy agreed to represent the Northwest and Cooper Aaxton, a leading member of Denver's BDSM community, represented the Rocky Mountains and Southwest. Washington, DC-area clubs failed to agree on a representative.[71]

As Barry Douglas noted, the SSCA's leaders first needed to create a functioning organization. Unfortunately, Douglas proved more hindrance than help when the SSCA's enlarged Interim Steering Committee (ISC) met at the International Mr. Leather contest in Chicago in May. Douglas repeatedly revived debates from Dallas, insisted the ISC restructure the SSCA without individual members, and that it assign projects to existing BDSM organizations rather than develop its own capabilities. The NLA, Douglas suggested, should "coordinate publications," while groups in Chicago and the Midwest would host an annual conference. New Yorkers had "the best political contacts and the most experience working with the broader gay and lesbian movement" and should lead the SSCA's political efforts.[72]

Responding to Douglas's complaint that both ISC co-chairs hailed from California, Jim Richards replaced John Ferrari as the ISC's male co-chair shortly after its May meeting. Debates over SSCA membership and voting structure, though, continued. Douglass and a few others wanted change, while members of Outcasts and other vocal advocates of individual membership opposed any change to the one-third, two-thirds voting arrangement reached in Dallas. Over the course of the next four months, repeated efforts at compromise failed. After losing a vote to dramatically restructure the SSCA, Douglas resigned in September and publicly condemned the SSCA as a failure. Clements and McGowan also resigned, leaving the ISC without any members from large, eastern men's organizations. While Jan Hall of Ohio represented the Midwest, several Midwestern men's organizations complained they lacked representation in the SSCA, perhaps indicating discomfort working with a woman.[73]

Poisoned by the vitriolic debates in Dallas, the SSCA never gained significant support. Criticism over the compromises achieved in Dallas never stopped. New critics attacked the SSCA for moving too slowly, unending efforts to satisfy Douglas and his supporters, and meeting behind closed doors, which it did to avoid chaotic debate. Repeated compromises failed to satisfy the SSCA's critics, but cost the SSCA support from other BDSM leaders. Without structure or membership, the ISC proved too small to accomplish anything. Its remaining leaders concluded the only way to advance their mission and save something from Dallas was to merge with the NLA. Its "strong local structure" and steady expansion," ISC members argued, would save SSCA, while the NLA would benefit from the SSCA's national contacts. A merger was the "most reasonable course of action" to create a functioning national BDSM organization.[74]

Douglas and other East Coast leaders expected the Dallas conference to produce an alternative to the NLA. Instead, the Dallas conference created the SSCA, a weak, ill-defined organization, which GMSMA's leaders hamstrung with constant criticism, driving it into the arms of the successful and growing NLA. It was the last thing they wanted, though a result generally welcomed by West Coast BDSM activists.

The NLA-SSCA Merger

While the SSCA's leaders struggled to build support, the NLA grew in size and ambition. Attendance at its annual Living in Leather conference grew. NLA chapters formed in Vancouver and Portland, Oregon. The NLA created a National Advisory Committee to oversee new chapter formation and mailed its monthly newsletter to BDSM organizations around the world.

The respective leaders of the NLA and SSCA met in Seattle at Living in Leather III (7–10 October 1988) and achieved consensus on most issues involving a merger, with minor issues resolved over the following year. The NLA's members overwhelmingly approved the merger just before Living in Leather IV (7–9 October 1989), hosted by its Portland chapter. A final meeting there, open to all interested parties, was prolonged. Those who participated missed some of the fun. This became a recurrent problem for the NLA as major meetings, held at Living in Leather, conflicted with demonstrations, seminars or parties. As Jan Lyon later noted, the NLA depended on people willing to miss parties and devote their time "to all those damn boring meetings." Attendees helped draft the organization's new statement of purpose and elected Jim Richards and Judy Tallwing McCarthy of the SSCA as the NLA's new male and female co-chairs. The new organization retained the NLA's name and assumed the SSCA's mandate.[75]

The merger forced the NLA to change, most importantly by ending the pretense it was a gay and lesbian organization. Encouraged by Maidhof, who promised "safeguards to protect all sexual orientations," the NLA officially became a "pansexual organization," open to people regardless of sexual orientation. *Sandmutopia Guardian* trumpeted the change. "A true national SM/leather coalition, open to and supportive of all, is clearly on its way!" The NLA's leaders estimated heterosexuals already accounted for 10–20 percent of their membership, a number they expected to grow.[76]

The NLA's new Statement of Purpose, which became a model for many BDSM organizations, called on its members:

> To establish and maintain a National/worldwide communication, information, education and support network for sisters and brothers of the Leather/SM/Fetish community.
>
> To promote with power and pride the rights of all adults to engage in Safe/Sane/and Consensual sexual expression.
>
> To increase communication and understanding among women and men in leather/SM.
>
> Political activism, visibility, and education to destroy stereotypes, misconceptions, and media misrepresentation about the Leather/SM/fetish family in the community at large.
>
> To provide through our publications, educational material, and "Living in Leather" conferences, a forum for the sharing of knowledge, viewpoints, and practices from a diverse network of women and men.
>
> To build, strengthen, and defend individuals, organizations, publications, and businesses within our community especially against threats to their freedom of expression, freedom of the press, their right to free association, and their right to equal protection under the law.
>
> To develop outreach to women, people of color, transgenderals, the physically challenged, and other minorities who have traditionally been discriminated against or poorly represented in the Leather/SM/fetish community.
>
> Fundraising for deserving projects, clubs, organizations, defense funds, and /or charities that have given direct service to the Leather/SM/fetish community.
>
> To fight for the decriminalization of all sexual acts between consenting adults.
>
> To preserve a record of our history, traditions, and culture.

The document reflected the objectives the Outcasts brought to the Dallas conference, particularly their call for outreach to people underrepresented in existing BDSM organizations, political activism, and education. The latter was a twofold mission. The NLA aimed to teach members of the BDSM community how to enhance their sexual activities while keeping them safe and educate the larger lesbian and gay community and mainstream society about BDSM to win acceptance as a legitimate sexual practice.

Leading members of the BDSM community settled on the NLA not because it was an ideal choice, but due to their inability to create a viable alternative to it. Accepting the Dallas organizational framework and assuming the SSCA's mantel helped the NLA grow rapidly over the next few years. Yet, the NLA's new organizational structure was cumbersome, balancing the needs of individual NLA members, local NLA chapters, and other local BDSM organizations affiliated with the NLA. Within a few years, its National Council, which represented these three constituencies, required almost a hundred members, representing about ten percent of the NLA's total membership.

As new NLA chapters formed, delegates from CHC, Dreizehn, GMSMA and Windy City Bondage Club resumed work on COSMOS as "an alliance of autonomous SM organizations," but without success.[77] It captured little attention and never organized a major event. Most BDSM organizations simply ignored it. The BDSM community's immediate future lay with the NLA.

GMSMA, though, remained very active. In 1989, it organized a large SM-Leather Contingent for the 20th anniversary of Stonewall parade. Douglas remained active in national efforts for gay and lesbian rights, speaking at numerous events and conferences, including the NGLTF's Creating Change conference. While many attendees of Creating Change II (1989) attacked BDSM, many others supported Douglas when he pushed back. Sadomasochists were winning a place for themselves at the table, but it required constant, sustained effort.[78]

★★★

The BDSM community's leading figures hoped to win recognition and legitimation of their sexual practices by mainstream society and secure a visible place in the struggle for gay and lesbian rights. Doing so, they realized, required uniting the community's disparate elements in a social and political effort. Echoing Gayle Rubin, their leaders argued it was "time to recognize the political dimensions" of their erotic lives and unite as a political force. The job of the NLA was to lead this effort by coordinating existing BDSM organizations and helping people with BDSM interests connect to this larger community. As Tony DeBlase emphasized, BDSM organizations were not "the Mormon Church." They did not proselytize or seek converts. They hoped, though, to recruit everyone already interested in BDSM activities, which sex surveys indicated could be one-tenth of the population.[79]

Despite the success with the March on Washington, Barry Douglas reported, it required "greater and greater effort" for members of the BDSM community to secure their "legitimate place in the lesbian and gay community." Yet when the BDSM community did mobilize and push back, its members secured places for themselves in their local communities. They needed to fight for inclusion, and a "strong national organization . . . would be a major asset in that fight."[80]

The Dallas conference left many issues unresolved. It particularly highlighted the lack of diversity among BDSM organizations. The group photo of the Dallas conference, which included only about half the attendees, shows only one unnamed African American. He and Silas McGowan were likely the only African Americans present. Jack Jackson, who died in 1985, was an important force in TES's early years, as was Billy Jefferson in the NLA's first years, but people of color remained rare among the leaders of BDSM organizations and in the community in general. Of the twelve IML winners by 1990, only one, Ron Moore

(IML 1984) was black. Viola Johnson was one of only a handful of women of color to attend Living in Leather III (1988).

As Mark Levine notes, "an air of authenticity hung around working-class men and men of color so that these men were often more highly prized for tricks" by the mostly white, middle class men who patronized leather bars and clubs like the Mineshaft. [81] Photographer Robert Mapplethorpe celebrated—or fetishized, depending on your perspective—African American men in his photographs. So, too, did several pornographic magazines, such as *Obeah* and *Black Amazon Digest*, which featured black women dominating white men. This exoticization of blacks did not translate into political power within BDSM organizations. While many Dallas delegates advocated reaching out to people of color, there was little discussion—either at the time or in the BDSM press afterward—as to how this would be accomplished or the complicating factors of the BDSM community's use of terminology, such as Master/slave, and iconography, such as slave collars and brands, rooted in the American history of chattel slavery.

Despite its many problems and omissions, the Dallas conference provided a framework on which the NLA's leaders hoped to build. They planned to be politically active, lobby for the right of people to engage in consensual sexual activities, and fight back against harassment of BDSM businesses, gathering places and practitioners. The majority of people who engaged in BDSM activities did not belong to any BDSM organization. Reaching out to them and educating them about the community and BDSM practice would grow the organized BDSM community and strengthen its political effectiveness. Promoting BDSM activities as safe, sane and consensual was essential to all these missions. By 1990, the NLA had almost 800 members and chapters in more than two-dozen US and Canadian cities. The NLA's annual Living in Leather conference, its newsletters, and local chapter events shaped the BDSM community around a set of core values epitomized by "safe, sane, consensual," pansexuality, and outreach to newcomers.

The centrality of "safe, sane, consensual" to the BDSM lexicon marked a significant change and highlighted the desire of BDSM activists to win acceptance and respectability, what sociologist David Evans labeled sexual citizenship, the right of free sexual expression. Darren Langdridge suggests that BDSM may be "too sexual, too erotic and therefore too transgressive for full citizenship."[82] For some BDSM activists, this was precisely the point. Just as a BDSM scene tested a top's imagination and the limits of the bottom's receptivity, BDSM itself offered a test of society's willingness to extend sexual citizenship to those considered most perverse. First expressed in Pat Bond's TES Creed, sadomasochists demanded the right to "pursue joy and happiness," freely "socialize with others of similar sexual orientation," and publicize their activities, sexual interests, and views without fear of professional or other repercussions.

Achieving those rights required shaping and constraining BDSM practice within the BDSM community and educating the broader public about BDSM. Often abbreviated as SSC, "safe, sane, and consensual" became the defining element in a determined effort to change BDSM and its public image. BDSM leaders hoped to educate their fellow enthusiasts to make BDSM practices "safe, sane, and consensual," while simultaneously demanding respectability from their critics and acceptance by mainstream society by demonstrating their safety, sanity and consensuality. This became both the community's definition of BDSM and a litmus test for appropriate behavior within the community. Its promotion in BDSM literature, by BDSM organizations, and at BDSM events helped formalize a process against which members of the BDSM community judged one another, dramatically changing the BDSM community in the late 1980s and early 1990s. The NLA and Living in Leather, in turn, became models for people who organized local BDSM organizations and conventions, which fueled the BDSM community's growth in the 1990s.

Notes

1 Michael Bronski, *A Queer History of the United States* (Boston, MA: Beacon Press, 2011), 179.

2 Pat Califia, "A Personal View of the History of the Lesbian S/M Community and Movement in San Francisco" in Samois (ed.), *Coming to Power: Writing and Graphics on Lesbian S/M 3rd Edition, Revised and Updated* (Boston, MA: Alyson, 1982), 271.

3 Califia, "A Personal View of the History of the Lesbian S/M Community and Movement in San Francisco" in Samois, *Coming to Power*, 272–3 and Gayle Rubin, "Valley of the Kings: Leathermen in San Francisco, 1960–1990," PhD diss., University of Michigan, 1994, 520.

4 Geoff Fergusson, "SM Networking: A Beginning," *GMSMA News* 2, no. 3 (June 1984), 8.

5 Nina Darnton, "How 9 1/2 Weeks Pushed an Actress to the Edge," *New York Times*, 9 March 1986, H1.

6 *DungeonMaster Yearbook* 1 (1983), 1; DeBlase, "What Is S&M?" 4 (May 1980), 1–2; Jack Fritscher, *Gay San Francisco: Eyewitness Drummer Vol. 1* (San Francisco, CA: Palm Drive, 2008), 393; "Leather Christmas," *Drummer* 19 (1977), 8–10; "The DS/SM Debate," *Growing Pains*, September 1982, 2–7; and "The DS/SM Debate," *Growing Pains*, October/November 1981, 3–8.

7 A.M. Chaise, "Pleasure-Pain vs Sado-masochism," *Fantasia* 18 (circa 1961), 9 and Carlson Wade, "The Secret World of Erotic Symbolism," *Exotica* 1 (1962), 49.

8 "All You Ever Wanted to Know about S&M and Then Some," *Gay*, October 1973, Sadomasochism Clipping File, Kinsey Archive; Alex Warner, "Feminism Meets Fisting: Antipornography, Sadomasochism, and the Politics of Sex," in Carolyn Bronstein and Whitney Strub, *Porno Chic and the Sex Wars: American Sexual Representation in the 1970s* (Amherst: University of Massachusetts Press, 2016), 256–7; Michael J. Mitchell, "Erotic S&M Among Gays," *Gay News*, 2 December 1976, 16–7; "Opening Statement of Pat Bond, Panel on Sadism and Masochism," at the Annual Conference of the National Institute for Psychotherapies, 29 October 1977, TES Files, LAAM; Barbara Ruth, "Cathexis," *Lesbian Tide* (May/June, 1977), 10; and Jack Fritscher, "The Catcombs," *Drummer* 23 (1978), 8–11.

9 LSM flyer, 1983, Lesbian Herstory Archives, SM Folder, in Gale Archives of Sexuality and Gender; 15 Association, "Policy and Behavior at SM Events," 1988, LAAM, DeBlase Papers, Box 39; Samois, *What Color Is Your Handkerchief?* (1979), 1–3; Alex Warner, "Feminism Meets Fisting" in Carolyn Bronstein and Whitney Strub (eds.), *Porno Chic and the Sex Wars* (Amherst: University of Massachusetts Press, 2016), 249–73; Sir Arthur, "Safewords: Con," *Prometheus* 8 (1977); and Daddy Warbucks, "Safewords: Pro," *Prometheus* 8 (1977).

10 Society of Janus, "Letter to San Francisco Chronicle and the Mayor," *Growing Pains*, April 1981, 4; "The DS/SM Debate," *Growing Pains*, October/November 1981, 3–8; "The DS/SM Debate," *Growing Pains*, September 1982, 2–7; "Open Discussion on SM Etiquette Through the Eyes of Janus," *Growing Pains*, October/November 1984, 4–6; and Dorothy Allison, "Notes and Letters," *Feminist Studies* 9, no. 2 (Autumn 1983), 601–2.

11 Donahue transcript 09292 (1982), 5, Kinsey Archive; Eric Van Meter [Jack Fritscher], "S&M: The Last Taboo, The Janus Society," *Drummer* 27 (February 1979), 36; Fritscher, *Eyewitness Drummer*, 393; and "Leather Christmas," *Drummer* 19 (1977), 8–10.

12 DeBlase, "What Is S&M?," *DungeonMaster* 4 (May 1980), 1–2; "CHC History," *Inferno* X (1981), 29; and Fledermaus [Tony DeBlase], "Up Front," *Sandmutopia Guardian & Dungeon Journal* 1 (Jan 1988), 4.

13 Don Miesen, "SM: A View of Sadomasochism," *Drummer* 87 (1985): 15–7, 100–3.

14 *Darling!* 1, no. 1 (HOM, 1988), 3 and *Mistress Quarterly* 1, no. 1 (HOM, 1983), 2.

15 Bill Brent, "Pat Califia Interview," *Black Sheets* 12 (undated, 1996 or 1997), 14–6.

16 Steve Stein, *Twenty-Five Years of Living in Leather: The National Leather Association* (Palm Coast, FL: Adynaton, 2012), 39–40, & 49–51; "GMSMA: The First 15 Years of Activism," at http://gmsma.org/newslink (accessed 23 June 2010); and David Stein, "Safe, Sane, Consensual," *Sandmutopian Guardian* 38 (2000), 13–7. Various draft versions of David Stein's article circulate on the Internet, all of which contain some inaccuracies.

17 Master Ed and kathleen, "The History of TES," *Prometheus* 24 (Winter 1996), 38–9; T. Weymouth, *Society of Janus: Twenty-Five Years* (San Francisco: Society of Janus, 1999), 13 & 30–1; Califia, "A Personal View of the History of the Lesbian S/M Community and Movement in San Francisco," in Samois, *Coming to Power*, 251–2; Pat Califia, *Public Sex: The Culture of Radical Sex* (San Francisco, CA: Cleis, 1994), 157; and Daniel Harris, *Rise and Fall of Gay Culture* (New York: Ballantine, 1997), 191.

18 Alex Warner, "'Where Angels Fear to Tread:' Feminism, Sex and the Problem of SM, 1969–1993," PhD diss., Rutgers, The State University of New Jersey, 2011, 69–70, 75; Carolyn Bronstein, *Battling Pornography: The American Feminist Anti-Pornography Movement, 1976–1986* (Cambridge: Cambridge University Press, 2011), 286; Skip A. [Aiken], "Don't Close the Closet Door Just Because There's Leather Inside," *Prometheus* 12; and Skip Aiken, "Bureaucracy and SM," *Drummer* 76 (1984), 76–7.

19 Skip A. [Aiken], "Don't Close the Closet Door Just Because There's Leather Inside," *Prometheus* 12; "First for Folsom," *Drummer* 79 (1984), 90; Rubin, "Valley of the Kings," 520; and Carol Truscott, "Interview with Jay Marston," *Sandmutopia Guardian* 7 (1990), 19.

20 "Controversy Over Mixed SM Group," *Chain Link* 2 (Summer 1987), 8.

21 David Stein, "SM's Copernican Revolution," in Mark Thompson (ed.), *Leatherfolk : Radical Sex, People, Politics, and Practice* (Boston, MA: Alyson Publications, 1991), 145.

22 *Urania News*, October 1985.

23 David Stein, "Celebrating a Decade of SM Pride," *GMSMA Newslink* (Winter 1991), 4–5 and "These Boots Are Made for Marching," *GMSMA News* 2, no. 3 (June 1984), 1.

24 "Gay Male SM Advocates," *DungeonMaster* 8 (1981), 5 and "March With Pride!," *GMSMA News* 1, no. 5 (June 1983), 1.

25 Fledermaus [Tony DeBlase], "On the Go," *DungeonMaster* 27 (1985), 6–7 and Amin Ghaziani, *The Dividends of Dissent: How Conflict and Culture Work in Lesbian and Gay Marches on Washington* (Chicago, IL: University of Chicago Press, 2008), 100–1.

26 Fledermaus to J.D, *Drummer* 103 (1987), 4 and "March on Washington Again," *Drummer* 102 (1987), 4.

27 Eric Van Meter [Jack Fritscher], "The Janus Society," *Drummer* 27 (February 1979), 34; and Weymouth and the Society of Janus, *Society of Janus: Twenty-Five Years*, 12–3; Stein, "SM's Copernican Revolution" in Mark Thompson, *Leatherfolk*, 145; Maidhof, "Top Priority," *ChainLink* 1 (Spring 1987), 2; "Secretary Scribbles," *Link* 1, no. 2 (undated 1987), 2; and "National March," *First Link* 1, no. 4 (undated 1987), 2.

28 SM-Leather Contingent brochure, SSCA Box, LAAM; Dave Rhodes, "March on Washington: These Boots Are Made for Walkin,'" *Leather Journal* 3 (November 1987–January 1988), 26–8; Fledermaus [Tony DeBlase], "How Many Fairies Can Dance on the Head of the Mall," *Drummer* 111 (1987), 4 and 69; "Secretary Scribbles," *Link* 1, no. 2 (undated 1987), 2; "National March," *First Link* 1, no. 4 (undated 1987), 2; and Barry Douglas, "For Love and For Life," *Drummer* 111 (1988), 91–2.
29 Steve Maidhof, "New vs. Old Leather," *Chain Link* 2 (Summer 1987), 9.
30 Ivo Dominguez, *Beneath the Skins: The New Spirit and Politics of the Kink Community* (Los Angeles, CA: Daedalus Pub. Co., 1994), 21 and Guy Baldwin, "A Second Coming Out" in Baldwin, *Ties That Bind: The SM/Leather/Fetish Erotic Style* (Los Angeles, CA: Daedalus, 1993), 31 (originally published in *Frontiers*, September 1989).
31 Stacy Dennen, "Janus at the National Lesbian/Gay March on Washington," *Growing Pains*, November 1987, 3; Juicy Lucy, "If I Ask You to Tie Me Up, Will You Still Love Me" in Samois, *Coming to Power*, 39; Jad Keres, "Violence Against S/M Women Within the Lesbian Community: A National Survey," March 1994, SM File, Lesbian Herstory Archive; and Wickie Stamps, "Trouble in Paradise: Michigan Women's Festival Bans S/M, but the Controversy Rages On," *The Advocate*, 28 August 1990, 57.
32 Dustin Logan, "Interview with Susie Shepherd, International Ms. Leather 1989," *Drummer* 140 (1990), 66–7 and Rubin, "The Leather Menace," in *Coming to Power*, 222.
33 Baldwin, *Ties That Bind*, 34, 37, & 40.
34 Goeff Mains, *Urban Aboriginals* (Los Angeles, CA: Daedalus Publishing, 2002), 30 and Dominguez, *Beneath the Skins*, 26–30.
35 "Washington Coverage," *GMSMA News*, Winter 1988, 6 and Barry Douglas, "GMSMA: The First 15 Years of Activism," circa 1995. http://gmsma.org/newslink/political.html (accessed through Archive.org, 10 April 2015).
36 "Washington Coverage," *GMSMA News*, Winter 1988, 4–6.
37 Fledermaus [Anthony F. DeBlase], "How Many Fairies Can Dance on the Head of the Mall," *Drummer* 111 (1987), 4 and 69; Dave Rhodes, "March on Washington: These Boots are Made for Walkin,'" *Leather Journal* 3 (November 1987–January 1988), 26–28; and "Stacy Dennen, "Janus at the National Lesbian/Gay March on Washington," *Growing Pains*, November 1987, 2–3.
38 Stacy Dennen, "Janus at the National Lesbian/Gay March on Washington," *Growing Pains*, November 1987, 2–3; David Rhodes, "Editorial," *Leather Journal* 3 (November 1987–January 1988), 6–7; and Carla, "Washington March Reflections," *Growing Pains*, December 1987, 2.
39 "Washington Coverage," *GMSMA News*, Winter 1988, 4–6.
40 Samuel R. Delany, *Times Square Blue, Times Square Red* (New York: NYU Press, 2019), 186 & 194.
41 Gayle Rubin, "May Day," *DungeonMaster* 33 (September 1987), 38.
42 Dave P. Siebert, "Safe-Sane Consensual: A Continuation of the SM-Leather Contingent of the March on Washington," publicity mailing, 7 December 1987, SSCA Box, LAAM; Stacy Dennen, "Janus at the National Lesbian/Gay March on Washington," *Growing Pains*, November 1987, 2–3; Summary of the S/M Community Organizing Seminar," DeBlase Papers, Box 41; and Anthony F. DeBlase to Members of the SSCA Interim Steering Committee, all Major SM Clubs, and Other Interested Parties, 4 September, 1988, SSCA Papers, LAAM.
43 Jim Richards, interview by Jan Hall, 6 July 2002, NLA Archives.
44 Stein, *Twenty-Five Years of Living in Leather*, 43–51; Dave P. Siebert, "Safe-Sane Consensual: A Continuation of the SM-Leather Contingent of the March on Washington," publicity mailing, 7 December 1987, SSCA Box, LAAM; and Registration Forms, Dallas Conference, SSCA Box, LAAM.
45 Dallas Conference registration forms, SSCA Box, LAAM; Minutes of NLA Board of Directors Meeting, 16 January 1988, NLA Archives; and David Meador, "Report on Dallas Meeting," undated, NLA Archives.

46 "Club Listings," *Sandmutopia Guardian & Dungeon Journal* 1 (January 1988), 7–8.
47 Fledermaus [Tony DeBlase], "Thoughts on the Way to Dallas," *DungeonMaster* 34 (1987), 4.
48 David Meador, "Report on Dallas Meeting"; Pat Califia, "Beyond Vanilla: National S-M/Leather Network Formed in Dallas," *Advocate*, 29 March 1988; and Dominguez, *Beneath the Skins*, 89–90.
49 Stacy Dennen, "Safe Sane Consensual Adults: Report on the Dallas SM Conference," *Growing Pains*, March 1988, 8–9; Dana Rosenfeld (of LSM) to Califia, 22 January 1988, SSCA Box, LAAM; Southern Kink Proxy Instructions, SSCA Box, LAAM; and Outcasts, "Proposals for the Dallas Leather and SM Conference," 25 January 1988, SSCA Box, LAAM.
50 Pat Bond, "Dallas—Perceptions of Reality," *Prometheus*, Early Spring 1988, 5–7, and 10–11; Douglas to Califia, 16 Feb 1988, SSCA Box, LAAM.
51 Dorothy Allison and Pat Califia, "The Dallas S/M & Leather Conference, February 12–14, 1988," SSCA Papers, LAAM.
52 "Some of the Issues to be Considered or Decided by the February 1988 Dallas Conference," SSCA Box, LAAM; "Preliminary Agenda for Small Groups," SSCA Box, LAAM; and Stacy Dennen, "Safe Sane Consensual Adults," *Growing Pains*, March 1988, 8–9.
53 Dennen, "Safe Sane Consensual Adults," 8–9.
54 David Meador, "Report on Dallas Meeting."
55 "Report from the Dallas Conference," *Urania Newsletter*, 22 February 1988; "Letter of Representation" to NLA delegates to Dallas Conference, undated, NLA Archives; Minutes, NLA Board Meeting, 16 January 1988, NLA Archives; and Dennen, "Safe Sane Consensual Adults," 8–9.
56 Dorothy Allison and Pat Califia to Lesbian Sex Mafia (NYC), Southern Kink (Atlanta, GA), Power Circle (Santa Cruz, CA), Sovereign Mysteries (Denver), Shelix (Northhampton, MA), "The Dallas SM & Leather Conference," 22 February 1988, SSCA Box, LAAM; "Report on Dallas Meeting—Summary of Notes supplied by David Meador," NLA Archives; and Carol Truscott, "Carol's Column," *Sandmutopia Guardian & Dungeon Journal* 2 (April 1988), 4.
57 Dennen, "Safe Sane Consensual Adults," 8–9 and Ice, "The Dallas Conference," *Bound and Determined Newsletter*, March 1988.
58 Stacy Dennen, "Safe Sane Consensual Adults: report on the Dallas SM Conference," *Growing Pains*, March 1988, 8–9.
59 Dominguez, *Beneath the Skins*, 92 and "Report on Dallas Meeting—Summary of Notes supplied by David Meador," NLA Archives.
60 Ice, "The Dallas Conference."
61 Ice, "The Dallas Conference."
62 Stacy Dennen, "Safe Sane Consensual Adults: report on the Dallas SM Conference," *Growing Pains*, March 1988, 8–9 and Fledermaus [Tony DeBlase], "Thoughts on the Way to Dallas," *DungeonMaster* 34 (1987), 4.
63 Jan Hall, Interview, (undated circa 2004), NLA Archives and "Safe-Sane-Consensual Adults," *DungeonMaster* 35 (1987), 32.
64 Pat Bond, "Dallas—Perceptions of Reality," *Prometheus*, Early Spring 1988, 5–7, David Stein, "Toward a National SM-Leather Network," *New York Native*, 14 March 1988, 16–7; David Stein, "Rough Stuff: Building a Community," *Drummer* 116 (May 1988), 38–9; and 10–1; Tony DeBlase, "Off the Top: Beyond Vanilla," *Drummer* 115 (April 1988), 4.
65 Ray Matienzo to Tony DeBlase, 23 September 1988, SSCA Box, LAAM; Ray Matienzo, "Dallas Disaster," *GMSMA Newslink*, Spring 1988, 10–1; and GMSMA to Members of the SM/Leather Community, 26 February 1988, SSCA Box, LAAM.
66 Carol T. [Truscott] and Joe Bridwell, "Male Call, *Drummer* 119 (July 1988), 6–7 and James L Bruce to Barry Douglas, 13 Aug 1988 and James L Bruce to Jan Hall, 28 August 1988, SSCA Correspondence, SSCA Box, LAAM.

67 Califia, "Adviser," *The Advocate*, 25 August 1992, 120.
68 Victoria Baker, "Some of My SM Heroes," *Sandmutopia Guardian* 14 (1993), 4.
69 Barry Douglas, "Washington Coverage," *GMSMA Newslink*, Winter 1988, 4–6; "News from NLA Affiliates," *First Link* 5, no. 1 (January 1990), 5; Bruce Marcus, "On the 'Edge' or Over the Line?," *GMSMA Newslink* (Summer 1991), 33–5; Laura Antoniou, "Letter to the Editor of GMSMA's *Newslink*," *First Link* 5, no. 10 (November 1991), 8; Jim Richards and Jan Lyon, "Reply to Bruce Marcus's Letter from NLA Co-Chairs," *First Link* 5, no. 10 (November 1991), 5 & 8; and David Stein, "Safe, Sane, Consensual," *Sandmutopian Guardian* 38 (2000), 13–7. Stein incorrectly claims the Washington Leather Contingents marched behind a "safe, sane, consensual" banner. The banner actually read "S/M-Leather Contingent."
70 Janus and SHELIX surveys, SSCA Surveys File, SSCA Box, LAAM.
71 Ferrari to ISC, 27 March 1988, ISC Progress Report #2 SSCA Minutes, 14 February, 28 May and 29 May, all in SSCA Box, LAAM.
72 Barry Douglas, "SSCA Meets in Chicago," *GMSMA Newslink*, Summer 1988, 7–9.
73 John Ferrari, "SSCA Progress Report," *Drummer* 118 (1988), 94; Anthony F. DeBlase to members of the SSCA Interim Steering Committee, all major SM Clubs, and Other Interested Parties, 4 September, 1988, SSCA Box, LAAM; Ferrari to ISC, 30 August 1988; Ferrari to ISC, 16 September 1988; and "Barry Douglas and Ty Clements Resign ISC-SSCA," *Leather Journal* 8 (November 1988–January 1989), 13.
74 Hall to ISC, 30 November 1988, SSCA Correspondence, SSCA Box, LAAM.
75 Jan Lyon, interview by Jan Hall, 6 July 2002, NLA Archives.
76 Retreat Agenda, 16 January 1988, NLA Archives; Special Meeting to Consider Revisions/Rewrites for NLA National Bylaws, 29 August 1988; Minutes, NLA Board Meetings, 10 and 14 October 1988, NLA Archives; "National Leather Assoc. Newsflash!," *Growing Pains*, October 1988, 8; Carol Truscott, "Carol's Column," *Sandmutopia Guardian & Dungeon Journal* 2 (April 1988), 5; and Carol Truscott, "National Leather Association's Living in Leather III," *Sandmutopia Guardian* 4 (January 1989), 30.
77 "COSMOS," *First Link* 3:3 (1988), 7 and "COSMOS," *First Link* 3:4 (1988), 6.
78 Barry Douglas, "The View from Out There," *GMSMA Newslink*, Winter 1989–1990, 2–3.
79 Gayle S. Rubin, "Thinking Sex," in Carole S. Vance (ed.), *Pleasure and Danger: Exploring Female Sexuality* (New York: HarperCollins, 1993), 310 and DeBlase, "Letter to the Editor," *The Inquisitor* 2, no. 11 (March/April 1992), 5.
80 Barry Douglas, "SSCA Meets in Chicago," *GMSMA Newslink*, Summer 1988, 9.
81 Viola Johnson, *To Love, to Obey, to Serve: Diary of an Old Guard Slave* (Fairfield: Mystic Rose, 1999), 171 and Levine, *Gay Macho*, 82.
82 David Evans, *Sexual Citizenship: The Material Construction of Sexualities* (London: Routledge, 1993); Jeffrey Weeks, "The Sexual Citizen," *Theory, Culture, and Society* 15 (1998), 25–52; Darren Langdridge, "Voices from the Margins: Sadomasochism and Sexual Citizenship," *Citizenship Studies* 10, no. 4 (2006), 373–89; and Dominguez, *Beneath the Skins*, 33.

5

A UNITED, POLITICALLY ACTIVE BDSM COMMUNITY, THE 1990S

Building on his experience from the 1987 March on Washington, Barry Douglas led an even larger SM/leather/fetish contingent for the 1993 March on Washington for Lesbian, Gay and Bi Equal Rights and Liberation on Sunday, 25 April. Marching behind an "S/M Leather Fetish" banner, more than five thousand people formed a black leather mass in the center of roughly one million marchers. They carried banners from their respective clubs, homemade signs, such as "Beat Me, Whip Me, Make Me March," and variations of "safe, sane, consensual." Several waved leather pride flags. Produced by Tony DeBlase to symbolize a united BDSM-leather community, the flag featured alternating black and blue stripes and a red heart in its upper left corner. As the leather contingent passed the White House, one woman yelled out "Can Hillary come out to play?," referencing the manipulated image of First Lady Hillary Clinton as a dominatrix in *Spy* magazine.

At night, SM/Leather contingent members filled local leather bars and packed dances sponsored by *Drummer*. Performers displayed their talents in live BDSM scenes featuring elaborate rope bondage and flashy, multi-whip floggings. One man culminated his scene by piercing his partner's penis and scrotum with dozens of needles. Several men presented dazzling scenes with violet wands. Sold as medical devices in the nineteenth century, the BDSM community rediscovered violet wands, which used low current, high-frequency electricity to produce a variety of sensations. Their buzzing sounds, occasional sparks, and glowing plasma lit up dim rooms and focused attention on the action, making them popular for public performances. The sighs and gasps of bottoms intermingled with buzzing wands and flashes of light, delighting the crowd. Not to be outdone, another man used a lighter and candles to carefully and systematically burn off his partner's body hair. People talked about these scenes for months afterward.[1]

The 1993 SM/leather/fetish contingent dramatized the BDSM Community's growth since the 1987 march. Its leaders again organized a pre-march conference, which established their agenda for the next decade. It featured panels on reducing domestic violence, combating censorship, and revising the American Psychiatric Association's Diagnostic and Statistical Manual of Mental Disorders (DSM), which categorized sexual sadism and masochism negatively as paraphilias. Susan Wright gathered support to repeal NOW's decade-old condemnation of BDSM. Others complained about police harassment of BDSM venues, criminal prosecution for BDSM activities, and obscenity prosecution of BDSM books and videos. Television shows disparaged BDSM practitioners, as did North Carolina Senator Jesse Helms who condemned sadomasochists as part of general attacks on sexual expression and the LGBTQ rights movement. Dennis Lee and Philip Douglas hosted a panel on BDSM people of color and afterward launched *Black Leather in Color* magazine. Despite the BDSM community's growing diversity, many people of color felt marginalized and representations of them remained rare in BDSM media. Lee and Douglas hoped to give sadomasochists of color a voice and reach out to those who had yet to find the BDSM community. Part of the problem, other panelists noted, was the sheer expense of clothes, membership fees and event costs, which excluded many from participation.[2]

The NLA continued hosting its annual Living in Leather conference, which comingled activism, education and fun—a format adopted by growing numbers of new, local BDSM conventions. Its leaders hoped to win inclusion for BDSM practitioners in LGBTQ organizations and political efforts, change how government and medical authorities perceived BDSM, and end the harassment of sadomasochists. Achieving these required uniting the BDSM community's diverse elements and reshaping BDSM practice to be "safe, sane, and consensual." Creating a safer, more welcoming environment for BDSM play, they thought, would remove the stigma associated with it and win social acceptance. So, BDSM activists established ethical behaviors emphasizing careful negotiation of BDSM scenes, clear communication during them, and using safe words to ensure the ongoing enjoyment of all participants. They standardized BDSM education around these concepts and disseminated them, along with a host of practical information, through hands-on demonstrations, guidebooks and technical magazines. As a result, growing numbers of Americans came to see BDSM as innocuous, "just another alternative lifestyle," as Rosie O'Donald's character declared in *Exit to Eden* (1994).

Uniting the BDSM Community

Merging with the SSCA accelerated the NLA's growth. New chapters formed in Arkansas, Atlanta, Chicago, Dallas, Denver, Detroit, Los Angeles, New England, New York City, San Diego, San Francisco, South Florida and Virginia. By the end of 1991, the NLA's 1,000 members made it the world's largest BDSM organization. It had 21 local chapters in the United States and Canada, and members in almost every U.S. state, as well as Finland, Germany, Great Britain and New Zealand. *Sandmutopia Guardian* encouraged "isolated SM/leather/fetish" people to join the NLA to connect with "the nation-wide community of SM/leather/fetish people" and launch local BDSM organizations. New local BDSM organizations, often modeled on NLA chapters, sprang up in such numbers that people had trouble keeping tracking them. They mandated safe BDSM practice, encouraged discussion, and hosted play parties, educational seminars, and conferences modeled on Living in Leather, including Leatherfest in San Diego, Beyond Vanilla in Dallas, and Beat Me in St. Louis. Most were open to everyone, but a few were restricted, such as Powersurge (1992), the first women's BDSM conference.[3]

While never the BDSM community's sole voice, the NLA became its forum for discussing, shaping and launching new initiatives. DeBlase joined its executive committee and became its central figures, advising co-chairs and incubating new initiatives. He promoted the Living in Leather conferences in his magazines and scheduled their seminars, ensuring they featured notable speakers, cementing Living in Leather as the community's premier educational conference.

The NLA encouraged cooperation and collaboration among diverse BDSM organizations and populations, working to bridge differences and create "a larger SM family that transcended orientational boundaries."[4] Laura Antoniou, Gerrie Blum, Mitch Kessler and several friends formed NLA Metro New York. They hoped to make a place for "women and men of all flavors and backgrounds from heterosexual 'club rats' … to gay leather-clad lifestylers"—a place where "people of differing styles and backgrounds and priorities" would share their experiences.[5]

The NLA's leaders worked to unite the BDSM community behind a dual educational effort, first educating members about BDSM technique, safety and negotiation, and then combating "SM phobia" by educating "vanillas," gay and straight, to depathologize BDSM by reframing it as safe, sane and consensual. This would end government and legal harassment of BDSM practitioners and win them inclusion in the struggle for lesbian and gay rights. Practically every BDSM organization adopted the phrase, which a new generation of how-to books, including John Warren's *Loving Dominant* (1992), Jay Wiseman's *SM 101* (1992), Pat Califia's *Sensuous Magic* (1993) and Race Bannon's *Learning the Ropes* (1993), promoted.[6]

So, too, did a slew of new BDSM technique magazines, including *Checkmate*, launched in 1993 by frequent *DungeonMaster* contributor T.A. Feldwebel, Robert Dante's *Boudoir Noir*, Califia's *Venus Infers*, *Kinky People Places and Things*, *Taste of Latex*, and many others. They followed *DungeonMaster's* format, prioritizing practical advice over erotic stories and photographs and stood in sharp contrast to both traditional pornographic BDSM magazines and expensive, glossy European fetish magazines including *O*, *Skin Two*, *Secret* and *Zeitgeist*, which resembled mainstream fashion magazine and devoted most of their pages to glamorous models in expensive, predominantly latex and rubber, fetish clothing.

Similarly, the growing community fueled a wave of erotic novels and anthologies. Written by and for members of the BDSM community, authors often set them within the contemporary BDSM community. Several of them, particularly Laura Antoniou, Pat Califia and Cecilia Tan, sought to shape the community itself. Califia addressed a host of practical and political topics in her fiction. "Fix Me Up" encouraged cooperation among diverse BDSM practitioners. Tan offered a discussion of safe words in *Telepaths Don't Need Safewords* (1992), while Antoniou covered a host of practical topics in her Marketplace trilogy (1993, 1994 and 1995), often contrasting the laidback behavior of casual sadomasochists with those who favored "high protocol." In her short story "A Familiar Ring," Antoniou discussed genital piercing, its aftercare, and common safety requirements. BDSM enthusiasts expected and appreciated realism, and a common literature helped unite the community.[7]

Becoming Pansexual

Uniting the BDSM community required uniting BDSM aficionados across divisions of fetish interest, gender, geography and orientation. Maidhof encouraged Living in Leather III (1988) attendees to set aside "personal, organizational, and regional differences," learn from each other, and "build a community" to "resist the erosion of our civil liberty to engage in any form of Safe, Sane and Consensual erotic expression." They had "too many enemies" to "afford internal squabbles."[8]

The NLA's leaders sought to maintain its "gay and lesbian ambience," while making it" accessible to non-gay perverts." Opening some play parties to all genders and orientations where "heteros, lesbians and gays indulged their pleasures next to one another," facilitated the transition. Their energy, one man enthused matched "any male-only leather run," and attracted people like one woman who explained, "my head is dyke, but my cunt is straight." She preferred intercourse with men, but BDSM with women. A straight man similarly explained in his personal ads he preferred men for his BDSM activities. Previously rare, mixed play parties became increasingly common, encouraged by Califia, Gabrielle Antolovich, 1990 IMsL and co-chair of NLA Los Angeles, and Victoria Baker, *Sandmutopia Guardian's* new editor, who championed "cross-orientation play" in several articles and presentations. Essentially, NLA leaders assumed that people who played together at Living in Leather would unite and politic together.[9]

Heterosexual and bisexual attendance at NLA conferences increased, becoming particularly evident at Living in Leather IV (October 1989). "As short a time ago as four years," one attendee commented, "leathermen and leatherwomen did not mix," and "most of us gays and dykes didn't know ONE kinky straight person." The NLA changed that. Bisexuals and heterosexuals played important roles in the formation of NLA chapters in Boston, Chicago and New York. Many of them adopted the outward markers of gay BDSM/leather identity, including leather caps and vests, boots, jeans and event pins, symbolizing "a united front."[10]

Efforts to unite the BDSM community exposed underlying tensions. While *Leather Journal* editor Dave Rhodes praised the NLA, arguing separatism hindered the "cause of sexual freedom and expression," he faced regular complaints from male readers for "excessive" coverage of women, highlighted by Susie Shepherd's appearance on issue 15's cover.[11] The major obstacle to growing NLA Metro New York, chapter president Mitch Kessler explained, was the perception among heterosexuals "that NLA is a gay organization" and "among lesbians and gays that NLA NY is a heterosexual organization."[12] Fellow New Yorker Leonard Dworkin complained many Living in Leather keynote speakers were "better known for their achievements in-and-for the gay community," lacked "connections to SM/Leather," and ignored, the NLA's "bi/het component."[13] Laura Goodwin, who won the 1991 Ms. NLA contest to become the organization's first bisexual titleholder, wondered whether heterosexuals were welcome among the NLA's senior leadership.[14]

The NLA's Denver chapter, which sponsored the Mr./Ms. Leather Colorado contest for several years, collapsed in 1992 due to tensions between its gay and lesbian members. Female members complained men controlled the chapter, mismanaged its finances and excluded them. A disgruntled male member, in turn, complained about pushy women and suggested NLA actually stood for "Nasty Lesbian Association."[15]

The NLA never wholly resolved these tensions, which mirrored the larger BDSM community. Gender and orientation divisions remained common. Many leather bars and events still excluded women. Canadian NLA member Paris Sea found herself regularly "berated over issues of gender, orientation, or language."[16] Yet, one should not dismiss the NLA's achievement. While never a majority, heterosexuals accounted for a growing percentage of its membership. Those most offended by the NLA's pansexual turn left the organization. The rest persevered. While the demographics of individual NLA chapters varied, by the mid-1990s membership as whole was roughly equally split between men and women, with some identifying as trans. Gay men and lesbians each accounted for about a third of its membership, while those identifying as heterosexuals, bisexual or pansexual accounted for the rest. At Living in Leather IX (1994), convention director Dean Walradt claimed most NLA members supported pansexuality. Promoting diversity and pansexuality, Jim Richards later noted, was the NLA's greatest success.[17] Its broad appeal helped it unite a diverse BDSM constituency—a unity expressed by the growing adoption of the inclusive acronym BDSM and symbolized by the leather pride flag.

The Leather Pride Flag

In the 1970s, some gay motorcycle clubs opened their runs by "trooping the colors" of attending clubs and singing the national anthem. Much as an earlier generation of gay men appropriated the "rituals of the dominant culture and invested them with new meaning" in masquerade balls, so too, did gay motorcycle clubs. By the 1980s, the practice of trooping the colors was "nearly universal."[18] The NLA adopted it for Living in Leather's opening ceremony in which diverse BDSM organizations marched. Later BDSM conferences in the United States did the same, often confusing foreign visitors.

Recognizing the tradition's importance, DeBlase created the leather pride flag, which he debuted at the International Mr. Leather contest in 1989, just in time for the Stonewall Uprising's twentieth anniversary. Encouraged by DeBlase, Susie Shepherd made and carried one in Portland's Gay/Lesbian Pride march. DeBlase sent flags to The Outcasts, Janus and GMSMA, whose members also carried them in pride parades the following week. The latter actually objected to the design and demanded a national committee to produce a symbol, which DeBlase refused because each "losing entry would have its champions," producing endless debate.[19]

DeBlase wanted the flag to symbolize—and catalyze—unity within the BDSM community, hence his distribution of the first flags to a men's group (GMSMA), women's group (Outcasts), and mixed group (Janus), as well as the pansexual NLA. As he explained in *Drummer*, the flag was "inclusive," encompassing "leather, rubber, SM, bondage," and any other "kinky" activities.[20] The flag's appearance across the county during Pride Month cemented its place as the BDSM community's primary symbol, displayed at conferences, marches and other events.

Making BDSM Safe

Making BDSM acceptable to wider society required defining and presenting it as benign. This required addressing the tension between the thrilling danger of BDSM scenes and the need for safety, which the status BDSM practitioners derived from "edge play" complicated. Loosely defined as scenes involving some risk, edge play could involve heavy whippings; cuttings or piercings that drew blood; erotic asphyxiation (breath play); or introducing knives (generally blunt), guns (generally unloaded), fire or similar items into a scene to add a tinge of fear. As BDSM cognoscenti pointed out, "heavy" and "edge" meant different things to different people. "One man's edge was another's daily life."[21] BDSM activists worked to reduce danger through education.

Safe BDSM practice developed over time. In the past, one woman noted, "we were just kind of doing it, and finding out as we went along." When people were hurt, "it was like, 'Oh, well, can't do that again.'" BDSM organizations pushed back against this, discouraging play while drunk or stoned, teaching safe play and restricting certain practices. While some pushed back, arguing draconian safety rules ruined their fun, the AIDS crisis added urgency to safety discussions.[22]

In the past, hosts kept an eye on activities at play parties. Problems were rare within small, intimate groups, but became an issue at larger gatherings where relative strangers engaged in BDSM. In the early 1980s, CHC established formal rules for its Inferno events, which dungeon monitors, who functioned somewhat like lifeguards on a beach, enforced. With more than 300 men, many of them playing with one another for the first time, they were essential. Instructions warned Inferno attendees to "check interests before proceeding, immediately observe genuine requests to stop," ask to join scenes in progress, and report problems to dungeon monitors. Tops should "force only those who want to be forced," and make certain of a bottom's "limitations and turn-offs." Bottoms, in turn, needed to make tops "aware of any medical issues" before play.[23]

Inferno attendees introduced dungeon monitors to their home clubs and the practice spread. The Seattle Dungeon Guild (SDG) introduced dungeon monitors to the NLA, which employed them at Living in Leather conferences and produced a dungeon monitor's guide on their use. "Without intruding into a scene," dungeon monitors should look "for possible problems," and provide "support to the top and reassurance to the bottom" by their presence. Local NLA chapters followed suit, as did ORGASM (Oregon Guild Activists of SM), a large, pansexual Portland group, and many others. The Dungeon Monitor Corps of NLA Metro New York compiled an "SM Etiquette and Party Manual," which influenced Hellfire, Paddles and other New York BDSM clubs.[24]

BDSM literature reflected increased safety concerns. *Sandmutopia Guardian* rated techniques from G (General Readership) through TG (Top's Guidance) to X (Highly Restricted) and XXX (Avoid). *The Lesbian SM Safety Manual* (1988) and *On the Safe Edge* (1993) focused exclusively on physical and emotional safety in BDSM scenes. Dungeon monitors took courses in CPR and professional dominatrices equipped their dungeons with safety devices to release customers quickly in the event of an emergency. BDSM pornography publishers Harmony and HOM introduced safety codes. HOM's "Rules of B&D" explained safe words, and warned "everyone's body is different and can't hold every position."[25]

Rules for BDSM parties became increasingly formal and detailed. Hosts often required attendees to sign statements indicating they read them, would abide by them, and were not undercover police officers or journalists. Rules required respectful interaction and confidentiality, specified prohibited BDSM or sexual activities (generally to avoid anything messy and enforce safe sex), and explained general courtesy, warning against "hogging equipment," maintaining "a reasonable distance from scenes," and not touching people without permission. Dungeon monitors embodied the "safe" in "safe, sane, consensual." They circulated among scenes and enforced rules, becoming an established institution whose absence people noted and criticized. Dungeon monitors eased encounters among relative strangers, facilitating play, and gave people confidence to seek new partners and explore new experiences.[26] Except in private homes or secluded areas, such as Inferno's woodland venue, penetrative sex was usually prohibited, particularly at events in hotels, bars and other spaces governed by local obscenity, indecency or prostitution laws. BDSM might be a prelude to penetrative sex, but that occurred after couples left the party. It was a big change from the Mineshaft.

Combating Domestic Violence

In 1989, the Lesbian Battering Intervention Project of Minnesota refused a donation from the Knights of Leather, a local women's BDSM group. Other women's shelters did the same, claiming BDSM caused domestic violence. The Knights' leader, Red Helbig, petitioned the NLA for help. "They think we're violent. They haven't bothered to check out safe, sane, consensual S&M."[27]

In the past, BDSM organizations warned members about dangerous tops, but rarely confronted the topic of domestic violence except to protest its conflation with BDSM. Helbig's complaint focused attention on the topic and catalyzed Jan Hall, a member of the NLA's executive committee, to make it a priority. At her encouragement, NLA co-chairs Judy Tallwing McCarthy and Jim Richards wrote the Lesbian Battering Intervention Project. "SM," they explained, is "a loving exchange of power between consenting adults," not "abuse and violence." If an activity "is not safe, if it is not sane, or if it is not consensual, it is not SM." Where there was abuse, they argued, there could be no consent. Those relationships were outside the bounds of legitimate BDSM.[28]

Differentiating BDSM from abuse and rooting out abuse within the BDSM community were important in their own right, but also essential to present a positive image of BDSM. The community had grown too large for word of mouth policing to reach everyone who needed help, and negative perceptions of BDSM often prevented victims from receiving help. "If we don't clean this mess up ourselves," Pat Califia warned, "it will be used against us by people who don't really care if our lives are free from danger."[29] The BDSM community needed to banish the "bullies" from the dungeon.[30]

The campaign against domestic violence reflected the BDSM community's increasingly formal structures as it transitioned from small, informal clubs and bars setting their own policies and individually policing behavior to a national community with shared values, institutions and expectations. Hall led domestic violence workshops at the 1991 and 1992 Living in Leather conferences and crafted the BDSM community's first domestic violence statement. Revised over the next few years, it pledged the NLA to educate the BDSM community about domestic abuse, its extent, and severity and work to reduce it by holding batterers accountable, helping victims, and encouraging them to take legal action. NLA members spoke to BDSM groups, as well as domestic violence programs and social workers, educating them on the "difference between consensual BDSM and domestic violence" and providing them educational pamphlets and transcripts of NLA workshops on BDSM and domestic violence. They compiled lists of shelters accepting BDSM women, assisted victims and worked to exclude abusers. Similar efforts targeted medical providers and local police departments, explaining BDSM, differentiating it from violence and domestic abuse, and encouraging "appropriate intervention" when warranted.[31]

Defining, Teaching and Expanding "Safe, Sane, Consensual SM"

BDSM organizations built on the legacy of *Leatherman's Handbook* and other BDSM guidebooks to move discussions of appropriate behavior beyond dressing and cruising to negotiating and enacting BDSM scenes, established new "mores and customs." Steve Maidhof found these "considerably different than those practiced for so many years by us 'old' types."[32] First used to justify their activities to outsiders, BDSM practitioners increasingly used "safe, sane, consensual" to regulate conduct within their community. While a useful phrase, its terms required definition. Numerous experts weighed in. "Loosely," *Drummer* columnist Guy Baldwin wrote, "SAFE" means "care is taken to prevent accidental or unwanted physical or psychological injury" or "transmission of disease"; "SANE" that participants are sober and "mentally in charge of themselves"; and "CONSENSUAL" that all participants can "influence the pace, intensity, and direction of an erotic encounter at all times," ending it at will.[33]

Consent required discussing limits and achieving a shared understanding of planned activities. But how far could a top push these limits? At what point did a bottom's consent to extreme activities become problematic? Should the community prohibit certain dangerous activities?

By the late 1980s, BDSM educators encouraged participants to move through a sequence of steps: negotiation, preparation, warm up, intensification, climax, cooldown and aftermath, addressing safety at each stage. Participants discussed what excited them, what they would do, and negotiated both the physical and mental limits of the scene, agreeing on forms of address, intensity and duration. They agreed on safe words, organized the play space and selected equipment. During the scene, the top ensured any restraints were securely attached, and checked periodically to see if the bottom's hands or feet had grown cold due to impaired circulation. After scenes, tops helped bottoms recover mentally and physically, perhaps wrapping them in blankets or holding them after particularly heavy scenes. Concern for a bottom's enjoyment became such that some dominants jokingly described themselves as "service-oriented tops." Others, though, complained about submissives who "topped from the bottom," belaboring them with instructions. Regardless, these scenes differed dramatically from those Sam Steward sought in the 1950s, which often lacked significant negotiation or safety concerns.

There were those, though, who played on the edge. At Living in Leather V (1991), several attendees arranged a public, bloody whipping. After carefully cordoning off an area with a screen of plastic wrap and securing the submissive to an X-frame, the flogging began, increasing in intensity as blood spattered the area and surrounding plastic. It continued until the submissive used her prearranged safe word. She described the experience as intense and ecstatic. While it disturbed a few witnesses, none complained. It provoked no controversy.

In contrast, the same conference's "Consensual Non-Consensuality" seminar angered many and inaugurated debates that clarified the community's "safe, sane, consensual" standard. The seminar leaders, all well-known edge players, discussed practices beyond the norms of edge play, including signing suicide notes before a scene, as Severin does in Sacher-Masoch's *Venus in Furs*, and provoking police officers to get arrested to experience "real confinement," something rumored of 1950s BDSM artist Steve Masters. Most of the seminar, though, focused on so-called "consensual non-consent" scenes, in which bottoms set parameters and then explained "given these parameters, don't pay attention to what I say after this." Often frightening to outsiders, in these scenes "no," might mean "yes," and tops ignored pleas to "stop." They involved pushing bottoms to their limits—and a bit beyond.[34]

Bruce Marcus, a leading member of GMSMA, heard about the seminar and objected. Calling it the "Death Workshop," he argued it violated "safe, sane, and consensual" and contradicted "what GMSMA and the rest of the organized SM-leather community" stood for. "Safe, sane, consensual" established an ethical standard requiring the community to draw a line and "proscribe certain behaviors" to differentiate themselves from accused murders like Andrew Crispos.[35]

Edge play had a long history of controversy. Almost from its origins, Califia noted, people used "safe, sane, consensual" to stigmatize others. People in fulltime BDSM relationships or who enjoyed "heavier trips" were often treated poorly by "mainstream" sadomasochists. If BDSM represented a "second closet," seminar moderator DeBlase posited, many edge players occupied a "third closet," keeping their activities secret even from many BDSM friends. So thoroughly had people embraced safe words, some "could not conceive of playing without them."[36]

Marcus's complaint sparked magazine columns and exchanges of public letters among leading activists. Seminar participant and Ms. NLA winner Ruth Marks complained Marcus advocated censorship. Audience member Casey Androzany warned sadomasochists, already perceived as "outlaws," should not create "outlaws among ourselves." Author Carol Queen argued similarly. Demarcating BDSM activities, would divide "an already marginalized community." Tolerance was essential. The "radical desires" of edge players should encourage everyone to "look deeply into the well of her/his own scary desires" and "examine where—and why—we chose to draw our limits."[37]

Seminar panelist Michael Decker participated in risky scenes as both top and bottom and explained their thrill. "I had a safety net because the penalty for taking a life is much greater than the whimsical notion of offering it." Yet, "knowing they didn't kill me, and the awe of what I gave them and they gave me transcends the puny stuff we call love." As *Drummer* editor Joseph Bean explained, Decker's edge play involved "playing with self-extinguishing and self-realization. It is playing with the realization of dreams and the destruction of fantasy."[38]

NLA Co-chairs Jan Lyon and Jim Richards insisted the NLA would not instruct workshop presenters on "what they may or may not say" and defended discussion of "controversial subjects." While important, "safe, sane, consensual" was mutable. Activities "safe for one person" might "not be safe for someone else." Non-consensual fantasies of kidnapping and forced submission featured in many scenes. Condemning them was problematic. "While we, within the SM lifestyle, consider our acts to be sane, many would disagree with us."[39] It was important, Laura Antoniou noted, "to discuss different levels of safety, sanity and consensuality," which the NLA had a "responsibility to facilitate."[40]

Despite the prestige of edge play's defenders, Marcus won the debate. Having argued BDSM excluded activities violating "safe, sane, consensual" in other contexts, the NLA's leaders implicitly accepted demarcations of safety, sanity and consensuality. While never admitting defeat, edge players' workshops became more restrained. Growing numbers of people applied "safe, sane, consensual" to condemn perceived excesses. Its rhetoric even spread outside the dungeon. One NLA member applied it to cigarette smoking, complaining that Living in Leather VI attendees were "non-consensually" subjected "to gasping, choking, coughing, asthma attacks."[41] Letters to *Drummer* expressed similar concerns about leather bars, and BDSM venues increasingly restricted smoking.

Jay Wiseman, who authored several BDSM technique manuals, became the most vehement advocate of increased safety. His first book, *SM 101*, included multi-page checklists and extensive discussions of safety, including arranging a "safe call" with friends when playing with strangers. Wiseman advocated CPR training for dungeon monitors, defibrillators for BDSM clubs, and banning a host of dangerous practices, particularly erotic asphyxiation (breath play). Warnings about the latter were routine. Avoid choke holds, nooses and playing alone, which reportedly killed dozens of people each year. It was such a controversial practice, *Sandmutopian Guardian* waited until its last issue to discuss it. On the rare occasion breath play scenes went badly, as in the death of Adrian Exley and suicide of Gary Leblanc, the top who accidentally killed him, they received extensive coverage in BDSM publications and renewed safety warnings.[42]

As Lisa Downing notes, Wiseman's polemics went beyond these safety warnings and often deployed the same rhetoric outsiders used to condemn all BDSM activities. Efforts like his "to dissociate SM from danger" encouraged "a policy of censorship" within the BDSM community on "activities involving erotic asphyxiation" and other types of edge play, which affirmed "safe, sane, consensual" standards. *Sandmutopian Guardian* editor Mitch Kessler made much the same point. "When custom-breaking sex" was involved, even customs breakers themselves were quick to condemn.[43]

The growing popularity of fire scenes led to several injuries. In the most common of these, tops applied a thin stream of rubbing alcohol along the bottom's torso or limbs, and ignited it. When done carefully, the flame streaked across, producing interesting sensations of cold and hot as fire consumed alcohol. In a dark room, the bursts of flame were dazzling. Title contestants introduced more complex and spectacular uses of fire, accidentally injuring partners and causing some property damage. In one incident, a man shaved his partner's genitals and then cleaned the areas with rubbing alcohol, some of which pooled in skin folds. When he later applied a violet wand, a spark ignited the residue of alcohol and severely burned the bottom's genitals. Not surprisingly, BDSM events soon banned fire play.[44]

The edge play debates took place within a framework of increasingly standardized BDSM education describing techniques of growing complexity. Experts demonstrated technique at BDSM events, encouraging emulation and elaboration. Attendees applied daytime lessons at nighttime dungeon parties and returned home to teach them in their local communities. BDSM publications standardized and presented this expertise, exploring increasingly sophisticated topics, such as processing pain in heavy scenes. "SM instruction" became better—and "more safety conscious"—than ever.[45]

Political Activism

After assuming the SSCA's political mandate, the NLA focused on three goals: acceptance by the lesbian and gay community, erasing the stigma associated with BDSM activities, and ending the censorship, legal harassment and prosecution of people for their BDSM activities. BDSM organizations raised funds for members facing criminal prosecution, lobbied local governments and federal agencies, supported national hate crime legislation, mobilized against anti-gay ballot initiatives, and fought the censorship of BDSM art, film and publications.[46]

Legal Defense

Participants in BDSM activities faced continuing legal problems. Revelations of BDSM interests alienated friends and family members, damaged careers, lost jobs and even custody of children. Police raids on BDSM events and gathering places remained common. Even BDSM scenes in "the privacy of the bedroom" violated "the law of most cities, states, and countries."[47]

On 20 December 1990, Boston police raided the Thunderhead Club, an informal group hosting BDSM events—some men's only, others mixed—in the basement of a private home. Two undercover officers infiltrated the event, waited until the party was in full swing, and opened the door to a squad of officers who rushed in. They arrested three of the three-dozen men present, claiming the five dollars charged at the door to cover snacks constituted prostitution and labeled BDSM paraphernalia "dangerous weapons." *Boston Globe* columnist Mike Barnicle supported the police, condemning partygoers as "disturbed men." You would, after all, have to be "disturbed to enjoy getting tied up tighter than a hostage while someone beat you with a stick."[48]

The event catalyzed the formation of NLA's New England chapter, which led fund raising efforts for the men's legal fees and wrote the *Globe*, protesting its bigotry, prudery, and its decision to print the names of those arrested and the Thunderhead's address. All three of the men charged received anonymous, threatening phone calls. While several local gay activists and newspapers condemned the police raid, including Michael Cronin of the Greater Boston Lesbian and Gay Political Alliance, other gay papers, such as *Bay Windows*, condemned the Thunderhead defendants. Helping sadomasochists, they argued, hurt the larger cause of gay and lesbian rights and wasted limited resources.[49]

Like the men arrested in police sweeps of gay bars, people arrested for BDSM often plea-bargained to misdemeanor charges to avoid the embarrassment, expense and time of a trial. The Thunderhead defendants refused. Funded by the BDSM community, which raised about $10,000, they mounted a successful defense. Prosecutors dropped the charges eight months after the arrests. Two years later, Los Angeles police raided the Dragonfly, a BDSM gathering place. They charged 16 people with lewd conduct and performing obscene acts. Twelve plea-bargained to lesser charges. Four others, two men and two women, supported by donations from BDSM organizations, successfully fought the charges. The trial ended in a hung jury, and the judge castigated prosecutors for wasting resources on frivolous charges.[50]

Many BDSM enthusiasts encountered child custody issues. DADS founder Laura Goodwin lost custody of her son for several months following her divorce when her ex-husband claimed her BDSM activities created an unsafe environment. It required repeated court hearings and substantial legal fees for Goodwin to regain custody, after which she moved to Connecticut and founded United Leatherfolk of Connecticut.[51]

In 1996, Child Protective Services of New York seized the children of Selina and Steven Houghton, a pseudonymous couple brought to police attention by a babysitting relative who found a videotape of their private BDSM scenes in a locked box and viewed it. Police charged the Houghtons with endangering their children, and the district attorney threatened to add additional charges after the Houghtons refused a plea bargain. The Houghtons contested the charges in criminal court while simultaneously litigating to regain custody of their children in family court, a prolonged and expensive process. The district attorney publicized the charges against them, and officers involved claimed the Houghtons were members of a "drug dealing motorcycle gang." Both Selina and Steven lost their jobs as a result.[52]

George Morrell, the TCC founder who a decade earlier faced criminal charges for hosting BDSM discussions and parties in his home, rallied to their defense. So, too, did Molly Devin and Philip Miler, authors of popular BDSM manual *Screw the Roses: Send Me the Thorns* (1994), psychologist Charles Moser, who called it "blatant discrimination against SM practitioners," and *Boudoir Noir* publisher Robert Dante.[53]

A few years earlier, Dante, then living in Houston, was accused of assault and pressured to plea bargain. He refused and was found not guilty following a three-day trial in which he successfully explained "safe, sane, consensual" and used the NLA's domestic violence statement to refute the prosecutor's argument that anyone involved in BDSM was dangerously violent. Dante urged the Houghtons to fight back and spearheaded fundraising efforts. The NLA called on its members and other BDSM organizations "to unite and send a strong message that our community will no longer be victimized by the legal system" or tolerate "storm trooper tactics by police to intimidate and ruin the lives of our law-abiding citizens."[54]

Faced with a determined defense, the prosecutor dropped most of the charges. The Houghtons agreed to see a therapist in exchange for the return of their children, but that deal fell apart when local police arrested them on new misdemeanor charges of child neglect. Yet, New York's Child Welfare Agency found no evidence of child neglect, helping the Houghtons reach a new agreement. They pled no contest to a misdemeanor charge in exchange for fines and community service hours for Steve. With that resolved, they successfully pressed their case, first in family court and then to the State Court of Appeals, which overruled the family court judge and returned their children after 14 months in foster care. Legal wrangling over their custody continued another year.[55]

BDSM organizations celebrated the children's return as a great victory. They raised more than $24,000 for the Houghtons, fully funding their defense. While the case set no legal precedents, it convinced BDSM activists a determined defense would force authorities to back down.

Confronting Censorship

BDSM imagery remained a common target of censorship. Encouraged by the Justice Department, local prosecutors targeted BDSM media, as did prosecutors in other countries. Canadian customs officials stopped John Preston's novels and other BDSM publications at the border, targeting Califia and other female authors, in particular. Local officials prosecuted bookstores, which stopped carrying BDSM titles. In Great Britain, the Obscene Publication Squad targeted BDSM materials. In the United States, stores became reluctant to carry even BDSM works without overt sexual content and illustrations, such as technique handbooks and magazines.[56]

Increasing censorship forced publishers to restrict content, which Barry Douglas declared the BDSM community's "most serious problem." The NLA encouraged members to report incidents of censorship, fight claims "pornography and SM" led to violent crime, and write newspapers and legislators to support sexual freedom. To avoid problems itself, the NLA wrapped its newsletters in innocuous covers, often cute animals. "An old hippo woodcut," its editor explained, was less "apt to have delivery refused by a small-town postmaster in Tennessee" than bondage drawings. In doing so, he emulated John Coutts' *Bizarre* magazine, which 30 years earlier similarly downplayed its contents.[57]

Numerous BDSM publishers encountered difficulty. DeBlase recognized that continuing repercussions from the Meese Report made many topics off-limits. Most distributors refused to carry publications with "any bondage, any hot wax, any piss," making *Drummer* unavailable in several states except by subscription. To Douglas's dismay, DeBlase toned down *Drummer*, profits from which supported *DungeonMaster* and *Sandmutopian Guardian*. Those magazines barely broke even, but were cornerstones of DeBlase's BDSM education and community building. Readers noted the changes and complained *Drummer* was becoming "soft core." Editor Joseph Bean explained they faced a "tide of repressive politics." Toning things down was the only way to keep *Drummer* on newsstands. He, too, urged readers confront "anti-sexual, anti-gay, and anti-leather/SM" media and government officials.[58]

The national debate over the work of photographer Robert Mapplethorpe, whose work occasionally featured sadomasochistic imagery, crystalized the BDSM community's anti-censorship efforts. Senator Jesse Helms attacked artists whose work featured homoerotic or sadomasochistic content. In carefully orchestrated events, he ordered all women to leave the room before showing Mapplethorpe's photos and other sexual art, condemning it to an audience reminiscent of 1950s stag film viewers. Congressman Bob Dornan similarly complained about art featuring "sadism, masochism, bondage, discipline, or torture disguised as some sort of sexual thrill." Dornan and Helms made Mapplethorpe "the Christian Right's *bete noire*" and led a conservative effort to ban National Endowment for the Arts (NEA) funding for sexual topics.[59]

In 1989, Philadelphia's Institute of Contemporary Art exhibited *The Perfect Moment*, a collection of 175 Mapplethorpe photos, five of which depicted "homosexual sadomasochism, including a self-portrait of Mapplethorpe in leather chaps plunging a bullwhip into his anus." The Corcoran Gallery in Washington, DC planned to host the exhibit later that year, but Jesse Helms forced its cancellation. The following year, Cincinnati officials, encouraged by the National Coalition Against Pornography, closed down *The Perfect Moment* and indicted Contemporary Arts Center director Dennis Barrie for obscenity, the first time a museum official faced such charges. A hung jury acquitted Barrie, but his trial further discouraged funding and exhibiting artists who explored sexual themes.[60]

Numerous BDSM organizations advocated for the exhibits. GMSMA and NLA worked with Peri Jude Radecic and the NGLTF to lobby the NEA to fund Mapplethorpe exhibitions and other BDSM artists. GMSMA hosted a packed meeting in New York, which rallied support.[61] The NLA raised funds for lobbying and issued a widely distributed statement crafted by Califia, who also organized a letter writing campaign criticizing the television show *Law and Order* for its "Prisoner of Love" episode, which spread "misinformation about S/M" and repeatedly referred to its practitioners as "pathological." Califia's statement argued against the censorship of "publishers, libraries, art galleries, bookstores, newsstands, or other outlets," demanded the Justice Department stop making "obscenity prosecutions a top priority," and end efforts to entrap adults purchasing pornographic materials. Safeguarding the BDSM community required a vigorous defense of "our right to speak, as explicitly as we wish, about our private and public lives."[62]

This anti-censorship effort led to the BDSM community's most colorful political foray. When Democrat Harvey Gantt challenged Jesse Helms in the 1990 North Carolina senate race, Bill Costimiris, president of the newly formed Tarheel Leather Club, launched a "Dump Jesse!" campaign. Susie Shepherd visited the club and convinced NLA Co-Chair Jan Lyon to launch the "Beat Jesse" campaign. Lyon and Shepherd arranged for t-shirts, buttons and other campaign trinkets, and encouraged BDSM organizations across the country to come together in "true leather unity" and defeat Helms whose virulent homophobia helped North Carolina chalk up "the highest gay-bashing rate in the United States." Many BDSM organizations joined the effort and supported ACT-UP's call to boycott Philip Morris and other corporations supporting Jesse Helms.[63]

Shepherd recognized most people joined BDSM groups for pleasure and worked to make the Beat Jesse campaign fun. She traveled the country, organizing pillow fights, skits and other events. ORGASM and other organizations hosted erotic art shows, but celebrity flog-a-thons became emblematic of the campaign. At these, a volunteer dressed up as Jesse Helms and berated the crowd by quoting his vituperative rhetoric. Attendees, in turn, bought raffle tickets or bid for the privilege of "safely, sanely & consensually" giving Jesse's stand-in the beating or spanking Helms so richly deserved. While Helms won reelection by a close margin, the campaign raised awareness and $7,000. Lyon and Shepherd encouraged BDSM practitioners to remain politically active and help create a "safe/sane/consensual world in which to live."[64]

Following "Beat Jesse," BDSM organizations focused on issues closer to home or more directly related to BDSM activities. The NLA and West Coast BDSM organizations campaigned against the 1992 Oregon Citizen's Alliance ballot initiative, which condemned "sadism, masochism, and homosexuality" and associated them with pedophilia. Members of LSM, TES and other New York SM groups organized an "I'd Rather Have an Orgasm" sex party, which raised funds for the effort. Members of NLA Denver and other Rocky Mountain BDSM groups campaigned against a similar Colorado initiative. Events in Britain, though, convinced American BDSM organizations to unite in their largest and most sustained political effort.[65]

Operation Spanner

Increasingly connected, British and American fetishists and sadomasochists influenced one another. British sadomasochists avidly read American BDSM publications, while Americans embraced fetish fashions glamorized by British magazines like *AtomAge* in the 1970s and *Skin Two* in the 1990s. Public BDSM clubs and organizations emerged later in Britain than the United States. Maitresse, a London dance club catering to kinky people, was among the first. It opened in the 1980s, but "was a fetish-scene, more than precisely an SM-club," a gathering place for "transvestites, transsexuals, SMers, gays, lesbians, heterosexuals, rubber-people, silk and satin-people, leather-people." Some professional dominants brought clients there and occasionally "beat willing straight men who would kneel in front of them, proffer them riding crops and beg to be lashed." One night, "a woman dressed as pony with a bit in her mouth" pulled "a guy in a horse buggy."[66]

By the mid-1990s, Maitresse had several competitors, including Torture Garden, Der Putsch, Submission and Club Whiplash. These British venues were not sex clubs. Unlike the Mineshaft or backroom bars, they prohibited sexual activity, enforced dress codes requiring genitals and nipples be covered, and kept activities quite restrained by American norms. Sex parties took place in private homes, and these attracted increasing police attention.

In 1987, encouraged by the Obscene Publications Squad, police in Manchester and other British cities launched Operation Spanner, targeting sadomasochists and BDSM publications and videos. Over the next two years, they raided men's homes and gay contact magazines, detained and questioned hundreds of gay men, and seized videotapes of private BDSM parties, which they used to identify suspects. In addition to flogging and other common BDSM activities, the videos showed a branding and one man nailing another's penis to a board. In 1989, officials charged 42 men who appeared in the videos with assault, unlawful wounding and related charges. In court, the defendants explained everyone at the parties consented. None of the activities resulted in injuries requiring medical treatment. The following year, Judge James Rant, like the judges in the 1967 Samuels Case in the United States, rejected this argument and convicted 16 defendants under the "Offences Against the Person Act." Eight received prison sentences, the longest for four and half years. The court cautioned 26 other defendants, the supposed victims, for "aiding and abetting assaults" on themselves. The ruling was so broad, legal commentators warned, it made tattooing and ear-piercing illegal.[67]

The Spanner defendants repeatedly appealed their convictions, which catalyzed the growth of BDSM organizations in Britain. NLA Co-Chair Chuck Higgins committed the NLA to support them. He sent British politicians information on "safe, sane and consensual SM," encouraged them to recognize "consensuality as a defense" and see BDSM as a legitimate sexual activity. While a March 1992 appeal reduced the Spanner defendants' sentences to three to six months, the court maintained "sadomasochistic libido" did not justify assault. The men appealed again.[68]

Higgins and other American BDSM activists feared Spanner-like prosecutions in the United States. Sadomasochism was not "protected under the law," nor was consent "available as a defense to its practitioners." Raids on private BDSM parties continued and local newspapers often published the names of those arrested. If American sadomasochists did not take "active measures" to protect their sexual rights, they would be prosecuted like the Spanner men.[69]

At Living in Leather VII (1992) in Chicago, Higgins led NLA members to the British consulate where they protested the Spanner convictions, spoke to American and British reporters, and pressed their case. Race Bannon, Guy Baldwin and Jan Hall worked to interest Amnesty International in the Spanner Case, but without success. Yet, a nationwide effort led by Higgins and Peter Fiske of the 15 Association raised $57,000 for the Spanner defense fund, covering most of the next appeal's cost. Higgins also convinced the International Gay and Lesbian Association to lobby for the defendants. He traveled repeatedly to Britain and worked with BDSM activists there, particularly the founders of Countdown on Spanner, the primary organization supporting the Spanner defendants and advocating the decriminalization of BDSM. Beginning in 1990, it organized fundraisers and an annual "SM Pride" march followed by a Dungeon in the Sky party. Modeled on American BDSM conferences, it featured a mix of educational and political seminars and evening entertainments.[70]

In March 1993, the Spanner defendants lost their House of Lords appeal in a three to two decision. Two years later, the European Court of Human Rights agreed to hear the pleas of three of the convicted men, who argued their sentences violated the privacy provisions of Article 8 of the European Convention on Human Rights. Tim Woodward, publisher of *Skin Two* and SM Gays, the largest British BDSM organization, formed the Spanner Trust Fund to support them, which American BDSM organizations helped fund. Ruling in February 1997, the European Court recognized the case involved "mutual sexual gratification," rather than violence, but refused to overturn the British court's decision. The court's Italian judge condemned sadomasochism as "unrestrained permissiveness" likely to lead to debauchery, pedophilia and torture.[71]

In the immediate years following the original Spanner convictions, police raided BDSM clubs and private play parties held in people's homes in Yorkshire, Herfordshire, Hoylandswaine and other British cities. Accompanied by dogs, 60 officers raided the Reflex Club in Sutton where undercover police witnessed a man dressed as a schoolgirl beaten hard enough to draw blood. In 1995, police raided heterosexual fetish club Whiplash and *Cul D'Or*, a spanking magazine. One bookstore owner was prosecuted for carrying *Modern Primitives*, Fakir Musafar's piercing and body modification magazine. These cases, though, mostly involved middle-class, middle-aged, heterosexual couples whom courts generally acquitted, as they did to customers of Reflex and Whiplash. Similarly, a man convicted of assault for branding his initials on wife's buttocks as part of their consensual BDSM relationship was sentenced only to conditional discharge (essentially a warning not to do it again) and then found innocent on appeal. Like David Reuben a generation earlier, British courts found heterosexual sadomasochists amusing, but condemned gay sadomasochists as dangerous.[72]

BDSM activists in Britain and in the United States highlighted the disparities between prosecutions of gay and straight sadomasochists, worked to "dispel myths about SM," and slowly changed legal attitudes. Prosecutions of gay sadomasochists declined in the late 1990s, and Britain's Law Commission proposed allowing consent as a defense if there was no lasting injury. The changing legal climate allowed Countdown on Spanner to redirect its efforts from legal defense and political protest to fun. As its leader Rob Grover explained in 1998, "we lost the case but won the war." That year, the London SM Pride march and Dungeon in the Sky party attracted a thousand participants.[73]

Revising the DSM

Ending the legal harassment of sadomasochists required redefining BDSM for health and legal professionals. In 1986, graduate student Kenny Boudreaux wrote

Drummer encouraging concerted action to change the pejorative definitions of fetishism, masochism and sadism in the American Psychiatric Association's *Diagnostic and Statistical Manual of Mental Disorders* (DSM). A decade earlier, Frank Kameny encouraged Gay Activists Alliance to challenge the DSM's classification of homosexuality as a "sociopathic personality disturbance." For Kameny, eliminating this characterization marked an essential first step to advance gay rights. The effort succeeded. After gay activists protested at its annual conference, contentious lobbying, and a vote of the entire APA, the 1973 edition (DSM II) eliminated the pejorative classification of homosexuality. The 1987 edition (DSM III-R) removed it entirely. Boudreaux advocated similar lobbying for BDSM, which was not a disorder and did not warrant "a diagnostic label." A few years later, Guy Baldwin renewed Boudreaux's call to revise the DSM.[74]

First published in 1952 and revised in 1968, 1973 and 1980, the DSM provided little specific discussion of BDSM activities, but nonetheless characterized them as pathologies and perversions. Psychologist John Money, who developed the idea of "love maps," mental templates of erotic desire developed in youth, successfully championed substituting the term paraphilia for perversion in the 1980 edition. Substituting one term for another, though, did not change DSM's pejorative characterization of sexual sadism, sexual masochism and fetishism. It classified these and other maligned sexual behaviors as mental illnesses. As Gayle Rubin noted, DSM offered "a fairly reliable map of the current moral hierarchy of sexual activities," a map stigmatizing "fetish, sadism, masochism, transsexuality, transvestism, exhibitionism, voyeurism," and other sexual practices.[75]

At Living in Leather VII (1992), Baldwin encouraged NLA members to lobby for revisions reflecting the realities of "safe and consensual SM and fetish play." Baldwin's partner, Race Bannon, a popular BDSM writer and educator, led the campaign. Since DSM's descriptions evinced no engagement with the organized BDSM community or even individual BDSM practitioners, Bannon encouraged BDSM practitioners to locate and compile "serious academic research" demonstrating people involved in "SM and fetish play" were not inherently mentally ill. Perhaps they could convince "the psychotherapeutic community" to change its views. So, unlike 1970s gay activists, BDSM activists chose to cultivate contacts among APA members and change minds one-by-one.[76]

The following year, Chuck Higgins and the NLA arranged for University of Arkansas psychologist Ralph Hammond to interview Living in Leather VIII attendees. He declared them "disappointingly normal" and advocated changing the DSM to reflect "Safe, Sane, Consensual SM." Bannon encouraged psychologists and psychiatrists within the BDSM community to write the APA. Baldwin approached several leading psychologists and psychiatrists. Ernest Greene, a pornographic film producer and member of Janus, cultivated Robert Stoller, who played a key role in earlier DSM revisions of homosexuality. Stoller interviewed Baldwin, Greene and other sadomasochists and concluded there was no singular perversion of sadomasochism. Rather, there were "many sadomasochistic perversions," which in turn informed many, "perhaps, all erotic fantasies."

Participants in BDSM scenes did "not brutalize, humiliate, or torture each other in their erotic play." The goal was to "tantalize and then satisfy." Charles Moser, who had long studied the BDSM community, similarly championed revision, which Bannon declared "would be a dream come true."[77]

That dream quickly became reality. DSM's 1994 edition (DSM-IV) substantially revised the definitions of "sexual sadism," "sexual masochism" and "fetishism." They were no longer considered mental illnesses unless they caused "clinically significant distress or impairment in social, occupational or other important areas of functioning." The same was true, though, of roughly half the paraphilias it listed. This makes it difficult to determine how much, if at all, lobbying by BDSM organizations influenced the proceedings, which reflected broad changes in psychiatry. Even Bannon admitted it was impossible to determine, since the APA made its decisions within committees sworn to secrecy. The same is true of the APA's earlier revisions in regard to homosexuality, about which debates continue. Did they simply reflect changing times and greater mainstream acceptance of homosexuality, as Michael Bronski suggests, or did gay activist lobbying make a difference, as others argue? On the other hand, was it not exactly that sort of lobbying—and gay and lesbian political activism in general, which changed public attitudes and influenced the APA?[78]

Clearly, though, the community's internal redefinition of BDSM as "safe, sane, consensual," influenced Stoller and some other revision supporters. *Checkmate's* editor declared the revisions "a terrific development for the kinky community." Yet, more work needed to be done. While the new language was "a good beginning toward greater understanding and acceptance of the 'kinky' individual," they still needed to work to change popular attitudes toward BDSM.[79]

While gay and lesbian activists celebrated the 1973 DSM revisions as a great victory, Abram J. Lewis argues many gays and lesbians dismissed their significance. Successive revisions to the DSM experienced a similar response in the BDSM community—hailed as great victories by activists, but largely ignored by rank and file members. Interest in a continuing campaign to remove BDSM entirely from the realm of paraphilias quickly faded. Bannon shut down his "DSM Project" and instead worked to compile KAP (Kink Aware Professionals), a directory of psychotherapeutic, medical and other health professionals who agreed "adults have the right to engage in all safe and consensual erotic behavior."[80]

Winning Acceptance by the LGBTQ Community

In the early 1990s, many LGBT rights activists still argued for the exclusion of leathermen, drag queens and others whose appearance visibly differed from the mainstream. Winning public acceptance, Marshall Kirk and Hunter Madsen argued, required appearing normal. They singled out sadomasochists, in particular, compared them to pederasts, and argued for their exclusion from the gay and lesbian community. Several large organizations took these warnings to heart, among them the Michigan Womyn's Music Festival, whose organizers regularly restricted or banned BDSM activities, attire and workshops and appeared, at times, to encourage harassment of leatherwomen at the festival.[81]

BDSM activists, in turn, argued the gay and lesbian community's internal divisions were a greater hindrance to achieving civil rights than attacks by bigoted politicians.[82] Arguably, the BDSM community's emphasis on unity across lines of gender, orientation and BDSM interest mirrored similar calls to unity by gay and lesbian leaders who successively broadened their approach to include people who identified as bisexual, transsexual or queer. The organizers of the 1987 March on Washington worked to assemble the largest possible coalition and growing numbers of lesbian and gay organizations adopted this approach. This necessarily required including leather and BDSM organizations, which could mobilize thousands of members and regularly raised tens of thousands of dollars for causes ranging from AIDS to helping victims of the 1989 San Francisco Loma Prieta earthquake, which devastated several BDSM businesses, including DeBlase's publishing offices.[83]

Pride march organizers increasingly welcomed visible leather and BDSM participation. In the 1990 Los Angeles pride parade, roughly 400 members from Avatar, Dykes on Bikes, Leather and Lace, NLA Los Angeles, Somandros, Trident International and other leather and BDSM organizations formed the parade's largest single contingent.[84] New York's BDSM organizations similarly worked together to assemble large contingents, as did those in Chicago, Dallas and Houston. San Francisco, though, was unique in accepting the participation and performance of a "precision whip drill team." Most parade organizers discouraged BDSM marchers from displaying whips and chains, or engaging in overt BDSM displays. BDSM organizations generally complied and formed ever larger parade contingents, such as that for the 1993 March on Washington.

BDSM organizations formed their largest contingent to date for the 1994 gay pride march in New York commemorating Stonewall's twenty-fifth anniversary. Before the march, GMSMA, LSM, NLA and other local organizations hosted the largest BDSM conference yet, the four-day International SM/Leather/Fetish Celebration, which affirmed "the role of sane, sane and consensual sadomasochism and power exchange," and promoted "freedom of sexual expression," and the "loving nature of S/M relationships." More than 2,800 people attended 65 daytime panels, which ranged from the practical, "SM Toys on the Cheap" and "Dungeon Etiquette" to the political, "the Right Wing and SM Images" and "Responding to Anti-Gay Ballot Initiatives." Many seminars reflected the increasing specialization and sophistication of BDSM play with seminars on steel bondage devices, accurately staging scenes in Victorian or other historical eras, elaborate Japanese rope bondage, suspension scenes in which tops secured bottoms with rope and hoisted them off the ground, and fulltime—often called 24/7—BDSM relationships in which BDSM interaction and power play entered everyday lives. They showcased the emergence of a new generation of BDSM educators, including Midori, a fetish fashion model and rope expert, and bullwhip experts Mary and Robert Dante. In the evening, attendees packed the Vault,

Hellfire, and other New York BDSM establishments where they not only played themselves, but watched the scenes of their community's best-known members, people whose books and articles they read, but never expected to see play in person.[85]

Checkmate editor Harold Cox praised the event, which raised more than $20,000 for the Spanner Defense Fund and various AIDS charities. It marked, he thought, a new level of cooperation among BDSM organizations. Seminar panelists reflected the community's diversity, a "cross-fertilization of different [BDSM] cultures," which benefitted everyone by advancing BDSM practice and uniting its practitioners politically. BDSM, Cox complained, was "the last outpost of discrimination. Far more than homosexuality, SM is subject to prejudice, hostility, and violence . . . Political harassment is constant." Resistance required a united effort.[86]

Several years earlier, the NLA created a speakers' bureau and began inviting members of the press to its events, such as Living in Leather IX, held the previous year in Toronto, which garnered favorable press along with condescending descriptions convention attendees, including a "man in the rubber French maid's costume teetering on high heels" and another "wearing a tiny black wrestling outfit and the kind of gas mask Dennis Hopper sucked from in *Blue Velvet*." Many of the International SM/Leather/Fetish Celebration's seminar leaders met with the press, among them was Cox who endeavored to debunk "the myths and negative stereotypes that have separated us from the vanilla community" and present themselves "as caring and community-minded individuals."[87]

The march itself tested the limits of BDSM tolerance and provoked controversy. The roughly 3,000 members of the SM/Leather/Fetish contingent displayed an array of banners, "lots of leather," variations of "safe, sane, consensual," and a fair amount of bare flesh. Tala Brandeis, a renowned whip expert, led the contingent cracking a 12-foot bullwhip, which she had done a year earlier in Washington and in several San Francisco marches. After about a half-mile, march officials appeared and demanded the whip cracking cease, provoking a debate among marchers. One person encouraged compliance, shouting out "what will the religious right do with the video footage?" Others added their voices to his, including GMSMA's Barry Douglas and Bruce Marcus. A shouting match erupted. Many supported Brandeis, some of whom wanted to unleash and crack their own whips. People opposed to whip cracking rushed Brandeis, forcing her to stop to avoid injuring them. Almost a hundred other marchers then formed a circle around her and linked arms to create a safety cordon. The march and whip cracking then resumed, culminating in demonstrations at the United Nations building.[88]

As Michael Bronski notes, the distinction "between claiming an outsider status and demanding acceptance as part of the 'normal' majority—has remained, in various forms, the defining division in the LGBT movement." The same division split the BDSM community, which was further divided between its gay and straight members. Gay and lesbian sadomasochists demanded a sexual citizenship recognizing both their sexual orientation and their BDSM proclivities and leather identity. While many heterosexuals supported this, particularly members of the NLA, many straight sadomasochists just wanted to be left alone. Carol Truscott encouraged initiatives and support groups to help "heterosexual SM people to come out," but without success.[89]

The whip cracking sparked considerable debate within the BDSM community. Pat Califia thought it highlighted differences between politically focused New Yorkers, who worked to present a restrained image of BDSM, and flamboyant San Francisco sadomasochists. New Yorkers saw "their role as building coalitions with more powerful groups and using financial leverage to compel them to support our cause." They undertook fund raising "with great dedication" seeing it as the BDSM community's "route to respectability and protection from harassment." In contrast, San Francisco sadomasochists expected marches to be fun, more party and street fair than somber demonstration. Rather than acceptance from mainstream society, they just wanted to be left alone.[90] Something essential to BDSM would be lost, they thought, by making it too respectable. One could not simultaneously embrace BDSM's outlaw mystique and present oneself as respectable. GMSMA and NLA leaders, though, hoped to do exactly that by shaping and normalizing BDSM—both its practice and its outward presentation—to win acceptance.

Outside the BDSM community, the event received surprisingly little publicity. March officials were more concerned Brandeis would accidentally injure someone than how media portrayed her whip cracking. The Lamda Report, an organization opposed to lesbian and gay rights did release a video, *Stonewall: 25 Years of Deception*, which linked gay sadomasochists to Nazism. While it encouraged Newt Gingrich and other conservative politicians to present all homosexuals as sadomasochists and condemn both groups, it failed to provoke new calls to ban BDSM contingents in pride parades. Instead, the BDSM conference and march proved effective demonstration of the BDSM community's political acumen and growing mainstream acceptance, the latter highlighted by a *New York Times* editorial arguing a "just society must offer the same protections to men in leather and chains as to those in Brooks Brothers suits."[91]

While favorable editorials in the *New York Times* were rare, appearance on daytime talk shows became common as BDSM activists engaged with the press. Gerie Blum and Mitch Kessler, the New York whipmaking couple and operators of the Utopian Network—one of the first BDSM friendly computer bulletin board networks—appeared on HBO's "Real Sex 6," "Inside Edition," "A Current Affair," "Evening Magazine" and several talk shows, including "Joan Rivers," where they received a generally positive reception, and "Geraldo," whose host compared them to child molesters. They later purchased *Sandmutopia Guardian* magazine from DeBlase, renaming it *Sandmutopian Guardian*. Professional dominants proved particularly popular on talk shows, among them Mistress Jacqueline who appeared with her favorite slaves on the Donahue Show to promote her autobiography and $1,000 domination fees.[92]

From *Cosmopolitan* to *Self*, women's magazines titillated readers with articles on fetishes and sadomasochism. Fetishes were "more common than you think," while BDSM offered ways to "assume control" of one's sexual life.[93] *Cosmopolitan* editor Helen Gurley Brown encouraged women to explore their kinky sides. "I don't think any woman should feel bad if she enjoys a sort of pseudoroughness in sex," including spanking, having her "wrists tied in silk scarves," or "playing out certain fantasies." Reporters from *Cosmopolitan* and *New York* magazine visited Paddles, New York's "couples friendly" BDSM club, and found not "sexual outlaws," but regular, middle-class people. Sighs of pleasure intermingled with sounds of beatings, echoing through the club's passageways. It was "slave auction night." Contrary to expectations, most of those auctioned were men "looking for domineering ladies." Rather than perverts, the reporter concluded, most of them just wanted to add a little excitement to their sex lives.[94]

Madonna shot photographs for her best-selling book *Sex* (1992) at New York's Vault. She staged most of them in its large, main room, which offered x-frames, benches and cages. Madonna, who adopted the persona of "Mistress Dita" for the book, appeared in a variety of BDSM attire, including a studded leather bikini with cut out nipples. She assumed both dominant and submissive roles, sucking toes, biting nipples and licking ass, was bound with rope and did the binding, flogged and was flogged. She claimed, there is "something comforting about being tied up" and letting "someone hurt you who you know would never hurt you."[95] Madonna continued her BDSM explorations in *Body of Evidence* (1993) in which her character is charged with slipping a man cocaine prior to BDSM sex, the combination of which killed him. It sold in video stores with an accompanying "Passion Pack" of candle, handcuffs, bubble bath and champagne flutes.

Anne Rice, author of popular vampire novels, discovered BDSM through her friendship with John Preston in the 1980s. Writing under pseudonyms, she published the *Claiming of Sleeping Beauty* trilogy (1983–85), based on the fairy tale, and *Exit to Eden* (1985), a novel set at a contemporary Caribbean BDSM resort. Garry Marshall, best known for *Pretty Woman* (1990), directed the 1994 film adaptation of her novel *Exit to Eden*. In contrast to prior films, *Exit to Eden* explained safe words and featured happy, middle class couples at a Caribbean BDSM resort where "all pairings" were "safe, sane," and by "mutual consent." While panned by critics, the film indicated significant engagement with the BDSM community. Jeanette Heartwood made the colorful whips featured in the film. While a comedy, the character Dr. Martin Halifax (Hector Elizondo) pushes back against those who mock BDSM, arguing people most deserve "freedom of choice" in the "most intimate of choices: sex." As Jeffrey Weeks notes, "a discourse of choice is a powerful dissolvent of old verities," and members of the BDSM community deployed it regularly, particularly women who worked to refute feminist critiques of sadomasochism.[96] Over time, their rhetoric of choice and "safe, sane, consensual" proved effective.

★★★

BDSM organizations changed how many sadomasochists met one another, learned about and engaged in BDSM. By the mid-1990s, hundreds of them operated in cities across the United States and Canada. Their members subscribed to BDSM technique magazines, attended regular meetings, demonstrations and play parties, and participated in local pride marches and other political events. Many of them traveled to participate in national events such as the Living in Leather conferences, the marches on Washington, and the Stonewall 25 events. Growing numbers hosted their own local BDSM conferences. "Safe, sane, and consensual" came to epitomize the BDSM community, which had little room for the outlaws celebrated in movies and literature a generation earlier.

The changes were so dramatic *Mr. Benson* author John Preston complained BDSM had "lost its edge." Instead of "trusting one person, a mentor," people relied on "impersonal how-to manuals." Formal clubs "directed by Robert's Rules of Order" like GMSMA displaced the "anarchistic sense of brotherhood" of motorcycle clubs. Instead of "breaking the rules," BDSM became rule-bound. The sexual world described by Preston in his novels, one of the purist expressions of Foucault's *ars erotica*, was gone, destroyed by BDSM organizations that "codified, measured, and packaged" BDSM.[97]

Instead of lustful rebellion, BDSM organizations promoted discipline and negotiation. They valued knowledge and expertise over sexual attractiveness and promiscuity and channeled desires for edge play in safer directions, emphasizing mastering complex skills. No bottom should have to put up with an unsafe or abusive top. As Pat Califia wrote, Mr. Benson did not "live here anymore."[98]

BDSM activists achieved greater visibility and participation in LGBT events and organizations and regularly presented seminars at the NGLTF's annual Creating Change conference. They proved effective fund raisers, supported community members facing criminal charges for BDSM activities, and helped change mainstream opinions of BDSM activities. Prosecutions for BDSM activities declined, as did pejorative portrayals in media. In contrast to *Cruising's* disturbed and dangerous characters, *Exit to Eden* presented sadomasochists as happy, middle class folk, "just another alternative lifestyle." Similarly, growing numbers of mainstream sex advice writers portrayed BDSM activities as fun. In *Gay Relationships* (1989), Tina Tessina described "light kink" as fun, as did Sharon Bakos in *Kink* (1995), though she echoed the BDSM community's warnings against edge play.[99]

BDSM activists united the disparate parts of their community and shaped BDSM practice to be "safe, sane, consensual." In terms of size, organization, and political effectiveness, the BDSM community's transformation was profound. As Patrick (formerly Pat) Califia noted,

> if you had told me in 1976 that someday the SM community would be able to mount an international fund-raising campaign like we did for Countdown on Spanner, or have a conference like Living in Leather, I would have laughed at you. We were too few, too weak, too self-hating, too disorganized for that to seem possible just 20 years ago.[100]

BDSM practitioners entered the twenty-first century a much less isolated subculture—one with a greater sense of identity and growing mainstream acceptance.

Notes

1 "The March on Washington 1993," *Leather Journal* 47 (1993), 10–20.
2 Bill Brent, "Marching, Cruising, and Channel Surfing," *Black Sheets* 2 (1993), 11–5; Barry Douglas, "SM-Leather-Fetish Conference Speech," *GMSMA Newslink*, Spring 1993, 6; Jesse Helms, "Only Morality Will Effectively Prevent AIDS from Spreading," *New York Times*, 12 November 1987, 22; Pat Califia and Robin Sweeny, *The Second Coming: A Leatherdyke Reader* (Boston, MA: Alyson Books, 2000), xiv; "Obscenity & Law Enforcement," *First Link* 5, no. 1 (January 1991), 11; Barry Douglas to Jan Hall, 22 March 1994, Hall Papers, March on Washington folder, LAAM; and Brame and Brame, *Different Loving Too*, 71.
3 "NLA National News," *First Link* 5:10 (November 1991), 1; "NLA Address List," *First Link* 4:4 (April 1990), 2; and Carol Truscott, "Living in Leather IV," *Sandmutopia Guardian* 7 (Jan 1990), 8.
4 Michele Buchanan, "Leather Is Thicker Than Blood: Identity Formation Among Organized SM Practitioners in New York City," PhD diss., New School University, 2004, 35–6.
5 Mitch Kessler, "From the Top: The Future of NLA: Metro New York," *The Inquisitor* 1, no. 3 (November 1990), 3–4 and Laura Antoniou, "Great Expectations," *The Inquisitor* 2, no. 10 (January–February 1992), 14.
6 "Help," *First Link* 1, no. 2 (undated 1987), 2; Steve Maidhof, "Leatherphobia," *Chain Link* 1 (Spring 1987), 2; Bet Power, "25 Ways to Combat SM-Phobia," Lesbian Herstory Archive; Stein, *Living in Leather*, 86, 126, and 154–5; Pat Califia, *Sensuous Magic* (New York: Masquerade, 1993); John Warren, *The Loving Dominant* (New York: Masquerade, 1992); Jay Wiseman, *SM 101* (San Francisco, CA: Greenery Press, 1992); and Race Bannon, *Learning the Ropes* (Los Angeles, CA: Daedalus, 1993).
7 Califia, "Fix Me Up," in *Melting Point* (Boston, MA: Alyson, 1993), 91–120; Laura Antoniou, *The Marketplace* (New York: Masquerade, 1993), *The Slave* (New York: Masquerade, 1994), *The Trainer* (New York: Masquerade, 1995); "A Familiar Ring," in *Scenes from the Marketplace* (Cambridge, MA: Circlet, 2013); and "Stealing Trash" at http://lantoniou.com/stealing-trash/ (accessed 15 January 2018).
8 Steve Maidhof, "Mr. & Ms. NLA," *Living in Leather III Souvenir Program*, 8; "New vs. Old Leather," *Chain Link* 2 (Summer 1987), 9; and "Top Priority," *Chain Link* 1 (Spring 1987), 2.
9 John Ferrari, "Leather May Day Celebration," *Sandmutopia Guardian & Dungeon Journal* 3 (August 1988), 34; Steve Stein, *Twenty-Five Years of Living in Leather: The National Leather Association, 1986–2011* (Palm Coast, FL: Adynaton, 2012), 54; *Knight* 4 (undated circa 1982), LAAM, DeBlase Papers, Box 29; Race Bannon, "International Ms. Leather 1990: Gabrielle Antolovich," *Drummer* 140 (1990), 67; and Victoria Baker, "Cross-Orientation Play," *Sandmutopia Guardian* 12 (1993), 16–7.
10 "Attention Hetero & Bi Folks," *First Link* 3, no. 1 (January 1989), 2; "Why Living in Leather," *First Link* 4, no. 7 (July 1990), 5; and "Black Rose Reports on LIL V," *Link* 5, no. 2 (February 1991), 8.
11 Dave Rhodes, "Editorial," *Leather Journal* 5 (February–April 1988), 6–7.
12 Mitch Kessler, "The Future of NLA: Metro New York," *The Inquisitor* 1, no. 3 (November 1990), 3.
13 Leonard Dworkin, "Letter to the Editor," *The Link* 9, no. 3 (June/July 1995), 9; Mitch Kessler, "The Pansexual Thing," *The Inquisitor* 10 (January/February 1992),

3–4; and "What Does the National Leather Association mean when it calls itself a Pansexual Organization?" *The Inquisitor* 12 (May/Jun 1992), 4.
14 Laura Goodwin, "We Are Us: Pride" *Quarter Link* 6, no. 4 (May 1992), 16.
15 Clipping from *Denver Blade*, 14 November 1990, 1 in NLA Denver folder, LAAM.
16 Paris Sea, Letter to the Editor, *The Link*, January 1999, 8.
17 Laura Pratt, "Birds of a Leather," *Eye Weekly*, 13 October 1994 and Jim Richards, interview by Jan Hall, 6 July 2002.
18 Joseph Bean, *International Mr. Leather: Twenty-Five Years of Champions* (Las Vegas, NV: Nazca Plains Corp., 2004), 33 and George Chauncey, *Gay New York: Gender, Urban Culture, and the Making of the Gay Male World, 1890–1940* (New York: Basic Books, 1995), 25.
19 DeBlase, "Off the Top," *Drummer* 131 (1989), 4; Barry Douglas, letter to the editor, and response by Tony DeBlase, *Drummer* 132 (1989), 5; and "Leather Pride Flag Turns 10!," *Lavender* 100 (26 March 1999) at https://leathercolumn.blogspot.com/1999/03/ (accessed 1 July 2019).
20 G.J.P., letter to the editor, and response by Tony DeBlase, *Drummer* 136 (1990), 5; Tony DeBlase, "The Leather Pride Flag," *The Link*, July–August 1999, 8–9; and Tony DeBlase, interview by Jan Hall, 1999, NLA Archives.
21 Bean, "Playing on the Edge," *Drummer* 148 (1991), 4 & 31–5.
22 Fish, "We're Not Knitting Doilies: Safe, Sane, Consensual and Beyond," *Brat Attack* 1 (1991); and Fish, "History is Just Good Gossip: Fifteen Years of Dykes Doing SM," *Brat Attack* 4 (1993).
23 "Group S&M Courtesy," *Inferno X* (1981), 15.
24 George Nelson, "Dungeon-Mastering," *First Link* 3, no. 9 (September 1989), 2; Laura Antoniou, "Great Expectations: Notes from the Editor," *The Inquisitor* 3 (1990), 18; and "NLA Chapter News," *First Link* 5, no. 5 (May 1991), 3.
25 Pat Califia, *The Lesbian SM Safety Manual* (Boston, MA: Alyson, 1988); Trevor Jacques, *On the Safe Edge* (Toronto: WholeSM, 1993); Sharon C. Bakos, *Kink: The Shocking Hidden Sex Lives of Americans* (New York: St Martins, 1995), 76; *Breast Bondage* 5 (HOM, 1982), 3; and *Hogtied* 4, no. 3 (1983), 3.
26 Carolyn and Steve Vakesh, "Hosting a Play Party," *Sandmutopian Guardian* 26 (1996), 10–3 & 44; and Charles Moser, "S/M (Sadomasochistic) Interactions in Semi-Public Settings," *Journal of Homosexuality* 36, no. 2 (1998), 19–30.
27 "Minnesota," *The Advocate*, 15 August 1989, 20: and Carol Truscott, "Lesbians Refuse SM Money," *Sandmutopia Guardian* 7 (January 1990), 11.
28 Ty Clements and Michael Terroy, "Sexual Assault Is NOT SM," *DungeonMaster* 35 (circa 1987/8), 7 and Jim Richards and Judy Tallwing McCarthy, "Letter to the Lesbian Battering and Intervention Project," 30 August 1989, *First Link* 3 (September 1989), 2.
29 NLA Executive Committee Minutes, August 1990, NLA Archives and Pat Califia, "A House Divided: Violence in the Lesbian SM Community," *Brat Attack* 1 (1991), 10–4.
30 Artemis Silverowl, "From Mr and Ms NLA International," *The Link* 8, no. 1 (January/February 1994), 2.
31 "Statement on Domestic Violence," *First Link* 5, no. 6 (June/July 1991), 3; "Domestic Violence—NLA Draws Distinctions," *Sandmutopia Guardian* 12 (April 1993), 4; International Leather/SM/Fetish Celebration program book; "Domestic Violence Project," *The Link*, January 2004, 3–4; and "NCAVP," *Domestic Violence Project Newsletter* 2, no. 1 (February 2007), 7–8.
32 Maidhof, "New vs. Old Leather," *Chain Link* 2 (Summer 1987), 9.
33 Guy Baldwin, "Second Coming Out," in Mark Thompson (ed.), *Leatherfolk : Radical Sex, People, Politics, and Practice* (Boston, MA: Alyson Publications, 1991), 176–7.
34 Carol Queen, "Playing on the Edge: A Look at Consensually Non-consensual SM," *Taste of Latex* 6 (circa 1992–93), 12.

35 Bruce Marcus, "On the 'Edge' or Over the Line?," GMSMA *Newslink* (Summer 1991), 33–5; "Marcus Response to Laura Antoniou," *Link* 5, 10 (November 1991), 8; and Edmund White, *City Boy: My Life in New York During the 1960s and '70s* (New York: Bloomsbury, 2009), 237.
36 "Pat Califia Is Quite the S/M Mover and Shaker," *Taste of Latex* 6 (circa 1992–93), 17 and DeBlase, "The Third Closet," *DungeonMaster* 29 (1985), 16.
37 Casey Androzany, letter to editor, *Link* 5, no. 5 (May 1991), 10; and Queen, "Playing on the Edge," 12.
38 Queen, "Playing on the Edge," 12; and Joseph Bean, "Playing on the Edge," *Drummer* 148 (1991), 4.
39 Lyon and Richards, "Response to Bruce Marcus," *Link* 5, no. 10 (November 1991), 5.
40 Laura Antoniou, "Letter to Bruce Marcus" and Bruce Marcus, "Response to Laura Antoniou," both in *Link* 5, no. 10 (November 1991), 8.
41 "LIL 6 Wrap-Up," *First Link* 5, no. 11 (December 1991), 6.
42 Wiseman, *SM 101*, 220–40; "Deadly Kicks," *Drummer* 56 (1982), 8; Mitch Kessler, "Breath Play Safety Rules," *Sandmutopian Guardian* 39 (2000), 60–1; and Jan Hall, "Play Safe," *The Link* July/August 2006, 1.
43 Lisa Downing, "Beyond Safety: Erotic Asphyxiation and the Limits of SM Discourse" in Darren Langdridge (ed.), *Safe, Sane, Consensual: Contemporary Perspectives Sadomasochism* (Palgrave Macmillan, 2008), 121 and Kessler, "The Appeal of Breath Control," *Sandmutopian Guardian* 39 (2000), 7.
44 Dave Rhodes, "Fire Scenes and Contestants Flambé," *Leather Journal* 61 (1994).
45 Joseph W. Bean, "Pleasure Not Panic: The Art of Welcoming Pain," *Sandmutopia Guardian* 11 (1993), 7–11 and Stein, "SM's Copernican Revolution" in Thompson, *Leatherfolk*, 154.
46 "ACT/REACT," *First Link* 3, no. 10, 2.
47 Wayne Gloege, "Editorial," *First Link* 5, no. 6 (June–July 1991), 15.
48 Mike Barnicle, "All for Knots, and Knots for All," *The Boston Globe*, 10 January 1991 and Ed Boyce, "Boston Police Raid Private S/M Club," *Gay Community News* 18, no. 26 (21–27 January 1991), 1.
49 "Police Invade Holiday Party and Harass Guests," *First Link* 5, no. 1 (January 1991), 2; "More on Thunder Head Raid," *First Link* 5, no. 3 (March 1991), 9; "Thunder Head," *First Link* 5, no. 5 (May 1991), 6; Wickie Stamps, "Boston Police Crack Down on the SM Community," *The Advocate*, 9 April 1991, 52–4; "NLA Status Report," *Living in Leather VI Program Book*, 11; Joseph Bean, "When Bashers Wear Badges," *Drummer* 147 (1991), 4 & 62; and "Wasting Our Time," *Bay Windows* 19, no. 3 (17–23 January), 2.
50 "The Thunderhead Raid," *First Link* 6, no. 8–9 (September–October), 3 and Barry Douglas, "They're Coming to Take You Away," *GMSMA Newslink*, Spring 1994, 5–7.
51 Dan Rider, "Colorado SM Leader Defeats Child Custody Challenge," *Growing Pains*, October 1987, 3.
52 Robert Dante, "The Houghton Case," *Boudoir Noir* 14, Summer–Fall 1996, 9–10 and Mitch Kessler, "Update on the Houghtons," *Sandmutopian Guardian* 27 (1996), 42–3.
53 Dante, "The Houghton Case," 10.
54 Robert D. [Dante], "SM on Trial in Houston," *Quarter Link* 6, no. 4 (May 1992) 10 & 19; "Houghton Update," *The Link*, July 1996, 3; and "Houghton Update," *The Link*, November 1997, 7
55 "Houghton Case Update," *Boudoir Noir* 16 (1997), 6–7 and "Update on the Houghtons," *Sandmutopian Guardian* 27 (1996), 42.
56 John Gallagher, "Strange Customs," *The Advocate*, 5 April 1994, 44; Ummni Khan, *Vicarious Kinks: S/M in the Socio-Legal Imaginary* (Toronto: University of Toronto Press, 2014), 205–8; Dana Collins, "'No Experts—Guaranteed!': Do-It-Yourself Sex Radicalism and the Production of the Lesbian Sex Zine Brat Attack," *Signs* 25,

no. 1 (Autumn 1999), 65–89; and "Angus Hamilton Interview," *O Magazine* 22 (1993), 45–8.

57 Barry Douglas, "State of the Organization," *GMSMA Newslink*, Fall 1990, 14; "Any Activists Out There?," *First Link* 3, no. 6 (1989), 2; "Secretary's Scribbles," *First Link* 3, no. 3 (1989), 7; and Julia Pine, "In Bizarre Fashion: The Double-Voiced Discourse of John Willie's Fetish Fantasia," *Journal of the History of Sexuality* 22, no. 1 (January 2013), 1–33.

58 Joseph Bean, "Put a splinter in the Lion's Paw," *Drummer* 151 (1991), 4.

59 Hartman, *A War for the Soul of America* (Chicago, IL: University of Chicago Press, 2015), 192–3; and Linda Williams, "Second Thoughts on *Hard Core:* American Obscenity Law and the Scapegoating of Deviance" in Pamela Church Gibson and Roma Gibson, *Dirty Looks: Women, Pornography, Power* (London: British Film Institute, 1993), 50 & 60.

60 Andrew Hartman, *A War for the Soul of America* (Chicago, IL: University of Chicago Press, 2015), 192–3.

61 Brian G. Newhouse, "Mappletorpe vs Congress: The Move to Outlaw SM Art," *GMSMA Newslink*, Winter 1989–90, 3–4; "Washington Coverage," *GMSMA News*, Winter 1988, 6; Barry Douglas, "GMSMA: The First 15 Years of Activism," circa 1995; and Jan Lyon, "Leather/SM Speaks to the Arts!," *First Link* 5: 12 (January 1992), 14.

62 Pat Califia, "Law and Order," *First Link* 5, no. 1 (January 1991), 4 and "Statement on Censorship," *First Link* 4, no. 11 (1990), 4.

63 Karen Kircher, "Interview with Susie Shepherd," *Leather Journal* 15 (1990); "Beating Jesse," *Drummer* 144 (1990), 42; Brian Baxter, "To Boycott or Not?," *GMSMA Newslink*, Fall, 1990, 28; Guy Baldwin, "Whipping Jesse: What Works and What Doesn't," *Leather Journal* 17 (no date), 9–10; and "TLC: Year with a Leather Club," http://www.coolcatdaddy.com/tlc.html (accessed 2 February 2019).

64 Jan Lyon and Susie Shepherd, "Beat Jesse," *First Link* 4, no. 8 (August 1990), 5; Lyon and Shepherd, "Beat Jesse Campaign," *First Link* 4, no. 12 (December 1990), 2; and Lyon and Shepherd, "Letter to the Editor," *Drummer* 145 (1990), 5.

65 "You are Now Illegal," *Quarter Link* 6, no. 4 (May 1992), 14; "Just Say 'No' to Bigotry," *Quarter Link* 6, no. 10 (November 1992), 14; LSM 20th Anniversary Booklet; and Bill Miranda Salzman, "A Message to the NLA Community from Mr. NLA," Living in Leather VII program (1992), 11.

66 Andrea Beckman, *Social Construction of Sexuality and Perversion* (New York: Palgrave Macmillan, 2009), 118 and Blue Blake, *Out of the Blue: Confessions of an Unlikely Porn Star* (New York: Running Press, 2009), Chapter 10.

67 Thompson, *Sadomasochism* (London: Cassell, 1994), 188–241 and W.G. [Wayne Gloege], "No Gay Witch Hunt?," *First Link* 5, no 2 (February 1991), 4.

68 "From Co-Chair Chuck Higgins," *Quarter Link* 6, no. 10 (November 1992), 15; Higgins, "NLA Spanner Defense and Education Fund," *The Link* 8, no. 1 (January/February 1994), 7; and David Smith, "House of Lords to Rule on Legality of Sadomasochism," *Gay News*, March 1992, 15.

69 Stephen, "Consent as a Defense to Assault: Sadomasochism and the Law," *Sandmutopian Guardian* 18 (1995), 8–9 and 39–40 and Bakos, *Kink*, 113–4.

70 Bakos, *Kink*, 114; Abe Bonowitz, "Amnesty International and the NLA," *Quarter-Link* 6, no. 10 (November 1992), 6–7; "From Co-Chair Chuck Higgins," *Quarter-Link* 6, no. 10 (November 1992), 15; "US Dollars Back Spanner Campaign," *The Pink Paper*, 22 July 1994, 5; and The Spanner Trust, at http://www.spannertrust.org/documents/spannerhistory.asp (accessed 8 July 2018).

71 Angus Hamilton, "Spanner Case Ends in Defeat," *Gay Times*, April 1997, 18.

72 Beckman, *Social Construction of Sexuality and Perversion*, 76–7; David Smith, "All S&M Sex Could be Illegal," *Gay Times*, January 1991, 5; "Angus Hamilton Interview," *O Magazine* 22 (1993), 48; James Cusick, "Jury Backs Right to Enjoy Bondage and Whipping," *Independent*, 30 March 1996; "Hot, Heavy, & Fun," *The Pink*

Paper, 8 September 1995, 21; and Angus Hamilton, "SM in Marriage OK," *Gay Times*, April 1996, 38.

73 Vi Johnson, "Good News," *The Link*, July 1996, 5; James Cusick, "Jury Backs Right to Enjoy Bondage and Whipping," *Independent*, 30 March 1996, at https://www.independent.co.uk/news/jury-backs-right-to-enjoy-bondage-and-whipping-1344743.html (accessed 30 June 2018); and Des de Moor, "Spanner Aftermath," *Sandmutopian Guardian* 30 (1998), 54.

74 Kenny Boudreaux, "*Drummer* Prompts a Challenge to DSM III," *Drummer* 90 (1986), 18 and Charles Kaiser, *The Gay Metropolis* (Boston, MA: Houghton Mifflin, 1997), 235–6.

75 Rubin, "Thinking Sex" in Carole S. Vance (ed.), *Pleasure and Danger: Exploring Female Sexuality* (New York: HarperCollins, 1993), 280.

76 "DSM Project," *First Link* 6, no. 2 (March 1992), 2 and Race Bannon, "The DSM Project," *QuarterLink*, Winter/Spring 1993, 21.

77 "DSM III: NLA/LIL Surveys," *The Link* 8, no. 1 (January/February 1994), 6; Bannon to DSM Project Participants, 1 June 1993, LAAM, DeBlase Papers, Box 39; Robert J. Stoller, *Pain and Passion: A Psychoanalyst Explores the World of S & M* (New York: Plenum Press, 1991), 27–9; Peggy J. Kleinplatz and Charles Moser, *Sadomasochism: Powerful Pleasures* (Binghampton, NY: Harrington Park, 2006); and Bannon, "The DSM Project," 21.

78 DSM Project, "For Immediate Release," undated mid-1994, LAAM, DeBlase Papers, Box 39; Michael Bronski, *A Queer History of America* (Boston, MA: Beacon Press, 2011), 218; Craig A. Rimmerman, *From Identity to Politics* (Philadelphia, PA: Temple University Press, 2002), 86; and Ronald Bayer, *Homosexuality and American Psychiatry: The Politics of Diagnosis* (Princeton, NJ: Princeton University Press, 1987).

79 "The DSM Project Moves On," *The Link* 8, no. 5 (November 1994), 13 and "The DSM Project," *Checkmate* 10 (February 1995), 3.

80 Abram J. Lewis, "We Are Certain of Our Own Insanity": Antipsychiatry and the Gay Liberation Movement, 1968–1980," *Journal of the History of Sexuality* 25 (January 2016), 83–113; Bannon to DSM Project Participants, 14 August 1994, LAAM, DeBlase Papers, Box 39; and "Metamorphosis: DSM to KAP," *Prometheus*, Fall 1994, 55.

81 Marshall Kirk and Hunter Madsen, *After the Ball--How America Will Conquer its Fear and Hatred of Gays in the 90s* (New York: Doubleday, 1989); Joseph Bean, "Off the Top: An Old Disease in a More Virulent Form," *Drummer* 134 (1989), 4–5; Stamps, "Trouble in Paradise," 56–8; "Michigan Women's Music Festival," *First Link* 4, no. 5 (May 1990), 9; and Pat Califia, "H.R.C.F. Letter," *First Link*, 4, no. 11 (November 1990), 9.

82 "Human Rights Campaign Fund Update," *First Link*, 5, no. 1 (January 1991), 10.

83 "Bay Area S/Mers Bottom to Mother Nature," *First Link* 3, no. 12, 2 and "Fundraising for San Francisco," *First Link* 4, no. 1 (January 1990), 3.

84 "New Coalition Building Techniques," *GMSMA Newslink*, Fall 1990, 30.

85 "New York City Leather Community Unites to Announce International SM/Leather/Fetish Celebration 1994," *The Inquisitor*, September 1993, 8 and Artemis Sliverowl, "Leather Celebration 1994," *The Link* 8, no. 3 (July 1994), 1 & 6.

86 Harold Cox, "After Stonewall 25," *Checkmate* 8 (August 1994), 2 and "Editor's Notebook: Many Preferences—One Scene," *Checkmate* 12 (August 1995), 4.

87 "Stonewall 25 Weekend," *Leather Journal* 61 (1994), 10–5 and Stein, *Living in Leather*, 96–7.

88 "Stonewall 25 Weekend," 14–5; Mark Frazier, "Thank you, New York!" *The Link* 8, no. 3 (July 1994), 10; and Califia, "Stonewall 25: Infighting among the Perverts," *Venus Infers* 2, no. 2 (June 1994), 4–11.

89 Bronski, *A Queer History of the United States*, 181 and Carol Truscott, "The First Editor of the Guardian Speaks Out," *Sandmutopian Guardian* 35 (1999), 49–50.

90 Califia, "Stonewall 25," 8.

91 Dona Minkowitz, "Tough Love," *The Advocate* 4 April 1995, 80 and "After Stonewall: Pride and Prejudice," *New York Times*, 26 June 1994, 16.
92 "Are They Crazy: Why Do People Tell All on Talk Shows?" *Cosmopolitan*, August 1992, 219; Gerrie Blum and Mitch Kessler, "Message from the Publishers," *Sandmutopian Guardian* 18 (1995), 4; and Mistress Jacqueline, *Whips and Kisses: Parting the Leather Curtain* (Buffalo, NY: Prometheus, 1991).
93 Levitt, Shelley, "The Scary Lure of Sadomasochism," *Cosmopolitan*, November 1992, 212–5; Brown, "Step into My Parlor," *Cosmopolitan*, November 1992, 14; and Andrea Raab, "Fetishes," *Self* 14, no. 4 (April 1992), 94–6.
94 Melinda Blau, "Ordinary People," *New York* 27 no. 47 (28 Nov 1994), 38–9.
95 Madonna, *Sex* (New York: Ediciones B, 1992), 18 & 21.
96 Jeffrey Weeks, *Invented Moralities: Sexual Values in an Age of Uncertainty* (New York: Columbia University Press, 1995), 28.
97 Preston, "What Happened," in Thompson, *Leatherfolk*, 214–5.
98 Pat Califia, "Are Bottoms Expected to Take Abuse in S/M Relationships?" *The Advocate*, 10 March 1992, 40 and "The Limits of the SM Relationship, or Mr. Benson Doesn't Live Here Anymore," in Mark Thompson, *Leatherfolk* (Boston, MA: Alyson, 1991), 221–32.
99 Bakos, *Kink*, xxiv & 321 and Letter to the Editor, *Drummer* 134 (1989), 7.
100 T. Weymouth, *Society of Janus: Twenty-Five Years* (San Francisco, CA: Society of Janus, 1999), 14.

6

SUCCESS AND FRAGMENTATION

The BDSM Community in the New Millennium

In 1999, the NLA's Fort Lauderdale chapter hosted Living in Leather XIV. Rather than displacing the local BDSM convention, Dungeon 401, the NLA held LIL the week afterward, creating the longest, if not the largest, BDSM event thus far: ten days of seminars, parties and other events. In his keynote address, Gay Baldwin suggested the primary mission of BDSM organizations should be winning mainstream acceptance. Madonna's book *Sex* sold upwards of 500,000 copies. BDSM appeared on cable television shows like HBO's *Real Sex* and *Sex in the City* and was used to advertise a host of products. BDSM activists, he argued, should build on this to make BDSM so socially and politically acceptable that activist organizations have nothing left to do. They should work themselves "out of a job."[1]

The BDSM community was actually closer to this achievement than Baldwin realized. Over the next few years, BDSM scenes—and even characters—appeared on popular television shows ranging from *Alias, Buffy the Vampire Slayer* and *CSI* to comedies like *Castle, Fraser, Friends* and *Will & Grace*. Miller Beer advertised at Living in Leather. Women's magazines answered readers' questions about BDSM and explained safe words. Not only had "S&M" gone mainstream, *Newsweek* suggested, but Americans liked becoming "a jaded culture of kink."[2]

More people than ever engaged in BDSM and suffered fewer consequences for doing so. Following two police raids on BDSM parties at the century's close, problems with police rapidly diminished, as did obscenity prosecutions. BDSM Businesses flourished. Yet, as BDSM gained popularity, many BDSM organizations experienced membership declines. Between people's acceptance of BDSM and the ease of finding play partners on the Internet, sadomasochists no longer needed to cruise leather bars or join BDSM organizations. They pursued their individual kinks, learned about BDSM, and found one another online. Some organizations dissolved. Many leather bars closed and most specialty BDSM magazines, including the much-revered *DungeonMaster*, folded. Its central institutions weakened, the BDSM community began fragmenting. In contrast, BDSM/fetish social media sites like CollarMe and FetLife attracted millions of members who outnumbered by orders of magnitude those who joined BDSM organizations, attended conferences like Living in Leather, or subscribed to *DungeonMaster*.

BDSM Organizations in the New Millennium

On 14 July 1998, Chicagoland Discussion Group (CDG) held its last meeting. It was just one of dozens of once active BDSM organizations that dissolved over the next decade. Almost every BDSM organization experienced membership declines, which resulted from several factors. First, and most importantly, the legal climate changed. In *Lawrence v. Texas* (2003), the Supreme Court overturned *Bowers*, which BDSM activists saw as a victory not only for gays and lesbians, but all sexual minorities. Declining prosecutions of people, organizations and businesses for BDSM activities confirmed this assumption. Second, many prominent BDSM activists either retired from active leadership positions or passed away, the latter including such luminaries as Tony DeBlase, Barry Douglas and JimEd Thompson. The cumulative loss produced a leadership crisis in many organizations. Third, even as surviving BDSM organizations emphasized fun and parties to retain and attract members, the Internet provided new ways for people to find one another. The NLA was particularly hard hit, and its leaders steadily handed off responsibilities to new organizations whose formation and growth they encouraged, most importantly the National Coalition for Sexual Freedom (NCSF), founded by Susan Wright.

A member of NLA, LSM and the New York SM Activists, Wright successfully lobbied NOW to remove the condemnation of sadomasochism from its Delineation of Lesbian Rights when revising the statement. In 1997, she founded the NCSF, which the largest BDSM organizations, Black Rose, GMSMA, NLA, TES and the Society of Janus, funded in exchange for seats on its board, The NCSF promised "to fight for sexual freedom and privacy rights for all adults who engage in safe, sane and consensual behavior." Focusing on "tolerance, privacy rights, and free speech," it became the leading advocacy group for adults engaged in "alternative sexual and relationship expressions," particularly, "SM/leather/fetish," swinging and polyamory. It received growing support from the BDSM community whose members accounted for most its officers.[3]

Declining Legal Threats

On 29 October 1999, police raided a BDSM play party hosted by San Diego's Club X at a local Masonic lodge. A former NLA chapter, Club X was a large pansexual organization. The party was their fourth of the year and 29th since their founding. They had never had problems with the police and had met with the vice squad the previous year for their Leatherfest X conference, which attracted more attendees than Living in Leather. Even though Club X posted security guards and required advance ticket purchases, police claimed the party was a public event and entered. They arrested five women and one man in the midst of BDSM scenes and charged them with "public nudity," "performing lewd acts in public" or both. Fearing another raid, Club X canceled Leatherfest XI, planned for March.[4]

The *Sandmutopian Guardian* publicized the raid, though editor Mitch Kessler suggested it was unlikely to produce a legal precedent. The BDSM community needed, he argued, something like the *Hardwick* case, which received wide publicity, was litigated by the ACLU, and heard by the Supreme Court. Unfortunately, Kessler wrote, defendants in BDSM cases, particularly when facing felony charges, usually accepted plea bargains.[5]

In this case, though, all six insisted on trial. BDSM organizations raised $20,000, fully funding their defense. Jurors, acquitted the first defendant after a four-day trial. Polled, they complained the case wasted time and resources. Deputy City Attorney Tristan Higgens-Goodall dropped the charges against the other five. Perhaps, Kessler conceded, the BDSM community could deter police harassment by fighting every case vigorously, which it did again the following year in Massachusetts. [6]

At 11pm on 8 July 2000, Attleboro, Massachusetts police forced their way into a BDSM party without a search warrant and arrested two of roughly 50 people in attendance. Like the Thunderhead raid a decade earlier, they charged host Ben Davis, for "operating a business without a license" and "keeping a house of ill fame." Davis had rented space for the party and charged attendees $25 to recoup his costs. Police also charged Davis with possessing dangerous weapons (various BDSM whips and paddles) and for "lending or selling articles for self-abuse" (a dildo, then illegal in Massachusetts). Police arrested Stefany Reed for "felony assault and battery" for spanking another woman with a wooden spoon. They confiscated guests' BDSM toys, as well as Davis's laptop from which they identified guests. Reed lost her job after her photo appeared in local papers, which covered the raid in detail, nicknaming it "Paddleboro."[7]

Police claimed they happened on the party by accident. Perhaps, party-goers suggested, the event's location across the street from police headquarters attracted attention. The New England Leather Alliance (NELA, formerly NLA New England) quickly raised $10,000 for the defense at its Fetish Fair Fleamarket, a popular weekend shopping event drawing 2,500 attendees twice a year. Among their bestsellers were bumper stickers reading "If Wooden Spoons Are Outlawed, Only Outlaws Will Have Wooden Spoons." Several people mailed wooden spoons to Attleboro police, explaining they were "surrendering their dangerous weapons."[8]

NELA and other BDSM organizations formed the Paddleboro Defense League, which hired a lawyer who argued police violated the U.S. Constitution's Fourth Amendment. "Police do not have the right to walk into any premises to essentially snoop around." Legal proceedings lasted two years, but ended in victory when the judge ruled the search illegal and dismissed charges. In sharp contrast to the 1990 Thunderhead raid, local reporters ridiculed Attleboro police for prudery and frivolous prosecution. Several championed the BDSM community's right to hold events. The *Hartford Courant* suggested Paddleboro would galvanize the BDSM community, doing "for fetishists" what Stonewall "did for the gay rights movement."[9]

After its trial, Club X worked with the Vice Squad whose new leader met with local BDSM organizations, explained the law, and encouraged them to communicate before hosting events, which they did. Boston and other BDSM organizations similarly reached out to police. Former NLA presidents Mark Frazier and Hardy Haberman produced *Out of the Darkness: The Reality of S&M* (2001), a short film explaining BDSM and "safe, sane, consensual" practice, which they mailed to police departments. Overall, BDSM organizations encountered fewer and fewer problems with law enforcement, which tended to be localized and quickly resolved. Assisted by the NCSF, for example, Baltimore-area BDSM organizations successfully challenged zoning laws classifying them as "Adult Entertainment" along with adult bookstores and strip clubs.[10]

Individual sadomasochists, though, occasionally ran into problems. Oliver Jovanovic, a Columbia University graduate student and game designer, met Jamie Rzucek, a student at Barnard College in an online chatroom. They corresponded for several months about their mutual BDSM interests and Rzucek's BDSM experiences with past boyfriends. On 22 November 1996, they met in person for a scene in which Jovanovic tied her up and dripped hot wax on her. Exactly what happened and what went wrong remains uncertain. Neither was a member of any BDSM organization and both lacked knowledge of "safe, sane, consensual" and similar norms. The two discussed their scene in emails afterward, Rzucek writing she enjoyed it. Several weeks later, though, she complained to police. Manhattan's district attorney's pressed charges. The trial judge excluded Rzucek's emails, and the jury convicted Jovanovic of assault, kidnapping and sexual assault. [11]

While the NCSF filed a brief on Jovanovic's behalf, the BDSM community otherwise remained silent. New York's BDSM organizations saw Jovanovic as an outsider who had never joined them or attended their events. Jovanovic served 20 months in jail before an appeals court overturned his sentence due to the emails' exclusion. While one judge favored upholding the assault conviction, labeling hot candle wax a "dangerous weapon," the majority held "Jovanovic had reason to believe, prior to their meeting, that they both had intended to participate in consensual, non-violent, sadomasochism." Still, they denied Jovanovic's claim that consent constituted a defense, which would have established a broad precedent. It became a textbook case of false accusation.[12]

The Jovanovic case highlighted how the Internet was changing BDSM. People with these fantasies could easily find one another without joining a BDSM group or acquainting themselves with any of the community's instructional literature or codes of conduct. Inexperience and unclear expectations were bound to cause problems. BDSM educators renewed warnings about playing with strangers, encouraging people to first meet and play in public.

Radio personality Laura Schlessinger warned about sadomasochists, cross-dressers and other deviants, and conservative organizations pressured hotels to ban BDSM. In 2002, the Southern Baptist Convention urged a boycott of Howard Johnson because its St. Louis airport hotel planned to host the sixth annual Beat Me in St. Louis conference. The American Decency Association urged a similar boycott of the Marriott chain for hosting a Leather Leadership Conference in California. The American Family Association forced the cancellation of Bondage and Beyond in Michigan by threatening to boycott Ramada Inn. A similar effort disrupted Black Rose's 2003 conference, one of the community's premier events, attracting more than 1,000 participants. Planned for the Princess Royale Hotel in Ocean City, Maryland, conservative organizations successfully lobbied city officials who threatened to revoke the hotel's liquor license, pressuring it to cancel the event. In remarkably short time, though, Black Rose's officers secured new venues in the Washington area, though their distance from one another required running shuttle busses. Facing similar pressure, Fetish in the Fall, planned for a New Orleans suburb, relocated to a new venue within the city.[13]

These efforts to deprive BDSM conferences of venues resulted from the community's greater size, the number of its local conferences—perhaps 200 in 2003—and the complacency of some conference organizers. When planning to host Living in Leather IV in 1990, Portland-area organizers wore fetish and leather attire to meet hotel staff and discussed in detail what would and would not take place at LIL. BDSM conference organizers relearned those lessons in 2003.[14]

The Michigan cancellation marked the only significant success of conservatives' boycott strategy. Events either relocated, as Black Rose did, or went on anyway, as in the case of My Vicious Valentine in Chicago, Beat Me in St. Louis, and Tribal Fire in Oklahoma City. When properly warned and prepared, large hotels resisted outside pressure. Renewed boycott threats a few years later failed as did a 2019 effort against Cleveland Leather Annual Weekend.[15] The boycott threats themselves highlighted changing legal attitudes. Most police departments no longer considered BDSM by itself a criminal issue. Paying money for sexual services or serving alcohol, though, changed matters.

Police still periodically arrested professional dominants, such as Michelene Nelson in Pennsylvania against whom prosecutors filed so many charges she faced seven years in prison for prostitution, running a house of prostitution and possession of "lewd and lascivious devices." Unable to prove she never had sex with clients, she pled guilty to lesser charges, paid a $2,500 fine, and received a year of probation. Such cases, though, were rare. Los Angeles professional dominatrix Stephanie Locke recalled the 1980s as "filled with paranoia and insecurities and police harassment," while the "1990s were great years." In one surprising case, jurors acquitted a dominatrix whose client died of a heart attack in the midst of a session.[16]

No major BDSM organization faced criminal charges after Club X. Even cases against informal BDSM play parties became rare. Sinner's Lounge, a suburban Boston BDSM club, lost its lease following publicity in local newspapers, but suffered no legal problems. Detectives cited Studio Heart, a private membership Orlando BDSM club for lacking a proper license for its staged BDSM performances. When police investigated a play party at the Diversions conference in Daytona Beach, they found nothing wrong, assured party hosts the BDSM activities they witnessed were legal, and left. They even considered citing the person who made the complaint, a belligerent hotel guest refused entry to the party. [17]

Police and courts also indicated a surprising ability to separate BDSM from criminality. In 2006, police in Paco County, Florida arrested a BDSM "lifestyle" master for prostituting his consensual slave, a fantasy from *Story of O* brought to life. After meeting online, the woman moved in with the accused, signed a 10-page slave contract, and began servicing clients he brought her. Police charged her with prostitution and him with several felony counts of "deriving proceeds from prostitution." Courts in other states similarly ignored slave contracts and other aspects of BDSM, focusing solely on legal issues.[18]

NCSF surveys in 2001 and 2008 indicated BDSM still figured in divorce cases (461 in 2001 alone). About 100 people involved in BDSM lost child custody cases, but the NCSF's reports are unclear as to the extend BDSM revelations influenced proceedings.[19] No case like that of Laura Goodwin or the Houghtons emerged in which people lost child custody solely for BDSM and turned to the community for help.

Obscenity prosecutions similarly declined. The Justice Department rarely made them a priority. Most cases focused on small producers making edgier films, particularly those challenging the "de facto ban on depictions of urination, defecation, fisting, incest, violence, and sadomasochism." Gay pornographer Michael M. Schein, for example, received an 18-month prison sentence for his water sports videos. He complained the Free Speech Coalition, established by the pornography industry to fund legal defense, ignored him.[20]

Pornography moved steadily online, which Congress sought to regulate by passing the Communications Decency Act in 1996 and updating U.S. Law Code 18, Section 2257 requiring studios to better record, particularly of performers' ages. Successive legislation and interpretation broadened 2257's mandate, provoking several failed legal challenges, including one supported by the NCSF (*Nitke v. Gonzales*, 2005). In 2005, the government's new Obscenity Prosecution Task Force applied these laws to many gay, BDSM, dating and other sexual websites. Among those convicted were filmmaker Max Hardcore, whose films were "more violent and more mean-spirited than nearly anything else on the market," and Karen Fletcher, whose "Red Rose" website offered fetish and BDSM short stories, a few of which involved underage characters. Max Hardcore served 30 months in prison for obscenity. Fletcher pled guilty to lesser charges in exchange for a $1,000 fine and probation.[21]

Numerous social and educational BDSM websites received warnings, including tribe.net. Fearing prosecution, most took down their web pages, as did many performers and small video producers, including Midori, a "fetish diva," popular BDSM educator and occasional actress. Suicidegirls.com announced it was "self-censoring materials over concerns about a possible obscenity crackdown." Having "lost the war against gays and lesbians," suggested BDSM activist Steve Sampson, "the SM community" was the "far right's" new target. Slave Girl Debbie, a member of several Los Angeles BDSM groups, warned: "First it was adult porn producers. Then BD/SM porn sites. Then online erotica sites. Then Pro-Domme sites. Then gay dating sites. Now our online communities. What's next?"[22]

Numerous commentators noted the incongruity of the Bush administration simultaneously defending its actual torture of terrorists incarcerated in Guantanamo, while prosecuting pornographers for simulated depictions of torture and consensual BDSM. Among those targeted was Insex, one of the first sites streaming BDSM films. Launched in 1997 by former college professor Brent Scott, it pioneered an unscripted, "gonzo" approach to BDSM filmmaking, which included live shows in which viewers suggested BDSM activities to enact. Scott pushed boundaries in his films, using dildos and eventually having sex with actresses himself. Fearing prosecution, which would bankrupt him, he first moved his web servers overseas, but then shut his operations down in 2006.[23]

Criminologist Andrea Beckman suggests "the contemporary exploitation of 'sexuality' as commodity has led to an apparent public tolerance" of BDSM, but this "tolerance turns out to be superficial, as old signifiers and stereotypes of 'SM' are still evoked within public discourse."[24] This was certainly the case in both government censure of BDSM websites and conservative boycotts of hotels hosting BDSM conferences. For the most part, though, BDSM organizations, events and websites simply adapted to the new legal reality. They operated more carefully, maintained proper records, constrained their content and proactively engaged with law enforcement and other relevant parties. This superficial tolerance satisfied most sadomasochists' needs, which posed a problem for BDSM organizations committed to winning greater tolerance.

The NLA's Decline

While several American BDSM organizations boasted members outside their immediate locales, only the NLA attempted to operate on an international scale. It founded chapters in Toronto, Vancouver and other Canadian cities, and led American fundraising efforts for the Spanner defendants in Britain. NLA Co-Chair Chuck Higgins travelled to Europe where he encouraged BDSM organizations to form. Yet, the NLA founded only one overseas chapter, in New South Wales, Australia. Led by Michael Primrose, it folded after a year, largely because Australians had little need for the NLA as they developed local BDSM organizations.

The NLA's overseas expansion efforts reflected its leaders' consistent optimism. Influenced by sex surveys showing widespread BDSM interest, they anticipated rapid membership growth. In the early 1990s, they established an office with paid staff, launched *Quarterlink*, an expensive glossy magazine modeled on *DungeonMaster*, and other expensive initiatives. Rather than attracting new members, they nearly bankrupted the organization, a problem compounded by an embezzling treasurer. Beginning with San Diego, several NLA chapters severed their ties and became independent. The NLA survived these crises, but financial constraints throttled its ambitions.[25]

Efforts to form a political action committee, failed due to lack of experience and funds. Initiatives to compile data on federal, state and local laws on consent and other issues relevant to BDSM activities repeatedly moved forward before collapsing due to project's scale and the lack of legally skilled volunteers. In 1999, new NLA president Spencer Bergstedt, a lawyer, declared this effort beyond the organization's means. Going forward, they would rely on and support the NCSF. [26]

As Gayle Rubin noted, "SM can be quite theatrical." People "starved of an appreciative audience often welcome the chance to enact their kinkiness on the social stage provided by an organization." The NLA provided a national stage for these theatrics, which compounded problems caused by squabbling local chapters, co-chairs with equal authority, and a cumbersome bureaucracy linking local chapters and affiliate organizations to its national leaders. When assessing the NLA's accomplishments at its tenth anniversary in 1996, Tony DeBlase complained about "administrative details, mainly involving petty feuds based upon regions, gender, orientation, or most often, personal differences in tactics, goals or even agendas," which prevented the NLA from building on its earlier successes.[27] So, too, did a high death toll among its leaders and general membership, highlighted by the deaths of founder Steve Maidhof in 1991. Between its mid-1986 founding and mid-1992, 56 NLA members died, a shockingly high number for an organization whose membership had just reached 1,000. Over the next dozen years, numerous other prominent members died, including Cookie Andrews-Hunt (1995), Leonard Dworkin (1998), Tony DeBlase (2000) and Dean Walradt (2003).[28]

The NLA restructured in the mid-1990s. It replaced co-equal co-chairs with a single president and reduced its bloated executive committees, but these changes overburdened remaining leaders who grappled with coordinating local NLA chapters and leading the BDSM community as a whole. Living in Leather attendance declined as other conferences came to rival it in the quantity and quality of celebrity speakers and ancillary events. TES organized its first conference in 1996 for its 25th anniversary. Over 1,300 people attended and it became an annual event.[29] Organizations in many other cities did the same, including NLA chapters in Dallas, Houston and Oklahoma City. New England's Fetish Fair Fleamarket proved particularly popular. The NLA was no longer unique. Its membership plunged to only 500 in 1998. Many prominent activists left, including Race Bannon who complained Living in Leather had "deteriorated," and the NLA's convoluted bureaucracy actually hindered its members' political organizing.[30]

Bannon's critique was overly harsh. No other BDSM organization played as active a role in combating domestic violence than the NLA, and the same was true of many of its other initiatives. The NLA played a central role in shaping BDSM practice and changing mainstream perceptions of BDSM. Yet, the NLA failed to respond to changes both within the BDSM community and society at large. Increasingly perceived as stodgy, it failed to attract and mentor younger leaders. Despite repeated pleas, its leadership failed to utilize the Internet or understand the changes wrought by its easy connectivity. Leonard Dworkin created the "NLA Friends" mailing list on his own, hoping it would provide a direct path for people to reach the NLA's leadership, incubate new ideas and encourage innovation. Instead, it became a forum for complaints.[31]

The NLA's Portland chapter, which hosted Living in Leather in 1996, 1997 and 1998, left the NLA in 1999. Seattle, the NLA's original chapter, departed the following year. Surprisingly low Living in Leather attendance in 1999 and 2000 left the NLA mired in debt. Its nadir came in 2001. Citing declining LIL attendance and reduced activism among its members, Spencer Bergstedt suggested the NLA had "outlived its usefulness" and moved for it to dissolve.[32]

Members rejected his motion. The NLA survived, but it lost influence and passed its missions to other organizations. After a final Living in Leather in 2002, the event went on hiatus. The NCSF assumed the NLA's legal missions. Tony DeBlase partnered with Chuck Renslow to create the Leather Archives and Museum, which became the community's official record keeper. Encouraging and nurturing BDSM activists fell to the Leather Leadership Conference. First held in 1997, it remained small. Only 200 people attended in 2015.[33]

The NLA, Tony DeBlase suggested, was "a dinosaur."[34] Unneeded, and increasingly unnoticed, its missions fulfilled or transferred, it had little unique to offer. It founded chapters in several mid-sized cities, including Colorado Springs, Colorado, Reno, Nevada, and Tulsa, Oklahoma. Members of its Domestic Violence Project remained active, and it created an annual award for BDSM writing to boost the stature of authors and offer an alternative to title contests.

Other politically active BDSM organizations experienced similar declines. Some collapsed entirely, including GMSMA. Unlike other BDSM organizations, GMSMA never hosted play parties, focusing exclusively on education and political activism. By 1999, when its membership hit 500, it had presented more than 250 workshops and demonstrations and raised over $200,000 for charities. Afterward, members drifted away. Like the NLA, its leaders were slow to see the potential of the Internet. By 2009, GMSMA lacked enough men willing "to step forward to lead the organization." Only 45 attended its last meeting.[35]

Most of New York's remaining leather bars and sex clubs also closed. The Vault, Hellfire, Spike and Manhole lost their leases due to gentrification and closed. So did J's Hangout, which hosted a few sex parties. "Wallyworld, another sex-party venue," folded in 1999 when "local party impresario Wally Wallace" died. Wallace had managed The Mineshaft and helped found LURE, "a bar dedicated to Leather, Uniforms, Rubber, Etcetera, which closed in April 2003."[36] The Eagle, with new owners and a new location, was among the few survivors. Leather Pride Night, once the highpoint of GMSMA's calendar, folded in 2015. Laura Antoniou noticed more and more people hooking up online rather than cruising bars. Part of the problem was bars themselves had changed. One could no longer "be overtly sexual" or "suck dick in a leather bar," Race Bannon explained. Paddles, which carefully policed activities and preserved its reputation as the "friendly" BDSM dungeon, also survived.[37]

The change was so noticeable Lori Selke asked: "Is SM on the Way Out?" While more people engaged in BDSM than ever before, most newcomers evinced only a casual interest. For some, sex columnist Dan Savage suggested, it was a fad, "an extreme sport" in which "participants boasted: 'Look how much I could take while that guy was beating me!'" Few newcomers were interested in activism. Then again, Gayle Rubin pointed out, "a lot of what we were fighting for, we've achieved." Joining a BDSM organization in the 1970s and early 1980s required serious commitment and dedication. In the new millennium, people had a "walk in, walk out" attitude. They tried BDSM for a while and left. While some complained casual newcomers were "diluting" the BDSM community and draining its energy, many older sadomasochists were weary from constant activism. As one woman commented: "This is my fun. I just want to spank butts. I don't want to weight it down." John Preston once argued there was no place for politics in "sacred, sexual space." A decade later, growing numbers of sadomasochists agreed.[38]

As threats to the BDSM community receded, its members focused on their own pleasure, fueling the return of dedicated BDSM play spaces at decade's end. By 2010, many large cities had public dungeons or other readily available BDSM play spaces, such as the Crucible in Washington, DC, or Seattle's Wet Spot. Not only larger than the Vault and other 1980s New York clubs, they were cleaner, better maintained and more lavishly equipped. Some BDSM organizations, such as Impact in Memphis, Tennessee or Sanctuary in Denver, Colorado, focused entirely on maintaining lavishly equipped multi-room dungeons for their members.

The membership declines of BDSM organizations coincided with diminishing sales of BDSM magazines, particularly those focused on education, activism and community building. As circulation fell, *Metropolitan Slave, Venus Infers, Brat Attack, Black Leather in Color, Body Play, Whap!, Equus Eroticus*, and *Kinky People, Places, and Things* ceased publication. DeBlase sold off his magazines in 1995, and the new owners struggled without DeBlase's deep connections to all corners of the BDSM community. *Drummer* ceased publication in April 1999, quickly followed by *Checkmate*, which had absorbed *DungeonMaster*. The *Sandmutopia Guardian* folded the following year. *Boudoir Noir* went on hiatus in 1999, published one last issue in 2001, and closed. European fetish fashion magazines, such as *Skin Two*, survived slightly longer, but also went under. After 2000, most people found BDSM information on the Internet rather than the pages of a magazine or the events of a local BDSM organization.

Contact magazines, which flourished into the 1990s and spawned such specialty publications as *Domination Directory International*, dedicated solely to promoting professional dominants, also disappeared. So, too, did the phone sex lines whose ads supported many sex magazines. Carter Stevens' *S&M News* sold from 21,000 to 28,000 quarterly issues on newsstands in the mid-1990s. While it had always included a few articles, erotic stories and pictorials, readers bought it for the contact ads. As professional dominants shifted their advertising to the Internet, profits plunged. Stevens pulled the plug to focus on video production.[39]

Rather than revitalizing the BDSM community with new members, growing mainstream acceptance and interest in BDSM coincided with declining circulation of BDSM specialty publications and membership losses in once central BDSM organizations. Most BDSM organizations abandoned their political activities and many reduced their educational programming as well, becoming primarily social organizations. Some of these, called "munches," simply announced gatherings at casual restaurants where attendees discussed BDSM in a relaxed environment with no visible fetish clothing, BDSM toys or organizational structure. Gerrie Blum had organized similar informal BDSM gatherings at her favorite casual New York restaurant in the 1980s, but the Internet made them easier to arrange and publicize.

The pathologization of BDSM, police harassment and other external pressures helped unite the BDSM community and encouraged its activism. In their absence, the community fractured back into smaller groups based on gender, orientation and fetish interest. Growing numbers of sadomasochists did not join formal organizations at all. Why bother when they could find play partners on the Internet?

The Internet

People quickly adapt new technologies to sex. The proliferation of personal computers and modems in the 1980s allowed fetishists, sadomasochists and other minority sexualities to extend their networks online. Many chatted on local bulletin boards. The more technologically sophisticated participated in FidoNet or similar networks, which linked local computer bulletin boards by storing each day's messages and forwarding them after midnight, when phone rates dropped. These systems networked local hosts across the United States and into other countries. Among them was SOBNET (Sexually Oriented Board Network), which focused mostly on swingers, but contained forums for BDSM discussion. By the mid-1980s, a few hundred sadomasochists talked to each other on SOBNET and shared experiences.

Gloria Brame, an active member on SOBNET, founded the BDSM support group Variations II on Compuserve in 1988. Then one of the most popular online services offering chat, discussion and messaging, Compuserve reached a large audience. BDSM chat areas soon sprang up on America Online, its leading rival. As the Internet became more accessible, sadomasochists gravitated to

Usenet discussion forums, including soc.subculture.bondage-bdsm and alt.sex. bondage, which by mid-1994 had "around 30 new topics and responses" each day. Some people discussed their relationships and reminisced about favorite BDSM experiences; others posted fantasies and erotic stories. Many asked questions, such as "How long can I safely leave clothespins on a friend's nipples?"[40] As people answered, alt.sex.bondage amassed a wealth of practical advice to which several leading BDSM educators contributed, including Laura Antoniou, Janet Hardy, David Stein, John Warren and Jay Wiseman. Participants debated a host of topics, including terminology, and it was from these conversations, which hearkened back to earlier Society of Janus debates, the term BDSM emerged.

David Allyn suggests relatively few couples actually engaged in swinging in the 1970s, and their number likely dropped in the 1980s. The Internet, though, reinvigorated swinging by making it "possible to locate thousands of couples with open marriages within a few seconds."[41] It similarly facilitated BDSM contacts as dedicated BDSM social networking sites emerged, including Alt.com, Bondage.com, CollarMe and FetLife. Founded in 2008 in Vancouver, British Columbia, FetLife became the most popular of them. It had 1.7 million users by 2013, 3.5 million in 2015, and almost 9 million in 2020. Even if only one percent of these users are active, they exceed by several-fold the combined membership totals of every BDSM organization in the United States, most of which have only a few dozen members. The Internet became the place sadomasochists found "someone to tell" and to meet for one-on-one BDSM activity.

Smaller sites devoted to particular BDSM interests also flourished, including The Slave Register (TSR), which allowed would-be slaves to register for official slave numbers, the most dedicated of whom had them tattooed on their bodies. TSR encouraged discussion of fulltime BDSM relationships, often called Master/Slave (or Master/slave) relationships. These varied greatly among couples, many of whom negotiated and signed detailed "slave contracts" specifying each partner's rights and responsibilities. In the strictest of these—at least as idealized by the participants—"the Master assumes total responsibility for the slave, and the slave offers total obedience and surrender."[42] Pursuit of this idealized BDSM relationship spawned a new organization, Masters and slaves Together (MAsT). While founded in 1987, MAsT did not experience significant growth until the late 1990s. It hosted its first conference in 1999, established chapters in several cities, and created an International Master/slave Contest.

The easy connectivity of services like FetLife is not without problems. Users complain of increasing censorship by site owners and users' predatory behavior. When FetLife members posted names of problem tops who pushed partners beyond agreed limits and ignored safe words, FetLife administrators removed their posts—even if they only revealed offenders' screen names. This ignited debates over the ethics of publicly accusing people and how to keep BDSM interactions safe.[43]

Part of the problem, Autumn Lokerson suggested, was that many BDSM newcomers, inspired by *Fifty Shades of Grey* and its ilk, jumped into the scene despite knowing nothing about it, particularly the norms of "safe, sane, consensual" interaction. FetLife not only failed to protect newcomers, but created "a false sense of safety in the community—primarily, by preventing identification of abusive members." "If I were a psychopath and looking for victims," she warned, FetLife would be "a great place to start."[44]

As complaints escalated, several people chronicled the growing problem, particularly Kitty Stryker, a model and blogger, who discussed her own experiences with tops who pressured her against using safe words and into activities she did not want, inflicting more pain than she desired because she "developed a fear of safewording, since it was so rarely treated with respect." Other women reported similar incidents with partners met online, which a 2014 NCSF survey confirmed. A third of respondents indicated their "pre-negotiated limit had been violated and/or their safeword was ignored during a BDSM encounter."[45]

Fearing litigation, credit card issuers and other FetLife business partners demanded change. In July 2017, FetLife deleted a host of content and message forums and banned discussion of alcohol and drug use, "race play or anything that might be construed as hate speech," scenes "causing permanent bodily harm," and those "depicting consensual non-consent, such as simulated rape or abduction." Stryker, amazed to be "on the side of capitalism," praised the action. "Perhaps if they had done as I had suggested years ago and self-policed the hate speech and harassment, this wouldn't have happened." FetLife, though, also maintained its ban on reporting consent violators.[46]

The tremendous number of sadomasochists interacting on the Internet limited the ability of any organization to keep people safe or speak for the BDSM community as a whole. Some FetLife users demanded protection; others reacted in anger against censorship and efforts to police conduct. Several dozen reacted angrily when they discovered the NLA's 20-year-old campaign against domestic violence, which they denounced for ruining their fun.

Frustrated users took matters into their own hands and created their own software application, the Predator Alert Tool for FetLife (formerly the FetLife Alleged Abusers Database Engine). It includes a database of allegations against FetLife members, scans users' profile pictures against the United States Sex Offender Registry and highlights user profiles with alleged consent violations. The need to keep people safe in an era without recognized authorities or any way to socialize the majority of BDSM newcomers forced a return to the policing by gossip common in the 1970s.

Acceptance

In 2001, popular television crime drama *CSI* introduced Lady Heather, an attractive, intellectually sophisticated professional dominatrix who became a recurring character, foil and sometime love interest of protagonist Gil Grissom. Afterward, dominatrices proliferated across television and movies, including Jennifer Garner in an *Alias* episode (2002), Kristen Bell in *Reefer Madness: The*

Musical (2005), Angelina Jolie in *Mr. and Mrs. Smith* (2005) and Eliza Dushku in a *Dollhouse* episode (2009). *Castle, Desperate Housewives, House* and other prime-time shows offered dominatrix episodes. British television show *Sherlock* even reimagined Holmes nemesis Irene Adler as a dominatrix. Patricia Payne offered "Sex Tips from a Dominatrix" (1999), and Ava Taurel, New York's best-known dominatrix, taught how to "Become a Dominatrix: For Fun, Love, or Profit" at the Learning Annex.[47]

BDSM returned to mainstream adult movies. John Stagliano's high-budget *Fashionistas* (2002) featured several BDSM scenes, appearances by BDSM community members and penetrative sex of every variety. It won a record 22 Adult Video News awards. Established BDSM filmmakers, in turn, introduced more sex into their films, including industry-leader GwenMedia. Its films continued to showcase all-female casts headlined Isabella Sinclair, expensive fetish costuming, and elaborate bondage, but added short scenes of penetration. Kink.com, a prolific producer of streaming fetish and BDSM films, similarly added more and more sex to its films, often exceeding the time devoted to BDSM activities.

Steven Shainberg developed a Mary Gaitskill short story into *Secretary* (2002), the first mainstream movie about BDSM to win critical praise and wide appreciation within the BDSM community. It offers a sympathetic portrayal of lawyer E. Edward Grey (James Spader) and secretary Lee Holloway (Maggie Gyllenhaal) who haltingly explore their BDSM interests. Troubled by guilt over his BDSM interests, Grey ends the relationship, driving Holloway to learn more about BDSM, contact the BDSM community, and save their relationship by seizing the initiative. After accepting her BDSM interests, she forces Grey to do the same. While the film avoids BDSM jargon like "safe, sane, consensual," it nonetheless portrays them in its final scenes. As Margot Weiss points out, rather than presenting BDSM as "real, raw, and dirty," something that challenges and disrupts established sexual boundaries, the film normalizes BDSM. Grey and Holloway marry and become a happy, outwardly normal, suburban couple.[48] This, perhaps, is why so many in the BDSM community liked it. They were tired of being portrayed as freaks.

BDSM appeared across television networks. *Family Guy, Friends* and *Private Practice* featured BDSM scenes or discussions of kinky sex. *Dharma & Greg* advised viewers: "Handcuff a guy to the bed and stick a ball gag in his mouth, and he's going to try harder."[49] *Buffy the Vampire Slayer* (1997–2003) reveled in BDSM subtext, offering such lines as "everyone's getting spanked but me."[50] Cable stations presented BDSM relationships spanning several episodes in *Billions, Californication* and *Transparent*. An episode of *Sex and the City* featured a BDSM restaurant, reflecting the emergence of restaurants and coffee shops, such as Seattle's Beyond the Edge Café, catering to BDSM folks. "Hush," an episode of *CSI: New York*, drew from casual perusals of House of Gord, which produced streaming videos featuring women in elaborate fetish costumes displayed and/or penetrated by mechanical devices reminiscent of Irving Klaw's illustrated books. Site owner Jeff Gord, who described his films as "forniphilia," was "disgusted and appalled" by its appropriation. He worried "vanillas" would "judge us by crap like this." Newcomers might jump right into dangerous play.[51]

In a 2001 episode of *Will & Grace*, a couple hires Grace to convert their home dungeon into a nursery. Building elaborate home dungeons was hardly new for BDSM cognoscenti. *DungeonMaster* and *Sandmutopia Guardian* regularly featured "Better Homes and Dungeons." Unlike Grace's clients, though, people stopped hiding them. Some touted them as features when selling their homes—even in such out-of-the-way (and presumably conservative) towns as Van Buren, Arkansas. Its owners were "convinced there's an underserved real estate market for couples who want a spicy space where they can connect." A Philadelphia couple, who first offered their home for sale, complete with dungeon, found it more profitable to rent out the dungeon. Others did the same, offering their dungeons on Airbnb, as did several bed and breakfasts.[52]

Sadomasochists had long claimed intense BDSM play produced altered states of consciousness. Nicknamed "sub space," they compared it to the "high" experienced by long-distance runners. *Runner's World* columnist Peter Sagal similarly compared the two, suggested "pain brings joy," and implied a dominatrix would improve his marathon training. Running podcaster Eric Schranz did Sagal one better by finding and interviewing a dominatrix who not only trained running clients, but ran ultramarathons herself.[53]

College campuses reflected this growing interest in BDSM with both increasing scholarship on BDSM and the formation of student BDSM organizations. In 1994, Columbia University students formed Conversio Virium (power exchange in Latin) and applied to be an official student organization. Refused recognition, then certified, and then decertified, the students appealed their case. Citing traditional protections of free speech, they received certification the following year. While Conversio prohibited BDSM play at on-campus gathering, it did host workshops and occasional BDSM demonstrations. Its success inspired students at several State University of New York campuses to host BDSM seminars, which Governor George Pataki condemned as inappropriate "expenditures of tax dollars." It was, *Newsweek* noted, "a rare note of complaint against creeping kink."[54]

Other college students followed suit. By 2017, roughly two-dozen BDSM organizations operated on US college campuses, including University of Chicago's Risk-Aware Consensual Kink, Cuffs at Iowa State University, the Harvard College Munch, Alternative Lifestyle Association at Washington University in St. Louis, KUFF at University of California, Santa Barbara, and the Kink Club at Berkeley. They mirrored other BDSM organizations by embracing "safe, sane, consensual," presenting educational seminars, and working to normalize BDSM. By emphasizing community building, safety and privacy, they positioned "kink as an identity, not simply a set of practices," and aligned themselves with campus LGBTQ organizations. Appeals for tolerance and free speech won over university officials. Faculty at the University of New Mexico, though, proved less tolerant after discovering a tenured colleague moonlighting as "Mistress Jade" for a domination service at which several graduate students also worked. Similarly, a University of Virginia vice chancellor was forced to resign following discovery of his CollarMe and FetLife profiles, ads seeking submissive women, and photos of his home dungeon.[55]

For the most part, though, tolerance was the order of the day. In 2002, Jack McGeorge, a retired US Marine and chemical weapons expert who managed his own security firm, volunteered to work as a United Nations weapons inspector in Iraq. An early member of Black Rose, McGeorge also wrote a guidebook for Master/slave relationships. Despite conservative protests about McGeorge's sexuality and negative *Washington Post* articles, Hans Blix, who led the United Nations Monitoring, Verification and Inspection Commission, dispatched McGeorge to Iraq.[56] For the most part, no one cared, which McGeorge apparently anticipated. He was one of a growing number of people who used his real name within the BDSM community and made no effort to separate his BDSM activities from his business identity. Another is Shanna Germain, who writes both role-playing games and BDSM handbooks. Most sadomasochists, though, remained at least "partly closeted."[57]

Published in 2011, E.L. James' *Fifty Shades of Grey* benefitted from this new fascination and familiarity with BDSM, becoming the decade's best-selling novel. Its surprise success puzzled critics and annoyed the BDSM community. Its leading members condemned protagonist Christian Grey as "an abuser" and pointed out James evinced no personal BDSM experience. Far from a "consensual BDSM practitioner," billionaire Grey manipulates Anastasia Steele, a naïve and sexually inexperienced recent college graduate, distracting her with lavish gifts while extending their BDSM interactions far outside his "Red Room of Pain." Steele's consent results from bribery, coercion and emotional blackmail rather than the informed, egalitarian negotiation the BDSM community expected.[58] Grey is an abusive, consumerist version of Mr. Benson. He pushes Steele beyond limits he never allows her to properly discuss, while manipulating her into signing a slave contract (and a nondisclosure agreement). His conduct epitomized what Kitty Stryker experienced at the hands of predatory tops.

The novel's popularity encouraged new discussions of consent within the BDSM community. The question, as Meg-John Barker points out, is whether consent is a sadomasochist's individual responsibility or the BDSM community's collective responsibility.[59] The latter, of course, is what the members of GMSMA, Janus, NLA, TES and numerous other BDSM organizations worked toward. As Pat Bond noted, efforts to root out abusers and troublemakers were often effective within small groups, but rules proved difficult to enforce as organizations grew larger. As BDSM became more popular, more people tried it without joining a BDSM organization, being socialized by it, and learning its norms of consent and negotiation.

Stryker launched a "Consent Culture" project to focus attention not only on outright consent violations, such as ignoring safe words, but how real-life versions of Christian Grey gained consent through manipulation or coercion, and silenced complaints about their behavior. It was to call attention to this problem that for many years Janus members favored the phrase "consensual, non-exploitative, and safe D/S." While important, Stryker's Consent Culture project gained little traction outside of established BDSM organizations, which already discussed these problems.

Fifty Shades' extraordinary popularity overwhelmed its critics and helped make erotica and sexual pleasure socially acceptable conversation topics. Even before the 2015 film, so many products referenced the novel *Bloomberg Businessweek* described a "'Fifty Shades of Grey Stimulus." Sales boomed as readers attempted "to replicate the characters' intricate bedroom scenes." The Adult Entertainment Expo encouraged retailers to capitalize on *Fifty Shades* by hosting BDSM workshops for newcomers. Makers of entry-level BDSM gear experienced as much as 50 percent sales growth. New firms entered the business and old ones diversified their offerings. Viktor, founder of New York BDSM support group DomSub-Friends, reported "one out of five people" coming to their events were inspired to explore BDSM by *Fifty Shades*. For a time, older members sported t-shirts reading: "I was into BDSM before Fifty Shades of Grey."[60]

Fifty Shades sold in excess of 100 million copies, spawned two sequels and encouraged dozens of other writers to pen BDSM-themed billionaire romances. Its success called into question BDSM's perversity. How could activities enjoyed by millions and read and fantasized about by tens of millions be perverse?

Indeed, social scientists increasingly questioned BDSM's perversity. Ten percent of *Psychology Today* readers, Marianne Apostolides suggested, experimented with BDSM. Many enjoyed it; some needed it. "S & M play" could help someone "fully connect with her sexual self in a way that has been difficult during traditional sex."[61] In 2000, the American Psychiatric Association (APA) formed work groups to consider revising the DSM for its fifth edition, particularly its discussion of paraphilias like BDSM.

The NCSF lobbied the APA to depathologize BDSM. Susan Wright contacted APA members, including Richard Krueger who led the Sexual and Gender Identity Disorders Work Group. She explained BDSM, answered questions, shared NCSF data and chronicled the discrimination and legal problems sadomasochists encountered. A petition to depathologize BDSM circulated among medical professionals gathered 3,000 signatures, among them Charles Moser and Peggy Kleinplatz who advocated normalizing most paraphilias. No clinical evidence existed, they argued, to support "equating particular sexual interests with psychopathology." Engaging in "atypical, culturally forbidden, or religiously proscribed" sexual activities did not necessarily make one mentally ill. Pamela Connolly found BDSM practitioners no more likely to suffer from depression or other "clinical disorders" than the general population. Three decades of sociological studies, Thomas D. Weinberg concluded, "showed SM practitioners to be psychologically and socially well-adjusted and functional."[62]

Krueger, though, argued for retaining the "Sexual Masochism" and "Sexual Sadism" diagnoses with minimal changes. They were needed, he said, to promote research and because of the "very small number of cases where masochistic fantasy and behavior result in severe harm or even death," particularly in breath play. While he recognized the "concerns of those in the S & M community regarding the misuse of the DSM to diagnose them," this could be addressed by "strengthening caveats circumscribing the application of the DSM."[63]

The debate ended in compromise. DSM-5 changed how it characterized paraphilias, defining them as "intense and persistent sexual interest other than sexual interest in genital stimulation or preparatory fondling with phenotypically normal, physically mature, consenting human partners." Paraphilias like sexual masochism or sadism could be diagnosed as either "benign interests" or "harmful disorders." Simply exhibiting paraphilias did "not necessarily justify or require clinical intervention." Only paraphilias causing "distress or impairment to the individual" or "whose satisfaction has entailed personal harm, or risk of harm to others" required clinical intervention.[64]

While NCSF engagement with APA members influenced their proceedings, the extent of this influence is unclear. Long before DSM-5 workgroups formed, many APA members favored depathologizing non-normative sexuality. As Edward Shorter notes, the various editions of DSM have always reflected contemporary cultural values. As these changed, so did the DSM. The APA's debates over BDSM reflected growing awareness of its acceptance (and apparent popularity) and questioned "the role of psychiatrists as society's moral gatekeepers." While Shorter suggested it was "time for psychiatry to bow out of the bedroom," the APA was unwilling to go that far and debates over BDSM continued.[65]

Legal scholar Ummni Khan agreed DSM-5 showed progress by "recognizing that a paraphilia is not in and of itself a disorder," but it still perpetuated "an essentialist viewpoint on sexuality, in its focus on genitals and preparation for intercourse as the signs of normalcy." She chronicled numerous studies in which "BDSM practitioners scored within normal ranges" and saw DSM-5's diagnoses of sexual sadism and masochism as "arbitrary, unjustly pathologizing," and "forensically problematic."[66]

Despite Khan's concerns, the NCSF celebrated DSM-5 as an important victory. Three percent of respondents to a 1998 NCSF survey lost custody of a child due to revelation of their BDSM activities. DSM-5, Wright reported, changed that. Despite its problematic language, the NCSF deployed it in several cases, successfully challenging the idea people who engaged in BDSM were necessarily bad parents.[67]

More Americans than ever, *Time* magazine reported, "experimented with sadomasochistic sex,"[68] as did marketing agencies, which released BDSM-themed television commercials. GwenMedia star Isabella Sinclair cracked her whip in a "Wonderful Pistachios" commercial, while comedian Kristen Schall joked about the pain of high-priced cell phone service in a T-Mobile spot. Cable television technicians and other trades people encountered BDSM paraphernalia in people's homes, including a caged man in a dominatrix's basement.[69] While some sadomasochists reported harassment and discrimination, others, like McGeorge, continued their careers unphased. Police raids became rare. Pressuring hotels to ban BDSM conferences failed. In 2005, the NGLTF even recognized the important role played by BDSM organizations in the LGBTQ rights struggle by creating a Leather Leadership Award to underline its commitment to an "inclusive community." Its leaders rejecting the idea "we will get ahead faster if we leave out, leave behind, or distance ourselves from those individuals and groups within our own community who might make those in power uncomfortable." Recipients of the annual award include Tony DeBlase, Dave Rhodes, Chuck Renslow, Guy Baldwin, Viola Johnson, Race Bannon and other BDSM luminaries.[70] The BDSM community finally had the recognition for which Barry Douglas, GMSMA, and so many other people and organizations had fought.

Fragmentation

As BDSM gained acceptance, the BDSM community fragmented. Mike Miksche complained leather bars lost their "overt sadomasochistic edge." Rather than gathering places for "rough personas, serious and perverse," New York's remaining bars were mostly "about dressing-up." Tony DeBlase meant the leather pride flag to symbolize a united BDSM/leather/fetish community, but following his death growing numbers of subgroups promoted their own flags and symbols, including Master/slave relationships, BDSM, rope bondage, puppy play and others. The BDSM community's unity, Pat Califia noted, was mostly "an illusion" created "by not talking about the differences between straight, gay, bi, women, men, white people, other people." By the late 1990s, it was "starting to wear pretty thin." After 2000, it fractured.[71]

By 2015, Laura Antoniou found the BDSM community "Balkanized," fractured into "tiny, discrete subcultures" with their own titles, "special language," and conferences, including Shibaricon, devoted to rope bondage, and the Master/slave Conference, one of several regional conferences devoted to fulltime BDSM relationships, which grew in popularity. Perhaps, Antoniou suggested, Fetlife and similar social media sites encouraged people to limit their interactions to those who share their interests.[72] Local BDSM conferences reflected their local communities, while specialty conferences focused on narrow subsets of the BDSM community. No national event took the place of Living in Leather as a forum bringing together diverse BDSM constituencies.

The community's Balkanization, decline of major BDSM organizations, and demise of BDSM technical magazines opened the door for people to challenge norms of conduct established over the last generation, including the much-revered phrase "safe, sane, consensual." From its origin, "safe, sane, consensual" had critics, said to include a woman at the 1987 March on Washington who amended her Leather Contingent "safe, sane, consensual" t-shirt to read "unsafe, insane, nonconsensual." While members of the BDSM community debated the precise definitions and boundaries of "safe, sane, consensual," the phrase itself proved useful and achieved near universal acceptance by the early 1990s. Disputes over the phrase—or its interpretation—increased over time, sometimes provoked by dungeon monitors or others troubled by heavy scenes or edge play at BDSM parties. One Chicago couple, Phantom and Femcar, engaged in such extreme humiliation scenes that dungeon monitors routinely broke up their fun. In response, they arranged to present humiliation demonstrations at major BDSM conferences, winning themselves a willing audience and uninterrupted play.[73]

Increasingly ridiculed as the "SSC Police," problems caused by overzealous dungeon monitors and community members encouraged alternatives to "safe, sane, consensual." In 1999, TES member Gary Switch introduced the most popular of these, "Risk Aware Consensual Kink." As Switch noted, "safe" and "sane" were very subjective terms. Heavy BDSM play inherently involves some risk, so why not acknowledge that? His phrase gained adherents as BDSM organizations promoting "safe, sane, consensual" lost influence, and the BDSM technical publications, which popularized it, ceased publication. Various other suggestions circulated, such as "Caring, Communication, Consent, and Caution," but only RACK garnered significant support. [74]

As philosopher Morten Nielson points out, SSC and RACK "express the same basic points," emphasize consent, and aim to provide "a sound moral framework for BDSM practices."[75] Nonetheless, their interpretation and use differ. Switch later explained RACK was deliberately confrontational. It implied a greater distinction with SSC than exists, one novelist Tiffany Reisz took to heart, explaining

> SSC is tamer. It's for the moms and dads in the suburbs with the furry handcuffs under the bed. RACK is for people more like us . . . People who do the rougher stuff, edge-play, no safe words, et cetera.

In other words, SSC was for newcomers and occasional sadomasochists, while the more experienced adhered to RACK.[76]

In practice, SSC remains the more popular term, which BDSM activists still use when explaining BDSM to outsiders. RACK is used much less frequently and only within the BDSM community. Switch's challenge to the notion of a single, unitary standard of BDSM behavior succeeded, in part, because the Internet allowed him to promote his ideas, bypassing magazine editors, convention organizers and other gatekeepers. RACK's popularity as a phrase also reflected a BDSM community with less to fear from outsiders and more willing to discuss exactly what they did in their dungeons.

Similarly, discussion of once taboo topics increased dramatically, including breath play, "consensual non-consent" scenes, and other types of edge play raised in the infamous "Death Workshop." The most dramatic of these—and certainly the one most noticed by academics—is race play.[77] These scenes involve using racial epithets, generally in a context of racism and racial power disparities, such as plantation slavery or a white police officer harassing a black suspect. They eroticize racial difference, which intensifies a scene's power dynamics. Sometimes they mirror historical disparities of power, but other times they reverse them as "revenge" fantasies, a topic alluded to in Antoniou's Marketplace novels.

As growing numbers of African Americans joined the BDSM community, some restricted their play to fellow people of color. Others played with—and submitted to—whites, often provoking comment and controversy, a topic explored in D. Alexandria's story "The First."[78]

Race play was not new. In previous decades, though, it was rarely discussed and generally done in private rather than at BDSM clubs or events. Living in Leather never offered race play seminars. While a few pornographic magazines featured black dominatrices, none of the best-known BDSM technical magazines published articles on race play. It was the most taboo of taboo topics, one broached only tentatively by *Black Leather in Color* in the mid-1990s.

While active in the BDSM community from its earliest days, African Americans remained marginalized within it. Mufasa Ali rarely saw other men of color in leather bars, or gay bars, in general. Writers in *Black Leather in Color* repeatedly pointed this out and explained the high cost of participation, be it clothing or conference fees, excluded many members of minority communities. Presenters at BDSM events often overlooked people of color in their talks. Even in workshops on flagellation, TES board member Guy deBrownsville noted, little was said "about the difference between white and black skin in terms of how it reacts." Presenters "talk about 'shades of red'" or other descriptors "that should be—but seldom are—modified when dealing with darker people." Caning for example, raises bright red welts on white skin, but pale welts on dark skin. Judging when "dark skin has been excessively flogged," Ali warned, can be difficult. Many in the community fetishized black bodies and people regularly approached deBrownsville expecting him to fulfill racial fantasies. Tensions over class and race tore apart Lesborados, the only Washington BDSM group for lesbian and bisexual women.[79]

Several friends of *Black Leather in Color* editor Antoinette dropped out of the BDSM community because others—black and white—declared their race play fantasies "unacceptable." Viola Johnson was almost unique in defending race play in the 1990s. Noting the hypocrisy of a community that accepted ideas of master/slave relationships and role-play, but ignored their "racial origin," she presented "racial or ethnic games" as just another kink, "an eroticized fantasy," in which she, a submissive African American woman, "can have it any way I want." Echoing Graylin Thornton, one of the few black titleholders, she proclaimed: "no longer is slavery an issue of pigmentation, but a matter of self-fulfillment. The brutality of the chains of the past are broken and replaced by the deepest forms of eroticism and respect." Johnson's article, though, attracted little attention outside *Black Leather's* readership.[80]

South Plains Leather Fest 2003 and TES Fest 2004 were among first BDSM conferences to present race play workshops. Mike Bond, a submissive, African American man promoted his forthcoming TES workshop as "Nigger Play: Free at Last!" Both content and title provoked controversy. Retitled, Bond presented his workshop at TES Fest with three white women to whom he enjoyed submitting. A prolonged discussion concluded with a demonstration in which a woman "planted in the audience heckled Bond," grabbed him and threw him down, and yelled at him. Some in the audience found it hot; others not so much. The thrill of transcending taboos, black top David Column explained, enhanced race play's erotic appeal. Why, he asked, was using the N-word in a scene was off limits, when calling women sluts and similar terms was routine BDSM role-play?[81]

These controversies discouraged discussions of race play until Mollena Williams raised its visibility by launching her blog, "The Perverted Negress" in 2007. Then living in San Francisco, she encountered few other black women at BDSM events. So, she played with white men and discovered this made many people uncomfortable. As Williams points out, the racial dynamic is unavoidable. Even without overt role-play and humiliation, the minute she submits to a white man in a public BDSM scene, race play has begun.[82]

Williams worked to carve out an acceptable place for race play while highlighting the BDSM community's continuing tensions over race. She is particularly fond of pointing out the historic origins of the slave auctions popular as BDSM fundraisers. Lauded for her efforts, Williams won International Ms. Leather 2010 and afterward presented workshops on race play at diverse venues, though she found the experience "nerve-wracking," never knowing how an audience will react. As she notes, it is "a struggle to say, 'This is genuinely who I am.'" Heavy race play makes others uncomfortable, but turns her on. "To say I can't play my personal psychodrama out just because I'm black," she argues, is itself racist. Her work again demonstrates how people could use the Internet to bypass traditional gatekeepers and challenge the BDSM community. Perhaps Rihanna's 2010 hit song "S&M," which describes bondage and flagellation, explains "pain is for pleasure," and proclaims "chains and whips excite me," helped Williams make her case.[83]

The BDSM community's carefully nurtured unity fragmented as magazines ceased publication and important institutions faded from prominence. In Boston, Tim Davis saw many organizations disintegrate from "internal personal differences or a lack of sustained volunteer support." Others pointed to losses from AIDS or the burn out of many long-term activists. The most important factor, though, was the Internet, which displaced "clubs as the main way to meet others."[84] No matter what other missions they embraced, BDSM organizations were fundamentally about connecting people. Sadomasochists no longer needed them to connect.

Guy Baldwin, an early proponent of mixed gender and orientation organizations, symbolized by his 1989 victory as Mr. NLA, reversed his position in the new millennium. Like Daniel Harris, who suggested "the consolidation of homosexuality through mass culture" would dissolve a gay "sense of collective identity," Baldwin worried gay sadomasochists lost something vital when primarily associating in pansexual organizations. Speaking to the NLA on its 25th anniversary, he argued against pansexuality. It was time for gay men to "go home, to each other, and to look after our own" in gay-only organizations.[85] More and more sadomasochists did just that, retreating into smaller groupings based on gender, orientation and fetish interest. While dozens of large BDSM conferences were held every year, none took the place of Living in Leather for bringing together the BDSM community's diverse elements in an environment fostering shared learning, mutual respect, and political unity and activism.

★★★

BDSM became increasingly commonplace in the twenty-first century, "so common-place, so banal," *Newsweek* noted, it was "used to sell beer."[86] *Fifty Shades'* success underlined BDSM's transition from taboo to "just another alternative lifestyle." More Americans knew more about BDSM than ever before. Paradoxically, this knowledge diminished the importance of BDSM organizations, publications and other institutions, which had shaped BDSM around a coherent set of behaviors and expectations exemplified by "safe, sane, consensual." Yet, *Fifty Shades of Grey*, the most popular sadomasochistic book since *Story of O*, showcased an exploitative relationship, outraging leading members of the BDSM community whose influence had so diminished few outsiders sought their opinions.

Surviving BDSM organizations depoliticized, shifting from fighting for their rights to party, to simply organizing parties for their members. As once central BDSM institutions faded away, some sadomasochists worried what they had lost. Complaints about inappropriate behavior and scenes gone wrong increased. New institutions like Fetlife, which connected and engaged millions, refused to establish or maintain standards of behavior. Apart from the NCSF, narrowly focused on legal action, FetLife members had few institutions to help them, and even fewer with any influence. Sadomasochists were better connected than ever before, but also more isolated with few places to turn for help.

Notes

1 "Guy Baldwin Addresses the NLA Convention," *The Link*, Jan–Mar 2000, 1 & 10–11.
2 Irma Kurtz, "Punishing Thoughts," *Cosmopolitan*, December 1999, 82 and Rick Marin, "Lick Me, Flog Me, Buy Me!" *Newsweek*, 29 December 1997, 85–6.
3 Wright, "S/M Policy Reform Project for NOW," 8 July 1999, Lesbian Herstory Archive and "The National Coalition for Sexual Freedom," *The Link*, January 1998, 3.
4 Madoc Pop, "And When They Came for Us . . . ," *Sandmutopian Guardian* 36 (2000), 18.
5 Kessler, "From the Editor's Desk: Commentary – X," *Sandmutopian Guardian* 36 (2000), 19.
6 Madoc Pope, "The San Diego Six" at http://www.madoc.us/sd6.php (accessed 15 May 2020); "The San Diego Six: The Views from There, *Sandmutopian Guardian* (2000), 40–1; and Patrick Califia, *Speaking Sex to Power: The Politics of Queer* Sex (San Francisco, CA: Cleis, 2002), 254.
7 "Another Play Party Runs Afoul of the Local Authorities," *Sandmutopian Guardian* 38 (2000), 39; "'Paddleboro' in Massachusetts," *Sandmutopian Guardian* 39 (2000), 52; Cindy Rodriguez, "Attleboro Sex Club the Talk of the Town," Boston Globe, 12 July

2000, B1 & B5; and Patrick Califia, *Speaking Sex to Power: The Politics of Queer* Sex (San Francisco, CA: Cleis, 2002), 248–53.

8 David Wedge, "Detectives' Presence in Sex Party Building Makes Some Wonder," *Boston Herald*, 14 July 2000 and Wedge, "Fetishists Defend Pursuit of Pain," *Boston Herald*, 16 July 2000, 1.

9 "S&M Prosecution Assailed," *The Link*, Spring 2001, 6; "'Paddleboro' Charges Fizzle," *Sun Chronicle*, 27 December 2001 at https://www.thesunchronicle.com/2001-in-review-paddleboro-charges-fizzle/article_1725aaee-88a3-56fb-801e-e11f96ad9924.html (accessed 16 January 2020); and Amy Pagnozzi, "Kinky Find a Cause in 'Paddleboro'" *Hartford Courant*, 9 March 2001 at https://www.courant.com/news/connecticut/hc-xpm-2001-03-09-0103091567-story.html (accessed 15 February 2020).

10 Mark Gabrish Conlan, "San Diego Leatherpeople, Police Meet to Discuss 'Leather and the Law,'" at https://la.indymedia.org/news/2001/10/11677.html (accessed 16 May 2020); "NELA's Medical Project," *The Link*, July 2004, 3; Seraphina, "Domestic Violence Project," *The Link*, October 2008, 20–1; and "NCSF Victory in Baltimore!" *The Link*, Fall 2000, 2.

11 Jand Fritsch, "Charges Dismissed in Columbia Sexual Torture Case," *New York Times*, 2 November 2001.

12 "Jovanovic Verdict," *Sandmutopian Guardian* 30 (1998), 56; "Oliver Jovanovic Conviction Reversed on Appeal," *Sandmutopian Guardian* 36 (2000), 40–2; and John O. Savino and Brent E. Turvey, *Rape Investigation Handbook* (Boston, CA: Academic Press, 2011), 276–7.

13 Jon Barrett, "Diss Jockey: Dr. Laura Discusses Her Position on Gay Rights," *The Advocate*, 15 February 2000, 28–35; Phyllis Labrach, "Sex-Oriented Convention Opens Today Despite Effort to Ban It," *St. Louis Dispatch*, 27 April 2002, 9; "Bound by a Boycott," *The Advocate*, 28 May 2002, 22; Chris Guy, "Fetish, Bondage Group Drops Convention Plan," *Baltimore Sun*, 7 October 2003; Black Rose 2003 Program Book, LAAM; Lolita, "BR Makes It Happen!" *Petal and Thorn*, March/April 2003, 1 & 5. Several scholars incorrectly report BR 2003 was cancelled: Margot Weiss, "Gay Shame and BDSM Pride: Neoliberalism, Privacy, and Sexual Politics," *Radical History Review* 100 (December 2008), 88; and RDK Herman, "Playing with Restraints: Space, Citizenship, and BDSM," in Kath Browne, Jason Lim, and Gavin Brown (eds.), *Geographies of Sexualities: Theory, Practices and Politics* (New York: Routledge, 2009), 89–90.

14 "Supreme Court Victory," *The Link*, July 2003, 1.

15 Killian Melloy, "Despite Right Wing Pressure, Straight BDSM Gathering Goes Forward," *Edge*, 10 February 2009 at https://boston.edgemedianetwork.com/story.php?ch=news&sc=&sc2=news&sc3=&id=87075 (accessed 1 May 2020) and Linda Harvey, "Help Stop BDSM Convention in Cleveland," *Mass Resistance*, 8 February 2019 at https://www.missionamerica.com/article/help-stop-the-bdsm-convention-in-downtown-cleveland-hotels-scheduled-for-april/ (accessed 20 June 2020).

16 "Professional Dominatrix Goes to Court in Bucks Country," *Sandmutopian Guardian* 30 (1998), 38; Goria G. Brame and William D. Brame, *Different Loving Too: Real People, Real Lives, Real BDSM* (British Columbia: Moon Grove Press, 2015), 121; and Raja Mishra, "Dominatrix Acquitted of Manslaughter, *Boston Globe*, 31 January 2006.

17 "Sinner's Lounge Forced to Close," *The Scarlet Leather* 3, no. 5 (1996), 3; "As Others See Us," *Sandmutopian Guardian* 33 (1999), 40–1; Lenny Savino "Sex Club Owners: Activities are Legal," *Orlando Sentinel*, 24 February 1999; and Susan Jacobson, "Sex Club Case Ends with Deal for Two Owners," *Orlando Sentinel*, 24 September 1999.

18 "Slave Contract Ends with Pair in Handcuffs," NLA, *Domestic Violence Project Newsletter* 2, no. 3 (October 2007), 20; and Jamal Thalji, Paso Sex 'Master' Gets No Jail Time, *St. Petersburg Times*, 16 July 2008; and Jen Chung, "Craigslist 'Sex Slave' Suspect

Claims Consensual S&M Relationship," *Gothamist*, 19 February 2011, at https://gothamist.com/news/craigslist-sex-slave-suspect-claims-consensual-sm-relationship (accessed 15 February 2020).

19 National Coalition for Sexual Freedom, "Violence and Discrimination Surveys," 2001 & 2008, at www.ncsfreedom.org/library/viodiscrimsurvey.htm (accessed 15 January 2015).

20 Chris Bull, "Cracking Down," *The Advocate*, 22 August 1995, 2–34.

21 Natalie Purcell, *Violence and the Pornographic Imaginary: The Politics of Sex, Gender, and Aggression in Hardcore Pornography* (New York: Routledge, 2012), 101 and Paula Reed Ward, "Woman Pleads Guilty to Obscenity for Child-Sex Story Site," *Pittsburgh Post-Gazette*, 7 August 2008.

22 Dennis McMillan, "BD/SM Internet Sites Under Attack," *San Francisco Bay Times*, 22 December 2005.

23 Eli Sanders, "Tortured Logic," in Felice Newman and Frédérique Delacoste (eds.), *Best Sex Writing 2006* (San Francisco, CA: Cleis, 2006), 23–32.

24 Andrea Beckman, *The Social Construction of Sexuality and Perversion: Deconstructing Sadomasochism* (Basingstoke: Palgrave Macmillan, 2009), 126.

25 Steve Stein, *Twenty-Five Years of Living in Leather The National Leather Association, 1986–2011* (Palm Coast, FL: Adynaton, 2012), 72–5.

26 "Board in Brief," *First Link* 3, no. 4 (April 1989), 1; Woody Bebout to NLA, 8 October 8 1991, NLA Papers, St. Louis Chapter, LAAM; "Law Project Needs Information," *The Link*, March 1997, 4; and Spencer Bergstedt, "President's Address," *The Link*, Spring 2001, 2–3.

27 Tony DeBlase, "LIL 10 Keynote Address," NLA files, LAAM.

28 Rubin, "The Outcasts" in Pat Califia and Robin Sweeney (ed.), *The Second Coming: A Leatherdyke Reader* (Boston, MA: Alyson Books, 2000), 345; DeBlase, "Keynote Address," LIL X, NLA Archives; "Honoring Our Dead," *First Link* 5, no. 12 (January 1992) 13; and "To Honor the NLA Dead," *Quarter Link* 6, no. 10 (November 1992), 19.

29 Master Ed and kathleen, "The History of TES," *Prometheus* 24 (Winter 1996), 38–9.

30 Race Bannon to David Scribner (Chair, NLA Membership Committee), 18 January 1994, NLA Files, LAAM.

31 Leonard Dworkin, "What Is This Thing Called the Internet" *Link* 9, no. 3 (June/July 1995), 13.

32 Spencer Bergstedt, "President's Address," *The Link*, Spring 2001, 2–3.

33 Stein, *Living in Leather*, 80–1 & 168.

34 Tony DeBlase, interview by Jan Hall, 1999, NLA Archives.

35 David Stein, "The Road Ahead: Time for Decision," *GMSMA Newslink*, Summer 1989, 25 and Eric Levin, "Unbuckling Straps: An Undoing of the NYC Leather Community" at http://www.bilerico.com/2009/07/unbuckling_straps_an_undoing_of_the_nyc_leather_co.php#7vQeY3bpQuslLhjb.99 (accessed 23 June 2017).

36 Steve Lenius, *Life, Leather, and the Pursuit of Happiness* (Minneapolis, MN: Nelson Borhek Press, 2010), 65 and Michael Musto, "Gay Leather Scene Tones Down from Hard-Core to Dress-Up," *New York Times*, 22 December 2015 at https://www.nytimes.com/2015/12/24/fashion/gay-leather-scene-tones-down-from-hardcore-to-dress-up.html (accessed 12 February 2020).

37 Tristan Taormino, host, "Interview with Laura Antoniou," Sex Out Loud (podcast), 11 January 2013; Mike Miksche, "In an Era of Closing Leather Bars and Harness-Wearing Poseurs, Where Are the Real Leather Men?," *Slate*, 29 June 2017 at https://slate.com/human-interest/2017/06/with-leather-bars-closing-and-poseurs-copying-the-aesthetic-where-are-real-leather-men.html (accessed 10 August 2017); and http://leatherpridenight.org/2015/06/lpnends/ (accessed 12 April 2019).

38 Lori Selke, "Is SM on the Way Out?," *On Our Backs* 14, no. 1 (June–July 1999), 28–9; Dan Savage, "Where Have All the Kinky People Gone?," *The Stranger*, 23 November

2000; and Preston, "What Happened?," in Thompson, *Leatherfolk: Radical Sex, People, Politics, and Practice* (Boston, MA: Alyson Publications, 1991), 211.
39 Sharon C. Bakos, *Kink: The Shocking Hidden Sex Lives of Americans* (New York: St Martins, 1995), 155 and Carter Stevens, interview by Rialto Report, April 2013 at https://www.therialtoreport.com/2013/04/21/podcast-07-carter-stevens-a-porn-renaissance-man/ (accessed 10 January 2019).
40 Richard Kadry, "Alt.sex.bondage," *Wired*, 1 June 1994.
41 David Allyn, *Make Love, Not War: The Sexual Revolution: An Unfettered History* (London: Routledge, 2001), 218.
42 Slave feyrie in Brame and Brame, *Different Loving Too*, 145.
43 Tracy Clark-Flory, "A BDSM Blacklist," *Salon*, 3 June 2012, at https://www.salon.com/2012/06/03/a_bdsm_blacklist/ (accessed 15 July 2020).
44 David Z. Morris, "How Kink's Largest Social-Networking Site Fails Its Users," *The Atlantic*, March 2015, at https://www.theatlantic.com/health/archive/2015/03/how-kinks-largest-social-networking-site-fails-its-users/385586/ (accessed 12 March 2015).
45 Kitty Stryker, "Safe/Ward, Safewords, and the Battle of Community Accountability," 30 January 2012, at http://kittystryker.com/blog/posts/safeward-safewords-and-the-battle-of-community-accountability/ (accessed 16 July 2020); "Safe/Ward: I Never Called it Rape," 7 July 2011, at https://www.slixa.com/blog/kink/safeward-i-never-called-it-rape/ (accessed 16 July 2020); and Susan J. Wright, Russell J. Stambaugh, and Derrell Cox, *Consent Violations Report* (NCSF, 2015).
46 Siri Kale, "Kinky Social Network FetLife Deletes Thousands of Fetishes to Stay Online," *Vice.com*, 25 January 2017, at https://www.vice.com/en_us/article/mbqe8a/kinky-social-network-fetlife-deletes-thousands-of-fetishes-to-stay-online (accessed 15 July 2020).
47 Pamela Lister, "I Was a Middle-Aged, Suburban Dominatrix," *Redbook*, August 1994, 64.
48 Weiss, "Mainstreaming Kink," 124, in Peggy J. Kleinplatz and Charles Moser (eds.), *Sadomasochism: Powerful Pleasures* (New York: Routledge, 2006), 103–32.
49 *Dharma & Greg*, episode 62, "The Trouble with Troubadour," aired 8 February 2000.
50 Call, "Sounds Like Kinky Business to Me": Subtextual and Textual Representations of Erotic Power in the Buffyverse," *Slayage: The Online Journal of Buffy Studies* 6 (Summer 2007).
51 Jeff Gord, email to houseofgord@yahoogroups.com, 5 March, 2005.
52 Kleinplatz and Moser, *Powerful Pleasures*, 109; Becky Bracken, "Will Sex Sell? Couple Hope BDSM Basement Will Bring Top Dollar for Family Home," *Realtor.com*, 12 May 2020, at https://www.realtor.com/news/trends/bdsm-basement-arkansas-home/ (accessed 1 August 2020); and Becky Bracken, "Whatever Happened to the 'Sex Dungeon' House in Pennsylvania?" Realtor.com, 12 November 2019, at https://www.realtor.com/news/unique-homes/what-ever-happened-to-the-sex-dungeon-house-in-pennsylvania/ (accessed 1 August 2020).
53 Morgan, "The Masochism of Urban Running," *Checkmate* 10 (1995), 6; Peter Sagal, "The Pain Truth," *Runner's World*, August 2011, 58–9; and Eric Schranz, host, "Ms. Monday Jones: BDSM and Ultramarathons," *Ultrarunner Podcast* (podcast), 21 December 2018.
54 Jennifer Bleyer, "Have You Been Naughty? Exploring the World of Corsets and Kink," *New York Times*, 20 March 2005 and Rick Marin, "Lick Me, Flog Me, Buy Me!" 85–86.
55 E. Coslor, B. Crawford, and B. Brents, "Whips, Chains and Books on Campus: How Organizations Legitimate Their Stigmatized Practices," *Proceedings of the Academy of Management, Annual Meeting*, 2017, 25; Peter Schmidt, "In Professor-Dominatrix Scandal, University of New Mexico Feels the Pain," *Chronicle of Higher Education*, 12 September 2010, http://chronicle.com/article/In-Professor-Dominatrix/124369/

(accessed 25 March 2011); and "University Chancellor, 64, Quits After Shocking Photos Exposed Him as Sex-Dungeon Master," *Daily Mail*, 23 August 2011, at https://www.dailymail.co.uk/news/article-2029196/University-Northern-Virginia-chancellor-David-Lee-64-quits-sex-dungeon-photos.html (accessed 25 June 2020).

56 Peter Tupper, *A Lover's Pinch: A Cultural History of Sadomasochism* (Lanham, MD: Rowman & Littlefield, 2018), 245–7; Kerry Lauerman, "A Taste of the Whip for Saddam," *Salon*, 4 December 2002, at https://www.salon.com/2002/12/04/un_sm/ (accessed 12 February 2020); and David Steinberg, "No Apologies: The Story of Jack McGeorge," *Comes Naturally*, 1 June 2003, at http://www.getunderground.com/underground/columns/article.cfm?Article_ID=809#selection-665.0-665.40 (accessed 10 June 2020).

57 Susan Wright, "Discrimination of SM-identified individuals," *Journal of Homosexuality*, 50, no. 2 (0062), 217–31.

58 Brame and Brame, *Different Loving Too*, 144 and Emma Green, "Consent Isn't Enough: The Troubling Sex of *Fifty Shades*" *The Atlantic*, 10 February 2015.

59 Barker, "Consent Is a Grey Area? A Comparison of Understandings of Consent in *Fifty Shades of Grey* and on the BDSM Blogosphere, *Sexualities* 16 (2013), 896–914.

60 Ruth A. Deller and Clarissa Smith, "Reading the BDSM Romance: Reader Responses to Fifty Shades," *Sexualities* 16 (2013), 932–50; David Sax, "The 'Fifty Shades of Grey' Stimulus," *Bloomberg Businessweek*, 24 May 2012; Lynn Comella, *Vibrator Nation: How Feminist Sex-Toy Stores Changed the Business of Pleasure* (Durham, NC: Duke University Press, 2007), 223; and Matt Haber, "A Hush-Hush Topic No More," *New York Times*, 27 February 2013.

61 Marianne Apostolides, "The Pleasure of the Pain: Why Some People Need S&M," *Psychology Today* 32, no. 5 (September/October1999), 60–5.

62 Tupper, *A Lover's Pinch*, 234; Charles Moser and Peggy Kleinplatz, "DSM-IV-TR and the Paraphilias: An Argument for Removal," *Journal of Psychology & Human Sexuality* 17 (2006), 91–109; Connolly, "Psychological Functioning of Bondage/Domination/Sado-Masochism (BDSM) Practitioners," *Journal of Psychology & Human Sexuality* 18, no. 1 (2006), 79–120; and Weinberg, "Sadomasochism and the Social Sciences: A Review of the Sociological and Social Psychological Literature," *Journal of Homosexuality* 50 (2006), 17–40.

63 Krueger, "The DSM Diagnostic Criteria for Sexual Sadism," *Archives of Sexual Behavior*, December 2009 and Krueger, "The DSM Diagnostic Criteria for Sexual Masochism," *Archives of Sexual Behavior*, March 2010.

64 American Psychiatric Association, *Diagnostic and Statistical Manual of Mental Disorders, 5th Edition (DSM-5)*, Volume 1, (APA, 2013), 685–7.

65 Edward E. Shorter, "Sexual Sunday School: The DSM and the Gatekeeping of Morality," *Journal of AMA Ethics*, November 2014.

66 Ummni Khan, "Sadomasochism in Sickness and in Health: Competing Claims from Science, Social Science, and Culture," *Current Sexual Health Reports* 9 (2015), 54 & 56.

67 Merissa Nathan Gerson, "BDSM Versus the DSM," *The Atlantic*, 13 January 2015 and Susan Wright, "Kinky Parents and Child Custody: The Effect of the DSM-5 Differentiation Between the Paraphilias and Paraphilic Disorders," *Archives of Sexual Behavior* 43 (2014), 1257.

68 John Cloud, "Bondage Unbound," *Time*, 19 January 2004.

69 Lauren Hough, "I Was a Cable Guy. I Saw the Worst of America," *Huffington Post*, 30 December 2018, 30 December 2018, at https://www.huffingtonpost.com/entry/cable-tech-dick-cheney-sex-dungeon_us_5c0ea571e4b06484c9fd4c21 (accessed 30 December 2018).

70 Dave Rhodes, "Race Bannon Presented NGLTF's 2013 Leather Leadership Award," *Leather Journal*, 28 January 2013, at https://www.theleatherjournal.com/news/national-news/item/360-race-bannon-presented-ngltf-s-2013-leather-leadership-award (accessed 15 June 2020).

71 Mike Miksche, "In an Era of Closing Leather Bars and Harness-Wearing Poseurs, Where Are the Real Leather Men?" *Slate*, 29 June 2017 at https://slate.com/human-interest/2017/06/with-leather-bars-closing-and-poseurs-copying-the-aesthetic-where-are-real-leather-men.html (accessed 10 August 2017) and "A Chat with Pat Califia, Part 2," *Black Sheets* 7 (1995), 17.
72 Laura Antoniou, "Stealing Trash," Presented at the Leather H.E.A.T. Conference, 19 April 2015, Los Angeles, CA, http://lantoniou.com/stealing-trash/ (accessed 25 April 2018) and Tristan Taormino, host, "Interview with Laura Antoniou," *Sex Out Loud* (podcast), 11 January 2013.
73 Steve Vakesh, "What Are Dungeon Monitors Good For, Anyway?" *Sandmutopian Guardian* 32 (1998), 49–50.
74 Gary Switch, "The Origin of RACK: RACK vs. SSC," *Prometheus* 37 (2001) and D. J. Williams, Jeremy N. Thomas, Emily E. Prior, and M. Candace Christensen, "From 'SSC' and 'RACK' to the '4Cs': Introducing a new Framework for Negotiating BDSM Participation," *Electronic Journal of Human Sexuality*, 17 (2014).
75 Morten Ebbe Juul Nielson, "Safe, Sane, and Consensual— Consent and the Ethics of BDSM," *International Journal of Applied Philosophy* 24 (2010), 285.
76 Tiffany Reisz, *The Angel: A Sexy Romance* (Don Mills, ON: Harlequin, 2012), Chapter 13.
77 See in particular Ariane Cruz, *The Color of Kink: Black Women, BDSM, and Pornography* (New York: NYU Press, 2016), and "Playing with the Politics of Perversion: Policing BDSM, Pornography, and Black Female Sexuality," *Souls* 18 (2016), 379–407.
78 D. Alexandria, "The First," in Laura Antoniou (ed.), *No Safe Words: Tales from the Marketplace* (Boston, CA: Circlet Press, 2013).
79 Karen Bullock-Jordon, "Death of the Lesborados," *Black Leather in Color*, Winter 1994, 9 & 36–7; Matt, Baume, "Inside the Changing Leather Scene," *Rolling Stone*, 18 August 2017; and Brame and Brame, *Different Loving Too*, 134–5.
80 Antoinette [Michelle Buchanan], "Editorial," *Black Leather in Color*, Summer 1994, 5 and Viola Johnson, "The Love That Dare Not Speak Its Name: Playing with and Against Racial Stereotypes," *Black Leather in Color* 2 (1994), 8–9.
81 Daisy Hernandez, "Playing with Race," *Colorlines*, 21 December 2004, at https://www.colorlines.com/articles/playing-race (accessed 24 April 2020) and David M. Column, "Race Play," 2004, at http://www.leatherweb.com/raceplayh.htm (accessed 20 June 2020).
82 Sandra Daugherty, host, "Edge Play with Mollena Lee Williams-Haas," *Sex Nerd podcast* (podcast), 16 March 2016; San Francisco Leatherman's Discussion Group, "Taboo Play—Mollena Williams, 24 August 2011, at https://www.sfldg.org/all-programs/taboo-play-mollena-williams (accessed 10 July 2020); and Mollena Williams, "BDSM and Playing with Race," in Rachel Kramer Bussel (ed.), *Best Sex Writing 2010* (San Francisco, CA: Cleis Press, 2010).
83 Williams, "For Today. . . I Win," 3 June 2009, at http://www.mollena.com/2009/06/i-win-i-rule/ (accessed 10 July 2020) and Zachary Woolfe, "A Composer and His Wife: Creativity Through Kink," *New York Times*, 23 February 2016.
84 Sue Katz, "The National Leather Leadership Conference," *Z Magazine*, August 2003, 23–4.
85 Guy Baldwin, "NLA Houston Keynote Speech," 17 April 2011 and Daniel Harris, *The Rise and Fall of Gay Culture* (New York: Ballantine, 1997), 62.
86 Rick Marin, "Lick Me, Flog Me, Buy Me!" 85.

CONCLUSION

From scattered networks of sadomasochists and the bars, businesses, and magazine publishers who catered to this small, maligned sexual practice in the 1950s, people with BDSM interests developed into a coherent community grounded in a shared literature, led by local and national organizations, and bound by shared principles epitomized by the phrased "safe, sane, consensual" promoted in the 1980s and 1990s. Applying this discourse of consent, they successfully changed popular perceptions by normalizing BDSM. Instead of fascists, murderers and outlaws, they became "just another alternative lifestyle," which—judging by the success of *Fifty Shades of Grey*—titillated the fantasies of millions.

Desire for sexual partners and like-minded people with whom to discuss their sexual interests encouraged sadomasochists to contact one another, their meetings facilitated by personal introductions, ads in contact magazines and leather bars. These networks fueled the development of the first dedicated BDSM organizations in the 1970s, which served the social and educational needs of their members and encouraged them to accept and explore their sexual interests. TES, Janus and other early BDSM organizations served as models for new BDSM, dozens of which sprang up in cities across the United States in the early 1980s, attracting more and more members. Instead of doormen turning away the unworthy, these new BDSM organizations welcomed newcomers. Anyone could join, which hundreds and soon thousands of people did.

TES, Janus, GMSMA, LSM and numerous other BDSM organizations displaced bars as the community's primary venues for education and socialization. They provided the impetus to create a national BDSM organization and solidified social and educational standards for incoming members epitomized by the phrase "safe, sane, consensual." As Jeffrey Weeks notes, they pushed "desire to the limits" while exploring "power and responsibility."[1] They taught members how to negotiate and engage in BDSM scenes, keeping them safe and pleasurable for all participants. Along with *DungeonMaster* and other BDSM technique magazines, they encouraged more sophisticated BDSM play, provided practical instruction on the use of implements ranging from candles and rope to whips and violet wands, and provoked serious discussions of the dynamics of BDSM scenes and the importance of freely given and ongoing consent in them.

In 1984, Pat Califia noted, "if you had a fight with two people, you could kiss your butt goodbye, and you probably weren't going to get laid, you know, for the next three years!" A dozen years later, though, "if you have a fight with those two people," you had "eight or nine other places where you can plug in and have a social life."[2] Hundreds of BDSM organizations operated by then, and new ones continued to form. Increasingly coordinated, BDSM organizations promoted tolerance and cooperation among constituencies separated by gender, orientation, BDSM interests, and tradition. While they represented just a fraction of the people who experimented with spanking, bondage or other BDSM practices in their sex lives, they nonetheless dramatically reshaped BDSM practice, changing how people thought about and engaged in BDSM.

This makes BDSM one of the best documented examples of the social construction of a sexual practice and community, the process of which was chronicled by BDSM organizations and documented in their newsletter, magazines and other literature. Within that community, knowledge and skill in BDSM technique became the most important "form of subcultural capital," which enhanced one's social position. Unlike swingers and members of other sexual communities, reporters, scholars and other observers all remarked with surprise on the average appearance of BDSM organization members. "People of all ages, sizes, and shapes do not hesitate to dress in skin-tight leather and rubber outfits or turn up in nude or half-nude states in order to explore themselves and others." The BDSM community welcomed everyone, including people with disabilities, the transgendered, and others often excluded from sexual communities. No longer, the reckless, beautiful men David Stein found at the Mineshaft, members of the BDSM community were ordinary members of the middle-class, distinguished only by their fetish attire and their courtesy, never pushing when reporters declined their advances.[3]

BDSM organizations focused increasing attention on political matters due to police harassment, pejorative characterization of sadomasochism by the press and medical establishment, and the AIDS crisis. These shared threats encouraged collective efforts among BDSM organizations to change public perceptions of BDSM to win acceptance by mainstream society and full inclusion in the struggle for LGBTQ rights, which the many gay and lesbian BDSM organizations sought. Transforming BDSM practice to be "safe, sane, consensual" provided a foundation for the community's political activism, and the phrase proved useful to explain BDSM to outsiders. BDSM activists raised funds for sadomasochists facing legal problems, lobbied psychiatrists to reassess their views of BDSM activities, and slowly changed popular perceptions of BDSM by normalizing it.

Movies mirrored changing popular perceptions of BDSM from sadistic murderers in *Cruising* (1980) and the abusive relationship of *9 ½ Weeks* (1986) to the hedonistic island resort of *Exit to Eden* (1994), and happily married (eventually) externally normal suburban couple in *Secretary* (2002). By 2011, when *Fifty Shades of Grey* became a surprise best-seller, BDSM was widely talked about and positive—or at least friendly—portrayals of its practitioners outnumbered the negative in movies and television.

While some decried DSM's continued description of sexual masochism and sadism as paraphilias, others celebrated its changed wording and acknowledgment that most sadomasochists were not mentally ill, others celebrated them as great victories. Similarly, critics who saw all BDSM as abuse remained, as did some old tropes, such as childhood abuse leading to adult sadomasochism and the common assumption that sadomasochists inherently pursue increasingly dangerous activities. Only the love of a "good woman" saved Christian Grey from treading this dangerous path. Yet, the majority of people seemed to find nothing wrong with BDSM. Sadomasochists themselves faced fewer legal, social and professional consequences for their sexual activities.

The trajectory of the BDSM community in the second half of the twentieth century was toward greater and greater organization, highlighted by the creation of the National Leather Association, its Living in Leather conference, and network of dozens of local chapters and affiliate organizations in the early 1990s. BDSM activists focused on the uniting the BDSM community across lines of gender, orientation and BDSM interests, taking models of interaction pioneered in San Francisco at Catacombs and making them national. Doing so both improved the quality of BDSM interactions and helped meld the BDSM community into an effective political force. The latter required shedding sadomasochism's outlaw image, which some opposed or later regretted. As International Mr. Leather 1979 David Kloss remarked, "it's nice to be accepted, but I kind of liked that sense of the forbidden, too."[4]

Changing perceptions of BDSM from forbidden to acceptable (and even fun) required education. TES, Janus and other early BDSM organizations focused much of their time and resources on educating members. Tony DeBlase, through his "Sandmutopia University" workshops, *DungeonMaster* magazine, and other endeavors, reached gay sadomasochists across the United States. Califia, Rubin and other Samois members did the same for women's groups, while many heterosexual and mixed gender and orientation groups developed from seeds planted by TES and Janus. Collected, practiced, shared and expanded, BDSM technique's growing body of knowledge provided a common foundation on which the BDSM community grew. Encouraged by the NLA, BDSM organizations coordinated their educational and political efforts. Many embraced pansexuality, working with—and even engaging in BDSM—people of different gender, orientation or fetish interest. This "pansexual BDSM community," Steve Lenius suggests, deserves much of the credit for encouraging gay and lesbian organizations to similarly broaden their outlook, by including bisexuals and transsexuals.[5]

At first focused internally, BDSM activists recognized the need to educate the general public about BDSM, not to recruit them for BDSM fun, as DeBlase warned, but simply to help them understand why some people enjoyed it. So, the BDSM community's educational and political efforts, both internal and external, ran in parallel. To attract more members, BDSM organizations shed their outlaw image. Shedding that image allowed them to reconfigure sadomasochistic sexuality to be "safe, sane, and consensual," which in turn helped change popular perceptions of their sexuality. They made BDSM both safe for practitioners and palatable to "vanillas." Instead of fascists and outlaws, BDSM became "just another alternative lifestyle."

While *Playboy* magazine suggested almost a third of its readers tried tying up their lovers,[6] most surveys indicate only about 10% of American adults are interested in at least some BDSM activities. Whatever their number, the vast majority of them confine their BDSM activities to fantasy, Internet chatrooms, their own bedrooms or perhaps a professional dominatrix. Those who join BDSM organizations and attend their events remain a small group, numbering in the thousands rather than the millions or tens of millions these surveys indicate. This disparity proved a continuing frustration to BDSM activists, but they still managed to advance their agenda.

Reconfiguring their sexual practices strengthened the political voice of BDSM activists who steadily advanced their agenda: inclusion in the LGBTQ rights movement, eliminating the legal and medical vilification of BDSM, and ending government harassment and prosecution of BDSM practitioners, businesses, events, organizations and media. Its decades-long discourses on consent influenced popular debates on the topic and spread to a host of specialized realms, including the players of role-playing games who discussed managing consent and extreme topics in their games, including playing an "X-Card" to halt proceedings when they became uncomfortable, a gaming equivalent of BDSM's safe word. Monte Cook Games even produced a short booklet on consent in gaming.[7] Well before *Fifty Shades of Grey* hit bookstore shelves in 2011, the BDSM community had achieved levels of social acceptance and sexual citizenship previously thought impossible.

The BDSM community's pursuit of acceptance through normalization has its critics, both inside and outside the community. Among the most ardent is Daniel Harris who denounces the community for a host of sins, both great and small. He condemns BDSM activists for their adoption of "the therapeutic jargon used to condemn them," their "calculatedly defensive rhetoric constructed out of the clichés of the human potential movement," and efforts to portray BSDM as "a wholesome form of self-actualization," benefitting "both the master and his slave." At times shockingly ill-informed, Harris is correct that BDSM activists worked to rebut feminist critics who saw BDSM as patriarchal violence, and appease "conservative gay men who preached the gospel of assimilation and strove to present a rosy-cheeked, choirboy image of the homosexual to mainstream America." Their efforts, though, were much more than "a massive PR blitz, an all-out snow job in which they caved into critics in order to recover their legitimacy," emasculated "everything the leather community once stood for," and changing "the entire nature of their sexual practices."[8]

In making his case, Harris conflates leathermen and sadomasochists, exaggerates the differences of BDSM activities between the nascent BDSM community of the 1960s and the political active community of the 1990s, and ignores the importance of women and pansexuality to the BDSM community (even criticizing Mark Thompson for titling his book *Leatherfolk* rather than *Leathermen*). The BDSM community changed in these years, but it was hardly the transition Harris presents from harsh, uncaring, sadistic masters and their battered victims to one of switches, play rooms, and fun, egalitarian BDSM. The latter was always present in BDSM encounters. The challenge for BDSM organizations, one they met successfully, was to banish from their membership those who failed to abide by their growing body of rules, central of which was "safe, sane, consensual" BDSM play. BDSM activists worked from a genuine desire to improve BDSM play and changed an informal, haphazardly educated community inadequately policed by gossip and word-of-mouth to one built around formal structures, educational expectations and behavioral norms. They enhanced BDSM play while making it safer. Mr. Benson, most realized, was best kept in the realm of fiction rather than celebrated as an ideal to emulate in their dungeons.

These changes, of course, also proved politically useful and BDSM activists' efforts to educate both BDSM practitioners and mainstream society often proceeded in tandem. Harris and other critics see normalization as somehow wrong. BDSM practice must necessarily lose something vital in the process. Most sadomasochists, though accepted this in order to achieve their larger goals, particularly ending police harassment and—for LGBTQ sadomasochists—acceptance by the larger LGBTQ community.

Paradoxically, growing mainstream acceptance of BDSM practices encouraged the BDSM community's fragmentation, a process accelerated by the Internet, which ravaged the finances of BDSM magazines allowed people to find partners for BDSM without recourse to BDSM organizations or leather bars. The institutions that nourished and grew the BDSM community for half a century lost their influence, a loss underlined by *Fifty Shades of Grey*, which ignored negotiation, explicit consent and other norms of conduct established and encouraged by these institutions.

The disparity between the number of people who joined BDSM organizations and those who engaged in BDSM activities—even if only occasionally—became more pronounced over time as FetLife and other social media sites attracted hundreds of thousands of members. Today's largest BDSM conferences, such as Frolicon, attract about 2,500 attendees, roughly triple what Living in Leather managed in its heyday. In contrast, about 400,000 people wander through the Folsom Street Fair and several million belong to FetLife. Kink.com, the largest producer of online pornographic BDSM videos, has more members than most

BDSM organizations and recently launched a series of educational videos, claiming an unmet need for BDSM instruction.

Meanwhile, of course, complaints continue about abusive tops and scenes arranged online gone wrong. While the NCSF continues its narrow mission of legal defense, no larger institution represents the BDSM community to outsiders or sets it political agenda. The BDSM community continues to change, but unlike the 1980s and 1990s, no one is leading that change.

★★★

Despite the surge in scholarship following *Fifty Shades of Grey's* surprise success, historical studies of sadomasochism and the BDSM community remain scarce. Much remains to for future researchers. Scholarly studies of leading figures in the BDSM community, particularly Tony DeBlase, Pat Bond, Cynthia Slater, Barry Douglas, Steve Maidhof and Chuck Renslow would be useful, as well as studies of influential BDSM organizations, particularly TES, GMSMA, CHC, LSM and Outcasts, as well as important writers like Larry Townsend, who recently died. The role of the NCSF as the community's legal voice certainly merits scholarly attention, as do relations among BDSM organizations in communities boasting several organizations, such as New York, Chicago, Los Angeles and San Francisco. While sources are scarce, studies of sadomasochists and their early networking in the 1950s and 1960s would be tremendously useful. While BDSM activists encouraged diversity and sought to build a large BDSM/Leather/Fetish coalition, tensions among its various constituencies remained. Studies of subcultures within the BDSM community, such as those pursuing Master/Slave relationships, would be interesting. The interactions of people of color within the BDSM community merit much greater attention, particularly how they simultaneously embrace a BDSM identity, while challenging the racial underpinnings of some BDSM role-play. While some have occupied prominent positions in BDSM organizations, many remain marginalized within a community that has never given serious consideration to issues of race.

Notes

1 Jeffrey Weeks, *Sexuality and Its Discontents: Meanings, Myths, and Modern Sexualities* (London: Routledge, 1990), 70.

2 "A Chat with Pat Califia, Part 2," *Black Sheets* 7 (1995), 17.

3 Nathan Rambukkana, "Taking the Leather Out of Leathersex: The Internet, Identity, and the Sadomasochistic Sphere," in Kate O'Riordan and David J. Philips (eds.), *Queer Online: Media, Technology, and Sexuality* (New York: Peter Lang, 2007), 73; Beckman, "'Sexual Rights' and 'Sexual Responsibilities' within Consensual 'S/M' Practice," in Mark Cowling and Paul Reynolds (eds.), *Making Sense of Sexual Consent* (Burlington, VT: Ashgate, 2004), 202; Melinda Blau, "Ordinary People," *New York* 27 no. 47 (28 November 1994), 38–9; and Sharon C. Bakos, *Kink: The Shocking Hidden Sex Lives of Americans* (New York: St Martins, 1995), 162.

4 Roy DeLaMar, "Twenty-five Years of Leather," *The Advocate*, 13 May 2003, 16.

5 Steve Lenius, "A Reflection on 'Bisexuals and BDSM: Bisexual People in a Pansexual Community'— Ten Years Later," *Journal of Bisexuality* 11 (2011), 420–5.
6 Sue Katz, "The National Leather Leadership Conference," *Z Magazine*, August 2003, 23–4.
7 Jaclyn Friedman and Jessica Valenti, *Yes Means Yes: Visions of Female Sexual Power and a World Without Rape* (New York: Perseus, 2008) and Sean K. Reynolds and Shanna Germain, *Consent in Gaming* (Monte Cook Games, 2019).
8 Daniel Harris, *Rise and Fall of Gay Culture* (New York: Ballantine, 1997), 186–7 & 190–2.

SELECTED BIBLIOGRAPHY

Manuscript Collections

Carter Johnson Leather Library (A travelling collection)
Leather Archives and Museum, Chicago, IL
Kinsey Institute, Bloomington, IN
Lesbian Herstory Archives, New York, NY
NLA Archives (in possession of NLA President)

Newsletters of BDSM Organizations

Atlanta SM Solidarity Newsletter
Avatar Newsletter
Bound and Determined Newsletter
Chain Link, First Link, QuarterLink, and *Link* (National Leather Association)
Dreizehn Newsletter
GMSMA Newslink and GMSMA News
Growing Pains (Society of Janus)
The Inquisitor (NLA Metro New York)
Mineshaft Newsletter
ORGASM Newsletter
Petal and Thorn (Black Rose)
Prometheus (TES)
Rose-n-Thorn (Black Rose)
Scarlet Leather (NLA: New England, later New England Leather Alliance)

BDSM and Adult Periodicals

Bizarre
Bizarre Life
Black Leather in Color
Black Sheets

Body Play
Bondage Life
Bound
Brat Attack
Checkmate
Cuir Underground
Drummer
DungeonMaster
Equus Eroticus
Exotica
Exotique
Fantasia
Fetish Times
Knight
Leather Journal
Leather Times
Marquis
Metropolitan Slave
O
On Our Backs
Penthouse
Penthouse Forum
Playboy
Sandmutopia Guardian
Sandmutopian Guardian (name changed with issue 18 in 1995)
Screw
Secret
Skin Two
SM Express
Taste of Latex
Urania News
Venus Infers

Books, Book Chapters, and Journal Articles

Achilles, Nancy. "The Development of the Homosexual Bar as an Institution." In John H. Gagnon and William Simon (Eds.), *Sexual Deviance*, 228–46. New York: Harper & Row, 1967.

Alexander, Jenny. "A Vampire Is Being Beaten: DeSade through the Looking Glass in Buffy and Angel." *Slayage: The Online Journal of Buffy Studies* 4.3, no. 15 (2004). http://offline.buffy.de/outlink_en.php?module=/webserver/offline/www.slayage.tv/essays/slayage15/Slayage_4.3.pdf [Accessed 15 May 2018]

Allen, Steven. *Cinema, Pain and Pleasure: Consent and the Controlled Body*. New York: Palgrave Macmillan, 2013.

Allyn, David. *Make Love, Not War: The Sexual Revolution: An Unfettered History*. London: Routledge, 2001.

Alwood, Edward. *Straight News: Gays, Lesbians, and the News Media*. New York: Columbia University Press, 1996.

Anderson, Misty. "Mr. Barvile's Discipline: Habit, Passion, and Methodism in the Eighteenth-Century English Imagination." In Patsy S. Fowler and Alan Jackson

(Eds.), *Launching Fanny Hill: Essays on the Novel and Its Influences*, 199–220. New York: AMS Press, 2003.
Antoniou, Laura. *Scenes from the Marketplace*. Cambridge, MA: Circlet, 2013.
———. *Some Women*. New York: Masquerade, 1995.
———. *The Marketplace*. New York: Masquerade, 1993.
Attias, Bernardo Alexander. "'Police Free Gay Slaves': Consent, Sexuality, and the Law." *Left History* 10, no. 1 (Fall/Winter 2004): 55–83.
Baim, Tracy and Owen Keehnen. *Leatherman: The Legend of Chuck Renslow*. Chicago, IL: Prairie Avenue Productions, 2011.
Bakos, Sharon C. *Kink: The Shocking Hidden Sex Lives of Americans*. New York: St Martins, 1995.
Baldwin, Guy. *The Leather Contest Guide*. Los Angeles, CA: Daedalus, 1993.
———. *Ties That Bind: The SM/Leather/Fetish Erotic Style*. Los Angeles, CA: Daedalus, 1993.
Bannon, Race. *Learning the Ropes*. San Francisco, CA: Daedalus, 1993.
Bauer, Robin. *Queer BDSM Intimacies: Critical Consent and Pushing Boundaries*. Basingstoke: Palgrave Macmillan, 2014.
Bean, Joseph W. *International Mr. Leather: 25 Years of Champions*. Las Vegas, NV: Nazca Plains Corp., 2004.
Becker, Howard S. *Outsiders, Studies in the Sociology of Deviance*. New York: The Free Press, 1966.
Beckmann, Andrea. "Deconstructing Myths: The Social Construction of 'Sadomasochism Versus 'Subjugated Knowledges' of Practitioners of Consensual 'SM.'" *Journal of Criminal Justice and Popular Culture* 8, no. 2 (2001): 66–95.
———. "'Sexual Rights' and 'Sexual Responsibilities' within Consensual 'S/M' Practice." In Mark Cowling and Paul Reynolds (Eds.), *Making Sense of Sexual Consent*, 195–208. Burlington, VT: Ashgate, 2004.
———. *The Social Construction of Sexuality and Perversion: Deconstructing Sadomasochism*. Basingstoke: Palgrave Macmillan, 2009.
Bernstein, Samuel. *Mr. Confidential: The Man, His Magazine & the Movieland Massacre That Changed Hollywood Forever*. New York: Walford, 2006.
Bienvenue, Robert Vincent. "The Development of Sadomasochism as a Cultural Style in the Twentieth-Century United States." PhD Dissertation, Indiana University, 1998.
Brame, Goria G. and William D. Brame. *Different Loving Too: Real People, Real Lives, Real BDSM*. British Columbia: Moon Grove Press, 2015.
Brame, Goria G., William D. Brame and Jon Jacobs. *Different Loving: An Exploration of the World of Sexual Dominance and Submission*. New York: Villard, 1993.
Bronski, Michael. *A Queer History of the United States*. Boston, MA: Beacon Press, 2011.
———. *Pulp Friction: Uncovering the Golden Age of Gay Male Pulps*. New York: St. Martin's Griffin, 2003.
Bronstein, Carolyn. *Battling Pornography: The American Feminist Anti-Pornography Movement, 1976–1986*. Cambridge: Cambridge University Press, 2011.
Bronstein, Carolyn, and Whitney Strub, eds. *Porno Chic and the Sex Wars: American Sexual Representation in the 1970s*. Amherst: University of Massachusetts Press, 2016.
Buchanan, Michele. "Leather Is Thicker Than Blood: Identity Formation among Organized SM Practitioners in New York City." PhD Dissertation, New School University, 2004.
Busby, Brian. *A Gentleman of Pleasure: One Life of John Glassco, Poet, Memoirist, Translator, and Pornographer*. McGill: Queens University Press, 2011.
Byrne, Romana. *Aesthetic Sexuality: A Literary History of Sadomasochism*. New York: Bloomsbury, 2013.

Califia, Pat. *Melting Point*. Boston, MA: Alyson, 1993.
———. *Public Sex: The Culture of Radical Sex*. San Francisco, CA: Cleis, 1994.
———. *Sensuous Magic*. New York: Masquerade, 1993.
Califia, Pat (ed.), *The Lesbian SM Safety Manual*. Boston, MA: Alyson, 1988.
Califia, Pat, and Robin Sweeney. *The Second Coming: A Leatherdyke Reader*. Boston, MA: Alyson Books, 2000.
Call, Lewis. *BDSM in American Science Fiction and Fantasy*. New York: Palgrave Macmillan, 2012.
———. "'Sounds Like Kinky Business to Me': Subtextual and Textual Representations of Erotic Power in the Buffyverse." *Slayage: The Online Journal of Buffy Studies* 6, no. 4 (2007). https://digitalcommons.calpoly.edu/hist_fac/48/ [Accessed 30 October 2020]
Canaday, Margot. *The Straight State: Sexuality and Citizenship in Twentieth-Century America*. Princeton, NJ: Princeton University Press, 2009.
Cardini, Leo. *Mineshaft Nights*. STARbooks Press, 2007.
Carney, William. *The Real Thing*. New York: G.P. Putnam's Sons, 1968.
Chapman, James. *Licence to Thrill: A Cultural History of the James Bond Films*. London: IB Tauris, 2008.
Chauncey, George. *Gay New York: Gender, Urban Culture, and the Making of the Gay Male World, 1890–1940*. New York: Basic Books, 1995.
Christy, Kim. *The Complete Reprint of Exotique: The First 36 Issues*. Cologne: Taschen, 1998.
Collins, Dana. "'No Experts -- Guaranteed!': Do-It-Yourself Sex Radicalism and the Production of the Lesbian Sex Zine Brat Attack." *Signs* 25, no. 1 (Autumn 1999): 65–89.
Comella, Lynn. *Vibrator Nation: How Feminist Sex-Toy Stores Changed the Business of Pleasure*. Durham, NC: Duke University Press, 2007.
Cowling, Mark and Paul Reynolds. *Making Sense of Sexual Consent*. Aldershot: Routledge, 2016.
Cruikshank, Margaret. *The Gay and Lesbian Liberation Movement*. London: Routledge, 1992.
Cruz, Ariane. "Beyond Black and Blue: BDSM, Internet Pornography and Black Female Sexuality." *Feminist Studies* 41, no. 2 (June 2015): 409–36.
———. "Playing with the Politics of Perversion: Policing BDSM, Pornography, and Black Female Sexuality." *Souls* 18, no. 2–4 (2016): 379–407.
———. *The Color of Kink: Black Women, BDSM, and Pornography*. New York: NYU Press, 2016.
Dangerous Bedfellows. *Policing Public Sex: Queer Politics and the Future of AIDS Activism*. Boston, MA: South End Press, 2008.
Dean, Tim, Steven Ruszczycky, and David Squires. *Porn Archives*. Chapel Hill, NC: Duke University Press, 2014.
Delany, Samuel R. *Times Square Red, Times Square Blue*. New York: NYU Press, 2019.
D'Emilio, John. *Sexual Politics, Sexual Communities: The Making of a Homosexual Minority in the United States, 1940–1970*. Chicago, IL: University of Chicago Press, 1983.
D'Emilio, John, and Freedman, Estelle B. *Intimate Matters: A History of Sexuality in America*. 3rd ed. Chicago, IL: University of Chicago Press, 2012.
Domínguez, Ivo. *Beneath the Skins: The New Spirit and Politics of the Kink Community*. Los Angeles, CA: Daedalus Pub. Co., 1994.
Downs, Jim. *Stand by Me: The Forgotten History of Gay Liberation*. New York: Basic Books, 2016.
Ehrenreich, Barbara, Elizabeth Hess, and Gloria Jacobs. *Re-Making Love: The Feminization of Sex*. New York: Doubleday, 1986.

Escoffier, Jeffrey. *Bigger Than Life: The History of Gay Porn Cinema from Beefcake to Hardcore.* Philadelphia, PA: Running Press, 2009.

Evans, David. *Sexual Citizenship: The Material Construction of Sexualities.* London: Routledge, 1993.

Foucault, Michel. *The History of Sexuality, Volume 1.* New York: Vintage, 1978.

Freccero, Carla. "Notes of a Post-Sex Wars Theorizer." In Marianne Hirsch (Ed.), *Conflicts in Feminism,* 306–25. New York: Routledge, 1990.

Freeman, Gilliam. *The Undergrowth of Literature.* London: Nelson, 1967.

Fritscher, Jack. *Gay San Francisco: Eyewitness Drummer Vol. 1.* San Francisco, CA: Palm Drive, 2008.

Gebhard, Paul. "Fetishism and Sadomasochism." In Jules H. Masserman (ed.), *Dynamics of Deviant Sexuality: Scientific Proceedings of the American Academy of Psychoanalysis,* 71–80. New York: Grune & Stratton, 1969.

Gertzman, Jay A. *Bookleggers and Smuthounds: The Trade in Erotica, 1920–1940.* Philadelphia: University of Pennsylvania Press, 1999.

Ghaziani, Amin. *The Dividends of Dissent: How Conflict and Culture Work in Lesbian and Gay Marches on Washington.* Chicago, IL: University of Chicago Press, 2008.

Gibson, Ian. *English Vice: Beating, Sex and Shame in Victorian England and After.* New York: Grove Press, 1984.

———. *The Erotomaniac: The Secret Life of Herbert Spencer Ashbee.* London: Faber & Faber, 2001.

Gibson, Pamela Church, and Roma Gibson, eds. *Dirty Looks: Women, Pornography, Power.* London: British Film Institute, 1993.

Greene, Gerald and Caroline. *S-M: The Last Taboo: A Study of Sado-Masochism.* New York: Grove Press, 1974.

Gregerson, Edgar. "The Sadomasochistic Scene." *Talk Delivered at the November 1969 Meeting of the American Anthropological Association,* New Orleans, LA, 1969.

Grumley, Michael. *Hard Corps: Studies in Leather and Sadomasochism.* New York: E P Dutton, 1977.

Hanley, Tim. *Wonder Woman Unbound: The Curious History of the World's Most Famous Heroine.* Chicago, IL: Chicago Review Press, 2014.

Harris, Daniel. *The Rise and Fall of Gay Culture.* New York: Ballantine, 1997.

Hartman, Andrew. *A War for the Soul of America.* Chicago, IL: University of Chicago Press, 2015.

Healey, Emma. *Lesbian Sex Wars.* London: Virago, 1996.

Heap, Chad C. *Slumming : Sexual and Racial Encounters in American Nightlife, 1885–1940.* Chicago, IL: University of Chicago Press, 2009.

Hennes, Peter. *Faeries, Bears, and Leathermen : Men in Community Queering the Masculine.* Chicago, IL: University of Chicago Press, 2008.

James, E.L. *Fifty Shades of Grey.* New York: Vintage, 2011.

Jacques, Mary Alison. "The Newspaperman and the Tabloid: Recovering the History of Philip H. Daniels and Justice Weekly." PhD Dissertation, McGill University, 2014.

Jacques, Trevor. *On the Safe Edge.* Toronto: WholeSM Publishing, 1993.

John, Sir. *The Q Letters: True Stories of Sadomasochism.* Buffalo, NY: Prometheus Books, 1993.

Johnson, David K. *Buying Gay: How Physique Entrepreneurs Sparked a Movement.* New York: Columbia University Press, 2019.

Johnson, V.M. *To Love, to Obey, to Serve: Diary of an Old Guard Slave.* Fairfield, CT: Mystic Rose Books, 1999.

Jorre, John De St. *Venus Bound: The Erotic Voyage of the Olympia Press.* New York: Random House, 1996.

Kaiser, Charles. *The Gay Metropolis*. Boston, MA: Houghton Mifflin, 1997.

Katz, Jonathan Ned. *The Invention of Heterosexuality*, 2nd ed. Chicago, IL: University of Chicago Press, 2007.

Khan, Ummni. "Sadomasochism in Sickness and in Health: Competing Claims from Science, Social Science, and Culture." *Current Sexual Health Reports* 9 (2015): 49–58.

———. *Vicarious Kinks: S/M in the Socio-Legal Imaginary*. Toronto: University of Toronto Press, 2014.

Kilpatrick, James Jackson. *The Smut Peddlers*. Westport, CT: Greenwood Press, 1973.

Kipnis, Laura. *Bound and Gagged: Pornography and the Politics of Fantasy in America*. Durham, NC: Duke University Press, 1998.

Kleinplatz, Peggy J. and Charles Moser. *Sadomasochism: Powerful Pleasures*. New York: Harrington Park, 2006.

Kroll, Eric. *The Complete Reprint of John Willie's Bizarre*. Koln: Taschen, 1995.

Krueger, Richard B. "The DSM Diagnostic Criteria for Sexual Sadism." *Archives of Sexual Behavior* 39 (2010): 325–45.

Kunzle, David. *Fashion and Fetishism: Corsets, Tight-Lacing and Other Forms of Body Sculpture*. Phoenix Mill: Sutton Publishing, 2004.

Lane, Frederick S. *Obscene Profits: The Entrepreneurs of Pornography in the Cyber Age*. New York: Routledge, 2001.

Langdridge, Darren. "The Erotic Construction of Power Exchange." *Journal of Constructivist Psychology* 18, no. 1 (2005): 65–73.

———. "Voices from the Margins: Sadomasochism and Sexual Citizenship." *Citizenship Studies* 10, no. 4 (2006): 373–89.

Langdridge, Darren, and Meg Barker. *Safe, Sane and Consensual: Contemporary Perspectives Sadomasochism*. New York: Palgrave Macmillan, 2008.

Langdridge, Darren, and Trevor Butt. "A Hermeneutic Phenomenological Investigation of the Construction of Sadomasochistic Identities." *Sexualities* 7, no. 1 (2004): 31–53.

Leigh, Michael. *The Velvet Underground*. New York: MacFadden, 1963.

Lenius, Steve. *Life, Leather, and the Pursuit of Happiness*. Minneapolis, MN: Nelson Borhek Press, 2010.

Lepore, Jill. *The Secret History of Wonder Woman*. New York: Vintage, 2015.

Levine, Elana. *Wallowing in Sex: The New Sexual Culture of 1970s American Television*. Durham, NC: Duke University Press, 2007.

Levine, Mark P. *Gay Macho: The Life and Death of the Homosexual Clone*. New York: NYU Press, 1998.

Lindemann, Danielle J. *Dominatrix: Gender, Eroticism, and Control in the Dungeon*. Chicago, IL: University of Chicago Press, 2012.

Litman, Robert E. and Charles Sweringen, "Bondage and Suicide." *Archives of General Psychiatry* 27 (July 1972): 80–5.

Madonna, *Sex*. New York: Ediciones B, 1992.

Mains, Geoff. *Urban Aboriginals*. Los Angeles, CA: Daedalus Publishing, 2002.

Marcus, Steven. *The Other Victorians: A Study of Sexuality and Pornography in Mid-Nineteenth-Century England*. London: Transaction Publishers, 2009.

Marks, Laura Helen. *Alice in Pornoland*. Urbana: University of Illinois Press, 2018.

McClintock, Anne. *Imperial Leather: Race, Gender, and Sexuality in the Colonial Contest*. New York: Routledge, 1995.

———. "Maid to Order: Commercial Fetishism and Gender Power." *Social Text*, no. 37 (Winter 1993): 87–116.

Meeker, Martin. *Contacts Desired: Gay and Lesbian Communications and Community, 1940s-1970s*. Revised edition. Chicago, IL: University of Chicago Press, 2006.

Miller, Nancy Ava. *Pervert*. Albuquerque: PepLove Press, 2009.

Miller-Young, Mireille. *A Taste for Brown Sugar: Black Women in Pornography*. Durham, NC: Duke University Press, 2014.

Moore, Alison M. *Sexual Myths of Modernity: Sadism, Masochism, and Historical Teleology*. Lanham, MD: Lexington Books, 2016.

Moore, Patrick. *Beyond Shame: Reclaiming the Abandoned History of Radical Gay Sexuality*. Boston, MA: Beacon Press, 2004.

Moser, Charles. "S/M (Sadomasochistic) Interactions in Semi-Public Settings." *Journal of Homosexuality* 36, no. 2 (1998): 19–30.

Muller, Eddie, and Daniel Faris. *Grindhouse: The Forbidden World of "Adults Only" Cinema*. New York: St. Martin's, 1996.

Musser, Amber Jamilla. *Sensational Flesh: Race, Power, and Masochism*. New York: NYU Press, 2014.

Naerssen, A.X. van. "Gay SM in Pornography and Reality." *Journal of Homosexuality* 13, no. 2–3 (Winter-Spring 1986): 111–9.

Nan, Mistress. *My Private Life: Real Experiences of a Dominant Woman*. Los Angeles, CA: Daedalus, 1995.

Newmahr, Staci. *Playing on the Edge: Sadomasochism, Risk, and Intimacy*. Bloomington: Indiana University Press, 2011.

Nielsen, Morten Ebbe Juul. "Safe, Sane, and Consensual—Consent and the Ethics of BDSM." *International Journal of Applied Philosophy* 24, no. 2 (2010): 265–88.

North, Maurice. *The Outer Fringe of Sex: A Study in Sexual Fetishism*. London: Odyssey Press Ltd, 1970.

Ortmann, David M., and Richard Sprott. *Sexual Outsiders: Understanding BDSM Sexualities and Communities*. Lanham, MD: Rowman & Littlefield, 2012.

Peakman, Julie. "Initiation, Defloration, and Flagellation: Sexual Propensities in Memoirs of a Woman of Pleasure." In Patsy S. Fowler and Alan Jackson (Eds.), *Launching Fanny Hill: Essays on the Novel and Its Influences*, 153–72. New York: AMS Press, 2003.

Pine, Julia. "In Bizarre Fashion: The Double-Voiced Discourse of John Willie's Fetish Fantasia." *Journal of the History of Sexuality* 22, no. 1 (January 2013): 1–33.

Preston, John. *Mr. Benson*. New York: Masquerade Books, Inc., 1992.

Purcell, Natalie J. *Violence and the Pornographic Imaginary : The Politics of Sex, Gender, and Aggression in Hardcore Pornography*. New York: Routledge, 2012.

Rambukkana, Nathan. "Taking the Leather Out of Leathersex: The Internet, Identity, and the Sadomasochistic Sphere." In Kate O'Riordan and David J. Philips (Eds.), *Queer Online: Media, Technology, and Sexuality*, 67–80. New York: Peter Lang, 2007.

Ramsland, Katherine. *Prism of the Night: A Biography of Anne Rice*. New York: Dutton, 1991.

Rechy, John. *The Sexual Outlaw: A Documentary*. New York: Grove Weidenfeld, 1977.

Reuben, David R. *Everything You Always Wanted to Know About Sex but Were Afraid to Ask*. New York: David McKay, 1969.

Rimmerman, Craig A. *From Identity to Politics: The Lesbian and Gay Movements in the United States*. Philadelphia, PA: Temple University Press, 2002.

Rubin, Gayle S. *Deviations: A Gayle Rubin Reader*. Durham, NC: Duke University Press Books, 2011.

———. "Elegy for the Valley of the Kings: AIDS and the Leather Community in San Francisco, 1981–1996." In Martin P. Levine, Peter M. Nardi, and John H. Gagnon (Eds.), *In Changing Times: Gay Men and Lesbians Encounter HIV/AIDS*, 101–44. Chicago, IL: University of Chicago Press, 1997.

———. "May Day." *DungeonMaster* 33 (September 1987): 36–7.

———. "Milestones of Modern Whipmaking." *DungeonMaster* 48 (1994): 22–3.

———. "These Boots Were Made for Walking Out." *On Our Backs* 9, no. 2 (November 1992): 5.

Rubin, Gayle S. "The Valley of the Kings: Leathermen in San Francisco, 1960–1990." PhD Dissertation, University of Michigan, 1994.

Rund, J.B. *Possibilities: The Photographs of John Willie*. New York: Belier Press, 2016.

Samois. *Coming to Power: Writing and Graphics on Lesbian S/M 3rd Edition, Revised and Updated*. Boston, MA: Alyson, 1982.

———. *What Color Is Your Handkerchief?* Berkeley, CA: Samois, 1979.

Schaefer, Eric. *Bold! Daring! Shocking! True: A History of Exploitation Films, 1919–1959*. Durham, NC: Duke University Press, 1999.

Scott, Henry E. *Shocking True Story: The Rise and Fall of Confidential, "America's Most Scandalous Scandal Magazine."* New York: Pantheon Books, 2010.

Seidman, Steven. *The Social Construction of Sexuality*. New York: Norton, 2009.

Seves, Richard Pérez. *Charles Guyette: Godfather of American Fetish Art*. 2nd ed. CreateSpace Independent Publishing Platform, 2017.

Shahbaz, Caroline, and Peter Chirinos. *Becoming a Kink Aware Therapist*. New York: Routledge, 2017.

Shortes, Carolyn. "'Cleaning up a Sewer': The Containment of S/M Pornography." *Journal of Popular Film and Television* 26, no. 2 (Summer 1998): 72–80.

Sigel, Lisa Z. "Fashioning Fetishism from the Pages of 'London Life.'" *Journal of British Studies* 51, no. 3 (July 2012): 664–84.

———. *Governing Pleasures: Pornography and Social Change in England, 1815–1914*. Piscataway, NJ: Rutgers University Press, 2002.

Spring, Justin. *Secret Historian: The Life and Times of Samuel Steward, Professor, Tattoo Artist, and Sexual Renegade*. New York: Farrar, Straus and Giroux, 2010.

Stein, Marc. *Rethinking the Gay and Lesbian Movement*. New York: Routledge, 2012.

Stein, Steve. *Twenty-Five Years of Living in Leather: The National Leather Association, 1986–* 2011. Palm Coast, FL: Adynaton, 2012.

Stoller, Robert J. *Pain & Passion: A Psychoanalyst Explores the World of S & M*. New York: Plenum Press, 1991.

———. *Porn: Myths for the Twentieth Century*. New Haven, CT: Yale University Press, 1991.

Stoller, Robert J., and I.S. Levine. *Coming Attractions: The Making of an X-Rated Video*. New Haven, CT: Yale University Press, 1993.

Stone, Lawrence. "Libertine Sexuality in Post-Restoration England: Group Sex and Flagellation Among the Middling Sort in Norwich in 1706–7." *Journal of the History of Sexuality* 2, no. 4 (1992): 511–26.

Streitmatter, Rodger. *Unspeakable: The Rise of the Gay and Lesbian Press in America*. Boston, MA: Faber and Faber, 1995.

Taylor, Gary Wilson. "The Discursive Construction and Regulation of Dissident Sexualities: The Case of SM." In Jane D. Ussher (Ed.), *Body Talk: The Material and Discursive Regulation of Sexuality, Madness and Reproduction*, 106–30. London: Routledge, 1997.

Taylor, Gary and Jane Ussher. "Making Sense of S & M: A Discourse Analytic Account." *Sexualities* 4, no. 3 (2001): 302–6.

Thompson, Bill. *Sadomasochism: Painful Perversion or Pleasurable Play?* London: Cassell, 1994.

Thompson, Mark. *Leatherfolk : Radical Sex, People, Politics, and Practice*. Boston, MA: Alyson Publications, 1991.

Townsend, Larry. *The Leatherman's Handbook II.* 4th ed. New York: Carlyle, 1983.

———. *The Original Leatherman's Handbook.* 4th ed. Beverly Hills, CA: LT Publications, 1993.

Tupper, Peter. *A Lover's Pinch: A Cultural History of Sadomasochism.* Lanham, MD: Rowman & Littlefield, 2018.

Vance, Carole S. *Pleasure and Danger: Exploring Female Sexuality.* New York: HarperCollins, 1993.

Warner, Alex. "'Where Angels Fear to Tread:' Feminism, Sex and the Problem of SM, 1969–1993." PhD Dissertation, Rutgers, The State University of New Jersey, 2011.

Warren, John. *The Loving Dominant.* New York: Masquerade, 1992.

Weeks, Jeffrey. *Invented Moralities: Sexual Values in an Age of Uncertainty.* New York: Columbia University Press, 1995.

———. *Sexuality and Its Discontents: Meanings, Myths, and Modern Sexualities.* London: Routledge, 1990.

———. "The Sexual Citizen." *Theory, Culture, & Society* 15, no. 3–4 (1998): 35–52.

———. *The World We Have Won: The Remaking of Erotic and Intimate Life.* New York: Routledge, 2007.

Weinberg, Thomas and G.W. Levi Kamel. *S and M: Studies in Dominance and Submission.* Amherst, NY: Prometheus, 1995.

Weinberg, Thomas, and G.W. Levi Kamel. *S and M: Studies in Sadomasochism.* Buffalo, NY: Prometheus Books, 1983.

Weiss, Margot. *Techniques of Pleasure: BDSM and the Circuits of Sexuality.* Durham, NC: Duke University Press, 2011.

Weymouth, T and Society of Janus, *Society of Janus: Twenty-Five Years.* San Francisco, CA: Society of Janus, 1999.

White, Edmund. *City Boy: My Life in New York During the 1960s and '70s.* New York: Bloomsbury, 2009.

———. *The Burning Library: Essays.* New York: Vintage, 1995.

Williams, Linda. *Hard Core: Power, Pleasure, and the "Frenzy of the Visible."* Berkeley: University of California Press, 1989.

———. *Screening Sex.* Durham, NC: Duke University Press, 2008.

Willie, John. *The Adventures of Sweet Gwendoline.* New York: Belier Press, 1999.

Wiseman, Jay. *SM 101: A Realistic Introduction.* San Francisco, CA: Greenery Press, 1998.

Woltersdorff, Volker. "The Pleasures of Compliance: Domination and Compromise within BDSM Practice." In María Do Mar Castro Varela, Nikita Dhawan, and Antke Engel (Eds.), *Hegemony and Heteronormativity: Revisiting "The Political" in Queer Politics,* 169–88. London: Routledge, 2011.

INDEX

For Product Safety Concerns and Information please contact our EU representative GPSR@taylorandfrancis.com
Taylor & Francis Verlag GmbH, Kaufingerstraße 24, 80331 München, Germany

www.ingramcontent.com/pod-product-compliance
Ingram Content Group UK Ltd.
Pitfield, Milton Keynes, MK11 3LW, UK
UKHW022020180926
475701UK00005B/946
* 9 7 8 0 3 6 7 4 7 6 8 0 9 *